# THE ART OF CATECHESIS

## What You Need to Be, Know and Do

## Maureen Gallagher

Foreword by
Archbishop Rembert G. Weakland, O.S.B.

PAULIST PRESS
New York/Mahwah, N.J.

*Photographs by Sr. Mary Luke Baldwin, SSND, A. Taidgh J. O'Neill, Mark Barthel and Maureen Gallagher.*

*Nihil Obstat*
Nancy A. Sell
Censor Deputatus

*Imprimatur*
+Rembert G. Weakland
Archbishop of Milwaukee

*Cover design by Tim McKeen*

Library of Congress Cataloging-in-Publication Data

Gallagher, Maureen, 1938–
    The art of catechesis : what you need to be, know and do / Maureen Gallagher.
        p.  cm.
    Includes bibliographical references.
    ISBN 0-8091-3778-X (alk. paper)
    1. Catechetics—Catholic Church.   2. Catholic Church—Education.
3. Christian education—Philosophy.   4. Christian education—Teaching methods.  I. Title.
BX1968.G28   1998
268'.82—dc21                                                                97-44070
                                                                                CIP

Published by Paulist Press
997 Macarthur Boulevard
Mahwah, New Jersey 07430

Printed and bound in the
United States of America

# Contents

# Abbreviations

| | |
|---|---|
| *CCC* | Catechism of the Catholic Church |
| *DV* | Dogmatic Constitution on Divine Revelation |
| *EACW* | Environment and Art in Catholic Worship |
| *GIRM* | General Instruction of the Roman Missal |
| *GS* | Pastoral Constitution on the Church in the Modern World |
| *LG* | Dogmatic Constitution on the Church |
| *MCW* | Music in Catholic Worship |
| *NCD* | Sharing the Light of Faith, The National Catechetical Directory |
| *SC* | Constitution on the Sacred Liturgy |

*Dedication*

This book is dedicated to all those who have had a major influence on my faith life, some of whom are named below:

To my parents, Mary and James Gallagher, who first taught me to believe in an all-caring God and made it possible for me to do it by showing me endless love and care, and to my grandmother who taught me "Here's the Church and here's the steeple…" and so much more by her presence.

To Kevin Lynch, C.S.P., for his many years of dedicated service in seeking out and publishing only high quality catechetical materials and for his genuine love of catechesis.

To Anne Marie Mongoven, O.P., Rita Claire Dorner, O.P., Kate Dooley, O.P., and Clare Wagner, O.P., who taught me a great deal about catechesis and liturgy and who have walked with me through many faith adventures.

To Jean Marie Hiesberger and Bob Heyer who as trusted friends, colleagues and front runners have inspired me and supported me in searching for lifelong catechetical "answers."

To Monsignor Francis E. Doherty and Father Robert Reardon for their insistence on excellent catechetical programming and for their work and support in making it happen.

To Archbishop Rembert G. Weakland, O.S.B., and Bishop Richard J. Sklba whose commitment to catechesis based on viable processes, sound Church teachings and quality liturgies have influenced my writing of this book.

To David Woeste, my husband and best friend, who has been a constant source of inspiration, courage, support and dedication, not to mention a great proofreader.

To all the catechists, liturgists and peers with whom I have had the privilege of working, for their generous spirit, inquiring minds, warm hearts and hard work.

# Foreword

*Rembert G. Weakland, O.S.B.*
*Archbishop of Milwaukee*

Of all the challenges facing the Catholic Church in the United States today perhaps the most pressing is that of handing on the faith to the next generation. Such a challenge always existed for the Church, but today's situation is different. We often forget that certain circumstances have come together here in the United States to make the problem of how to transmit our faith unique to our generation. It is a unique moment because in the past the Church could rely on the general Catholic culture of the ethnic group to which a Catholic family belonged to help support and transmit its teaching. Those ethnic enclaves have for the most part disappeared. Today the general culture in which our people live is often antagonistic to the faith, projecting and affirming ideas totally contrary to those we believe in. Moreover, in the past the Church could rely on the strength of the family structure to support its mission. The family was truly the *locus* where catechetics took place. One learned the beliefs of one's faith and how they were lived out, as it were, from one's mother's milk. Nowadays one cannot count on such fundamental social structures as the family. Thus catechetics faces a new challenge, that of broadening its scope to include reaching out to the whole family. Finally, a whole generation of Catholics grew up during a period of intense change, often violent and disruptive, in both society and Church. These people did not themselves receive solid catechetical training. Now, in their own attempts at parenting and talking about the faith, they feel like the blind leading the blind—at least as far as teaching the faith and transmitting it is concerned.

1

Moreover, the implications of today's challenge to catechetics are more profound, and the stakes seem much higher. Catholics are now becoming an integral part of the dominant culture of the United States. Not only are they being formed by that culture but they also have the unique opportunity of playing a more and more decisive role in forming and transforming that culture. But they cannot adequately assume that role and responsibility as disciples of Christ without themselves being formed and steeped in the Catholic tradition.

In the light of this demanding situation, one can rightly ask: What tools are available to assist the catechists of today in their task? There are, indeed, many books or manuals available to help them in presenting the faith in a systematic way. These are graded from one to twelve, covering the grade school and high school years. Moreover, these books are, for the most part, excellent, especially those re-worked in the light of the *Catechism of the Catholic Church*. These newer editions have sought to remedy the deficiency of some older text books that minimized the content of the faith while trying, with good intention, to make the learning experience for the young Catholic pleasant, and not a chore. In that attempt they often failed to emphasize content, feeling that it would be handed on by the parents or the extended family. That did not happen. Thus arose the need for a catechism that would be primarily a storehouse of doctrine. Every catechist should be armed with that *Catechism of the Catholic Church* and refer to it frequently. But it remains a reference tool, too large for any catechist to absorb or synthesize totally. Nor can one teach from it, as useful as it may be. Plunging into the graded material can also be a bit overwhelming. Where does one begin? Who can give an overview of what the whole ministry is all about? Who can help the catechists, not just the students?

What is needed, therefore, is a book that the pastor can put into the hands of a new catechist, one that helps that person get a feel for the whole, one that does not lose sight of the practical aspects of the task. At the same time it must be a book that synthesizes the material in such a way that the catechist can envision what the whole enterprise is all about. The wedding of the content of catechetics with the methods used in the past is what today's catechists need. On the level of content nothing can be taken for granted. Concepts such as the Catholic approach to scripture or the nature of the Church must be laid out clearly. But since all the material cannot be absorbed at once, the catechist, before settling down in the grade assigned to him or her, must be able to see how the parts form a whole.

Convinced that imparting information is not the sole aim of his or her ministry, the catechist must show how all that information is integrated into life and life's decisions. Catechetics, then, implies formation, not just information.

In this regard, one of the most difficult aspects of catechesis in our day is that of reconciling revelation, on one hand, and human experience, on the other. Revelation is a deductive process, given by God, handed down to us humans. Experience begins with us, our daily encounters with God through people, events, and life's vicissitudes. In reconciling these two important approaches, Dr. Gallagher relies on the important theology of Karl Rahner, S.J., and his many writings. Perhaps some readers might not be as convinced of the validity of the way in which Rahner has made his synthesis, but his is one of the most significant theologies of our time and one that has influenced many catechists in the contemporary post-Vatican II Church. It has the advantage of not minimizing the importance of human experience in the here and now. Faith must be lived out and not remain just an abstract concept.

Our Catholic population also lives in a world that is highly dominated by a fundamentalist usage of scripture. Thus there arises the need for catechists to be well-informed on the Catholic approach to God's Word. The catechist today must have both a knowledge of scripture and the courage and freedom to use it well. This book is a fine introduction to such a Catholic approach.

Given our American pragmatic mind and the need we have in our culture for clear processes and for aides in presenting material, Dr. Gallagher has included many helpful suggestions for methods that can make the material come to life for our younger population, so inductive and experiential in their educative approaches to life. Drawing from her many years of teaching and catechizing, she can add those myriad insights, so needed by a new catechist, on how to present the material in an ever fresh way. Thus, catechetics will not be seen as just another academic discipline but as a part of one's prayer life, of one's spiritual and moral growth. These insights, as she points out, can be adjusted to every age level.

Fortunately, Dr. Maureen Gallagher has brought together all these approaches in one book. First of all, it is written in the framework of the documents of Vatican Council II and has caught the spirit of renewal that this Council wanted to bring about. Secondly, it brings together in a synthetic way the best of all the catechetical material, such as the *Catechism of the Catholic Church,* that has been produced since Vatican Council II. Thirdly, it integrates scripture and catechetics in a way not always found in pre- or post-Vatican II manuals. This perspective complements much that is found in the *Catechism of the Catholic Church.* It also ties catechetics into the Church's liturgy and social teaching in a way that is much needed today and so often neglected. This latter aspect is one of the greatest merits of this work.

This is the right book for every catechist who undertakes the difficult task of helping form people in the faith. It can be a special blessing for parishes looking for just the right book to give their volunteer catechists who are approaching this ministry for the first time—probably with some anxiety about what the whole enterprise entails. It is aimed at catechists themselves and keeps their needs, not just that of the learners, in mind. In the best of the post-Vatican II tradition it weds content and method, just as one would wish. I hope and pray it will give catechists a good basis upon which to build their own understanding of the faith to be transmitted, point out the tools available to them in assuming the task of catechizing others, and stimulate their creativity and insights on new and useful approaches that do not diminish the content of the faith.

Lastly and perhaps most important, I hope it also generates some enthusiasm and excitement about the Catholic faith. Only with such enthusiasm is the faith transmitted. The catechist must be full of solid and genuine enthusiasm. In transmitting the faith the lack of personal conviction is easily spotted. Faith, as we all know, is contagious and cannot be taught—only caught. After reading and using this book as a *vade mecum,* a catechist will have all the tools needed to feel confident in approaching this ministry. Let him or her be inspired with great enthusiasm to instruct and challenge both self and others.

# Introduction

*The Art of Catechesis* is designed to assist catechists in becoming artists in helping others grow in faith. Art portrays the interrelationship of form and meaning in such a way that the form becomes the meaning. While this may sound abstract at first, once it is explored, the interconnectedness between art and catechesis becomes clear. Artists have materials to use which enable them to express some inner reality and meaning. Some artists use paint and canvas; others stone and metal; some use ink on paper; others employ musical scales, staffs and notes; some use fabrics and objects from nature. Artists always portray meaning by using something. Catechists do the same thing. They use the Bible with all its imagery and style. They use liturgy with the richness of its symbols and rituals. They use the lives of the people who have gone before them and the experience of people today. They use the tradition of the Church. They use the teachings of the magisterium. While the forms and the materials of the artists and the catechists may be different, the artistic process is similar.

Art has many levels of meaning. On examining a painting, one gets an initial impression. Thinking about the painting and perhaps looking at it from another perspective gives a new interpretation. Works of art also have social and spiritual dimensions. They can be discussed, compared, criticized, praised and valued. The artist observes the signs of the times, reflects on them and then presents them for the viewer or the listener to absorb, reject, question or accept. Artists explore space and then present an aspect of the exploration for a viewer. Sometimes the view is an aerial one; sometimes a close-up; sometimes a simultaneous, multi-faceted view. Modern art, for instance, does not have a static point of view; it presents concurrent

points of view. Artists fill old formulas with new life. The Impression-
ists are said to have taken the rules of the Renaissance painters, but
used them with a new spirit which reflected a new era.

Catechists are called to be creative as they help unfold the meaning of various aspects of faith. The symbolic actions of the liturgy are
available for catechists as they constantly seek ways to have those they
catechize experience the symbols, probe their meaning and interpret
them today. The challenge of helping those catechized appreciate that
the presentation of gifts will be transformed and will transform the
assembly calls for no less artistry than that required of a great painter.
Catechists invite the participants to look at a scripture passage from
several points of view as they try to understand its meaning. The profound meaning of the scriptures and the liturgy can only be facilitated
by one who sees "more than meets the eye." Catechists interpret the
signs of the times in the light of faith and clarify them for those whom
they catechize.

Both artists and catechists see beyond the ordinary. Artists and
catechists express the profound meaning of life with its spiritual and
social dimensions. The work of artists and catechists call for interaction
among those participating. Both present material from different points
of view, under different light. Artists and catechists both deal with the
expression of truth, and the expression that calls for some kind of a
response. The catechist, just like the artist, uses traditional forms and
breathes new life into them.

For catechists the challenge to show the interrelationship between
the experience of the participants, the biblical experience, the liturgical
experience, the experience of the saints, and of the Church throughout
the ages, calls for the imagination of an artist. To know how to put the
various aspects together in a way that reveals meaning to a particular
group at a specific time in history is a major artistic achievement. The
artist takes what is and expresses it in a way that brings new meaning.
The catechist takes what is in the treasury of the Church, including the
lives of its members, and presents it in such a way that faith is engendered. The catechist cannot "make" someone grow in faith. Faith is a
gift from God. However, catechists can, through use of their imaginations, foster growth in faith by the way they engage those catechized
with the richness of the Christian heritage. The artist does not pump
information into people. The artist absorbs a great deal of knowledge
and thought and reflects on it in light of experience before rendering it

in an artistic form. The catechist does the same thing. Catechists begin with their own experience of God in their lives and their own questions and reflections on this experience.

However, they must also know the scriptures, the liturgy, the teachings and history of the Church, the lives of the saints, the role of religious imagination, psychology, good methods of interaction, and so on in order to be able to catechize. Their tools are different than those of the artists. Catechists need to reflect on all these things just as artists reflect on reality before they present it. Catechists need to be people of faith, ever growing to be more faith-filled.

This book is written to provide a solid knowledge base as well as practical ideas for catechists. It is designed in such a way that catechists are called to stop and reflect on their own experience, the experience and teachings of the Church as they relate to their lives and their role as catechists.

*The Art of Catechesis* is fashioned to promote building of community among catechists, proclaiming of the message of Christianity in an effective and accurate way, leading people in prayer and motivating people to service. The book is meant to whet the appetite of catechists so that they may explore in greater depth the rich heritage of the Church. Finally, the book is written with the hope that it will stimulate faith growth in the catechist and subsequently in the lives of those catechized. Catechesis is the art of knowing how to put various aspects of scripture, tradition and liturgy together in a stimulating and provocative way, so that those catechized might bring meaning to their lives in the light of the Good News of Jesus Christ.

**"Catechesis: To Echo the Word of God."**

# 1

# Understanding Catechesis and Those You Catechize

Just as visual artists need to know what being an artist is all about and what mediums are at their disposal, so catechists need to have a sense of what it is they need to be, to know and to do as they explore the artistry of catechesis.

## WHAT IS CATECHESIS?

Catechesis is an essential ministry in the Church. Its primary goal is to help people grow in faith (CCC 5). Growing in faith is a lifelong process. It calls for us to be attuned to God's presence in our lives, to be able to name that presence in terms of our tradition, the faith of the Church, and to respond to God's call to build the Kingdom here on earth so that a more just society will exist. Catechesis is about helping people recognize and understand God's revelation in the Judeo-Christian tradition. This is an on-going process, a gradual unfolding.

God's revelation happens in the lives of human people. Abraham was called from a rather stable and apparently successful life to risk a new journey of God's undertaking. Moses was doing his job, tending sheep, when God revealed that God was a personal God, not a god of nature. Mary was not anticipating being the mother of Jesus when she was asked by God's messenger to be the handmaid of the Lord. The Bible is full of stories of God working through the ordinary events of people's lives to reveal the mysteries of faith. Revelation is complete in the apostolic age. It reached its fullness in Jesus Christ. The mysteries of God, however, are continually manifested today in the daily events of our lives (DV 2, 4; CCC 66).

We look for the signs of God's continual manifestation in human experiences, the Bible, the Church, the lives of people in the Church, and the liturgy. In one way, the scriptures, the Church and the liturgy help verify our own experience of God in everyday life. In other words the presence of God permeates human existence. In case we are not sure that God is speaking to us we can compare our experience with those of the people who have gone before us. The similarities encourage us to recognize God in our own lives and respond in ways like the heroes and heroines of the past. This is not to say that the Bible, Church and liturgy themselves cannot be revelatory events, but the power of God's revelation is found in the convergence of our life experiences, scriptures, Church and liturgy. Such ideas will be explored throughout this book.

## GETTING IN TOUCH WITH OUR OWN FAITH EXPERIENCE

If the primary goal of catechesis is to foster growth in faith, then before we consider helping others grow in faith, it is important to reflect on our own faith lives. Many of us were baptized as infants. At baptism we were initiated into the death-resurrection mystery of Jesus Christ. We were given rights and responsibilities: rights to be active members of the believing community; responsibilities to spread the Good News that we are loved and redeemed people. When we become involved in the catechetical ministry of the Church we are living out our baptismal commitment.

Most of us probably recall learning something about God as children. For many, religious pictures, statues, or crib sets first caught our imaginations. Parents introduced us to some religious stories, taught us simple prayers and took us to Church. In a sense, we absorbed their values and their faith.

Catholic schools or catechetical sessions further contributed to our knowledge and love of God and our on-going initiation into the Christian community. As we grew through adolescence into young adulthood, questioning and searching confirmed us on our faith journey.

Each of our faith stories is different. The moments of awareness of God's presence, of God's revelation, and our response to these events have a ring of uniqueness for each of us. While the individual stories carry their own special characteristics, similar patterns often emerge. As people grow in faith they internalize the faith-filled stories and values of others. Scriptural stories, for instance, become part of one's own frame of reference. As it matures, faith becomes less segmented and more integrated into life experiences.

Reflect on some major life events. In your imagination or on a separate piece of paper, name the road signs in your life journey.

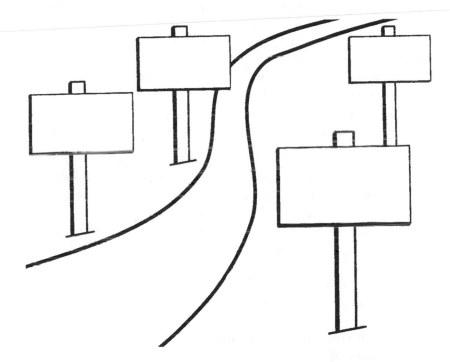

*What image of God or Jesus do you associate with each event?*
*(Example: God as an old person in the sky with flowing robes,*
*God as a judge, Jesus as a friend, etc.)*
*How has your image of God changed?*
*To what do you attribute this change?*

## JESUS AS THE PERSON OF GREAT FAITH

The *Catechism of the Catholic Church* (CCC) points out that Jesus Christ is at the heart of catechesis (CCC 426). As catechists we are called to reveal the person of Jesus, the Christ. We do this by helping people understand the meaning of Jesus's life, death, resurrection and glorification. To obtain insights into these great events we need to grapple with the significance of Jesus' words and actions as he walked the earth. The Church teaches that catechesis strives to bring people into "communion" with Jesus Christ so that they can share in the life of the Trinity (CCC 426). In order to bring people into a life united with Christ, catechists need to be in union with him themselves. They must see Jesus as someone who was faithful to God while at the same time addressing the issues of his day.

Jesus set a wonderful example of what it means to be faithful to God. His bonding with God becomes a model for us. Jesus' life of faithfulness was made up of many of the same things which fill our lives. Some of what Jesus spent his life doing includes: affirming people, sharing meals, making friends, challenging people, forgiving people, defending the rejected, teaching, preaching, praying, and traveling.

> *Imagine that you were with Jesus on his journey. Then think about how you do some of the same things Jesus did in his life. Remember that artists are people who make connections and in so doing help others see anew.*
> *Use the following chart to see the interconnections between your life and the life of Jesus.*
> *In what ways is your life a lot like Jesus' life?*
> *How does it differ?*
> *What did Jesus reveal about his life that is also true of your life?*
> *How could you create a dynamic like this for use with those whom you catechize?*

Twenty centuries after Jesus, a renowned German Jesuit theologian, Fr. Karl Rahner, continued to clarify for us that it is in the everyday that we experience God—that God is revealed to us. It is the everyday that is grace-filled. Rahner describes grace as occurring when we laugh, cry, stand up for what is right, hope against hope, refuse to be embittered by the stupidity of life, etc. Images of God's pervasive presence in

| Much of Jesus' life of faith included doing the following things: | Think of a time when you have done these things. Create your chart. |
|---|---|
| **Affirming people** | |
| **Sharing meals** | |
| **Making friends** | |
| **Challenging people** | |
| **Forgiving people** | |
| **Defending the rejected** | |
| **Teaching** | |
| **Praying** | |
| **Traveling** | |
| **Dying/Rising** | |

such ordinary experiences are found throughout scripture. However, it takes faith to see and to respond to God's graciousness. The gift of faith acts like a lens showing us added dimensions to life, helping us to see more than what meets the eye, enabling us to see the sacred in the secular, the holy in the profane. One of the graces of being catechists is that we have added opportunities to reflect on our faith lives and nurture them as we prepare to foster the faith growth of others.

*List the five most important things you believe about yourself.*

1.

2.

3.

4.

5.

*List five important things you believe about Jesus Christ.*

1.

2.

3.

4.

5.

*Compare your responses with the Apostle's Creed.*
*How is what you wrote similar to what is in the creed?*
*How is it different?*
*List five things you do because you believe in yourself and*
*God's presence in your life.*

## CATECHETICAL CHALLENGES

One of the great challenges in catechesis is to go beyond simply knowing the creed and the doctrine of the Church to knowing how to open up the Church's treasures so that they speak to modern people. Pope John XXIII opened the Second Vatican Council by saying: "Our task is not merely to hoard this precious treasure, as though obsessed with the past, but to give ourselves eagerly and without fear to the task that the present age demands of us—and in so doing we will be faithful to what the Church has done in the last twenty centuries.... But this authentic doctrine has to be studied and expounded in light of the research methods and the language of modern thought. For the substance of the ancient deposit of faith is one thing, and the way in which it is presented is another." Today, using the resources of Vatican II and our own insights, we are called to excite people about being part of an alive, dynamic Church which seeks to continue its faithfulness in building God's kingdom.

## LITURGY AND SCRIPTURE

The Second Vatican Council did a great deal to open up the Church's liturgical and scriptural treasures. Pope John Paul II noted in his preface to the *Catechism, Fidei Depositum,* that the use "of doctrine in catechesis must be biblical and liturgical. It must be sound doctrine suited to the present life of Christians." In saying this the pope was reiterating an insight of the early Church Fathers.

Saints like John Chrysostom, Ambrose and Augustine in the fourth and fifth centuries gave helpful hints to catechists. They emphasized three points. First, catechesis needed to be a "concrete, living and thrilling thing." Second, Christian doctrine was God's message of salvation, a distillation of Sacred Scripture and liturgy. Third, God's message comes through God's word and God's action. As with the early Church, the Church of today is called through catechesis to help nurture other people's faith to become living and active through the light of instruction.

## PROBLEMS ENCOUNTERED BY CATECHISTS

Some think that applied psychology is something the Church has discovered in the last fifty years. But in the fourth century, St. Augustine wrote a wonderful guide which is full of psychological insights which can be applied to today's catechetical efforts. He showed concern for catechists because he felt that they are prone to five dangers. The first of these is the feeling of being ineffective, of not doing a good job. Augustine's answer to this feeling was threefold: (1) you never did as bad as you think you did; (2) endure—or, as we would say today, "hang in there!"—for love's sake; (3) do the best you can and let God speak through you.

The second danger was boredom from repetition. As catechists might say today, "Same old, same old…!" Augustine's solution was to see things through the eyes of love and to realize that catechists were helping people move from death to life. He wanted catechists to persevere because he saw what great work they were doing.

Augustine's third danger was apathy. He knew what it was like to look at blank faces and receive little reaction. Today people who catechize adolescents often feel that they are not getting through to them. Augustine noted how hard it was to keep on going when the hearer was not touched. His way of working with this was to find out what was the underlying problem. In other words why was the listener apathetic? Was the person timid? If so, bond with him or her to give confidence. Did the person have trouble understanding? If so, speak more clearly, more simply and more briefly. Allow the person to lay objections out freely and don't respond defensively. If the person was not bright, then be compassionate and focus on essential truths designed to "inspire awe." A final bit of advice was for the catechist to say "much on his behalf to God" rather than say too much to the person about God. That means the catechist needs to pray for the person, but not lay heavy intellectual expectations on him or her.

The fourth danger Augustine identified was an "up-set mind." For him this meant a catechist was preoccupied with other things, or wished to be somewhere else. In modern times we may say that the catechist is stressed out. Augustine's advice is to do the best you can, knowing that sometimes you do not have control over outside influences. The best laid plans may fall apart through no fault of our own.

The fifth danger is "grief of heart" resulting from some scandal, either self-caused or involving others. Basically Augustine says, "Get over it and get on with the mission." Joy is needed for catechists to be effective. If catechists are joyful in their work, the message will be "delivered more easily and received more gratefully."

## THOSE CATECHIZED

Augustine also had some advice concerning those being catechized. The first thing he said was to take them at their word. Don't second-guess their motives. The second bit of advice was to tailor what was taught to the abilities of the ones catechized. If the people are well educated, do not "annoy" them by going over what they already know. Use the experience of the people as a springboard to help them make connections with the scriptures and the sacramental life of the Church. Augustine exhorts those catechized to plumb the depths of scripture to look for various levels of meaning. He also emphasizes the need to appeal to the emotions of those catechized, because as he says "there is no voice to reach the ears of God save the emotion of the heart." Augustine's last point rings very true today. Augustine believed that love was the ultimate purpose of catechesis. He states: "This love, then, is that to which you may refer all that you say, so give all your instruction that those to whom you speak by hearing may believe, and by believing may hope and by hoping may love." In this, he points to the necessity to adapt catechesis to the needs of the people being catechized. Both the *National Catechetical Directory, Sharing the Light of Faith* (NCD 181) and the *Catechism of the Catholic Church* (CCC 24) state that adaptation is essential in catechesis.

## KNOWING THOSE WHOM YOU CATECHIZE

Effective catechists know the people they are catechizing. They know about their capabilities, their interests and their needs. They know how to adapt material to the culture, age and spiritual maturity of those whom they catechize (CCC 24). They take people where they are and help them to see and respond to God in their lives.

Jesus was the master catechist. He helped people see, recognize and respond to God's presence in their daily lives. Jesus never introduced ideas which did not relate to people's lives, which did not connect to an authentic question. He never taught concepts that required a new vocabulary or were related to abstract ideas. Jesus pushed the people to see things differently and to act differently in very profound ways, but to do this he appealed to their own experience and helped them to see the manifestation of God in that experience. Jesus challenged people to search for meaning and purpose in life. His own search led to his being faithful to God.

Based upon the principles Jesus used in catechesis, what do we need to know to minister as catechists? We will examine six concepts to guide our thinking: (1) children belong to families and it is in families where they first experience God; (2) children develop gradually through adolescence into adulthood; (3) faith growth often parallels human development; (4) "every form of catechesis is oriented in some way to the catechesis of adults" (NCD 32); (5) when Jesus catechized, he integrated his message with community life, service and prayer; and (6) cultural, racial and gender diversity needs to be taken into account when catechizing.

### 1) Taking a Family Perspective

The children we catechize come from families. It is families who have the primary religious influence on them. Parents provide their children with their first experience of God. They do this by caring for their youngsters. By feeding, bathing, clothing and playing with their children, parents make it possible for children ultimately to believe in a God who cares for them, nurtures them and is present to them.

Parents need to be affirmed in their role and to be helped to see that by being good parents they are helping their children know God and to be faith-filled. Both single-parent and two-parent families contribute to their children's positive self-concept by providing a healthy

Christian environment. There is no greater gift that parents can give their children than healthy self-esteem. Faith, hope and love grow from the solid foundation of a wholesome self-concept. Such a characteristic is arrived at through trusting relationships. These are first experienced through parents' consistency in the way they bring up their children. As children's needs for food and warm clothes and attentive care are met on a regular basis, they learn they can trust people. This familial trust is the basis for the virtue of hope. The point is if children can trust people, then they can more easily believe in and trust a loving God.

As children grow they learn from their parents that they are competent. By providing a stimulating and safe environment, parents help children develop talents which can be used throughout a lifetime. They play with blocks to gain large muscle dexterity. They learn to ride bikes and gain muscle coordination. They discover artistic talents by using crayons, markers, chalk and paints. All these experiences are often taken for granted but they form the foundation which will empower a person to ultimately contribute to building the reign of God on earth.Compared to parents, we as catechists play a subsidiary role in helping children grow in faith. Keeping in mind that children belong to a family system will help us to be effective. It is in and through the family system and the Church community that they grow in faith. Our role is to affirm parents and to build upon the foundation they have laid. We can do this by getting to know the parents of the children we catechize and consciously involving them in our programs.

> *How many of the parents of those you catechize do you know?*
> *How might you get to know all the parents?*
> *What message do you think parents need to receive from you as*
> *a catechist?*
> *How might you deliver the message?*

## 2) Understanding Human Development of Children and Adolescents

To catechize we need to understand patterns of growth in children. As St. Thomas Aquinas said centuries ago, "Grace builds on nature." To help children grow in faith we must be familiar with their natural stages of physical, emotional, intellectual, social and spiritual growth.

| Approximate age | Physical | Emotional | Intellectual | Moral/Faith | Social |
|---|---|---|---|---|---|
| Age 3–5 Preschool | High activity level, eye-hand coordination improving. | High need for security/love. | Great spurts in language development. | Reward/punishment; loves God. | Like to play with adults, people, animals. |
| Age 6–8 Primary | High activity levels. Short, quiet periods possible. Improved eye-hand coordination. | Growing awareness of others. | Reading and writing. Brain growth spurts continue. Like to draw and paint ideas. | "You scratch my back and I'll scratch yours." Drama and myth important in faith development. | Interest in home, neighbors and school. |
| Age 9–11 Intermediate | Possible plateau before pre-adolescent growth spurt. | Emotional life more stable due to ability to reason. | Plateau 9–10. 10–12 more abstract reasoning. | Doing things to gain acceptance; initial movement toward law and order. Faith points toward action. | Group is important. |
| Age 12–13 Preadolescent | Wide range of individual differences. | Strong emotional life. Moody, self-conscious. Need for peer acceptance is becoming very important. | Both concrete and abstract reasoning possible. | Continuation of previous levels. Continuous movement toward law and order. Faith is related to objective information about religious persons. | Hero and heroine identification strong. Team effort important. |
| Adolescent 14–18 | Differences continue. Psychosexual development is occurring. | Insecurity and sometimes "know it all" attitude prevail. Over-sensitivity is common. | Problem solving and self-awareness are prevalent. Idealism and justice issues are important. | Continuation of above, plus awareness of rights of others and personal values. Faith takes on an inter-personal focus. | Maturing friendships. Strong peer influence. |

This chart briefly points to developmental phases of child and adolescent growth. While different levels are tagged with specific ages this does not mean that every five-year-old or nine-year-old is going through all the developmental stages of five- or nine-year-olds at a particular age. It merely means that many children in a certain age bracket share many of the same developmental characteristics.

*Picture the age group you catechize. Study the charts presented. Use the table below to name specific actions which you have noticed which are similar to the characteristics on the chart. If you catechize adults, use your own experience to fill in the table.*
*Example: Primary child = Physical—cannot sit still very long.*

| Age | Physical | Emotional | Intellectual | Moral/Faith Social |
|-----|----------|-----------|--------------|--------------------|
|     |          |           |              |                    |
|     |          |           |              |                    |
|     |          |           |              |                    |

### 3) Phases of Development, Faith and Catechesis

The implications of understanding developmental psychology and faith growth are important for planning. For instance, the preschool catechists will be successful if they plan many and varied short activities, some of which should include physical activity. The love of God, people and animals should be the focus of the faith dimension of the time spent together in catechetical sessions. Stories which call for participation through gestures are appropriate for these high energy children. Stories such as the Good Samaritan or how Jesus loved children, or vivid, up-beat phrases from the psalms such as "Shout to God with cries of joy!" can be used effectively.

Sharing is an important moral characteristic to work on with preschool children. Having large sugar cookies which need to be shared is but one way to give the youngsters an experience of sharing.

Sharing crayons or markers is another way to provide opportunities for cooperation and self-giving.

Prayer should revolve around praise and thanksgiving. The preschool catechist will be very ineffective if he or she talks too much, makes the children sit too long, presents content which cannot possibly be understood or makes children memorize adult prayers. Learning to pray simply is important. Initiating a child into how to talk to God in prayer is appropriate. Prayers like "Jesus, I love you," "Help me to be good," are easy forms to help little ones begin to pray. Thanking God for food is another way to help a child develop a prayer life. Preschoolers can be taught basic communal prayers such as the Sign of the Cross and the Glory Be. The latter should be taught with gestures and a lot of time should not be spent trying to explain it. Let it be simply a prayer of praise to God. Both of these prayers begin to get children in touch with the Trinitarian mystery which will constantly unfold.

Successful primary catechists also take into account the high activity level of their children, but they can begin to introduce brief, quiet periods into the children's experience. Thirty seconds of closing one's eyes and thanking God in one's heart is appropriate for a primary child. The child is slightly less egocentric than the preschool child and is now becoming somewhat more aware of others' needs. Reinforcing sharing one's possessions is important. Dramatic skits based on simple Gospel stories are appropriate activities for this age group, as are demonstrations of ways to show kindness and caring to others. Such activities help the primary child become aware of the stories which nourish the community.

Intermediate-grade children have more control over their energies and are experiencing greater emotional stability than those of primary youngsters. This is due to their increased ability to reason. Early on in this middle grade period they like doing things to gain the acceptance of adults. Their faith life is enriched by the stories and rituals of the tradition as well as by actions. They like making surprises for people like elderly shut-ins or singing as a group at the local nursing home. They take pride in ecological projects. Children at this level have a sense of justice that is based on law and order. Not lying, stealing, cheating, fighting or disobeying authorities need to be reinforced as well as positive efforts to show love of one's neighbor.

Pre-adolescent children experience a wide range of physical differences. Some will enter puberty as much as three years before others.

With the onslaught of puberty comes a strong emotional life. This is often accompanied by periods of moodiness and self-consciousness. At this stage law and order take on new importance in terms of moral development. Faith growth is related to new information about religious ideas. Particularly appealing are new facts about religious heroes and heroines. This is related to the hero-heroine identification which pre-teens have with rock stars or TV celebrities. Group projects are effective for this age.

Adolescents continue to experience many changes. Emotional changes accompany biological changes in early adolescence. Many teens also go through a phase of negativism where they are "bored" and there is "nothing to do around here." This phase often opens up to a time when they begin to discover others as "others." Romantic "crushes" are common during these times. Adolescents often become awakened to justice issues and attack institutions for not being very concerned about justice. For many reasons teens sometimes become distant from the institutional Church and prefer to reinvent Church to suit themselves. Effective catechesis at this stage will include both social justice projects as well as insights into self-understanding, spirituality and connectedness to the larger community.

> *Name key catechetical experiences which you think would be appropriate for the youth with whom you work.*
> *Explain the reason you think these will be effective catechetical approaches for the age group with whom you are working. What imaginative approaches could you take in working with young people to help them see how faith enhances their lives?*

### 4) Adult Catechesis

Catechesis is a lifelong process. Adults are capable of a full response in faith, which keeps on growing. They have the maturity to understand more deeply than younger people the mysteries of God, the redeeming Christ and the Spirit and to witness these mysteries in their lives. While there has been an increase in adult participation in formation activities, such as parent and family programs, marriage enrichment programs, Rite of Christian Initiation of Adults process, small groups and some Bible study, there is still a great deal more that should happen (NCD 9, 40). Because of the complexities of daily life, the sophistication of knowledge, and the vast amount of change that is happening, interpreting the signs of the times in light of the Gospels is a challenge most fitting for adults.

Most people agree that there needs to be much more adult catechesis, but these same people wring their hands and say, but how can we get people to come to them? Because adults are very busy, with many events and causes begging for their time, adult catechetical activities must be well-planned and well-marketed. The following ten principles provide a useful framework to examine what contributes to successful adult catechesis.

1.  Adults are attracted to programs or activities when they are treated with respect and made to feel that they have something to contribute. Adults come with a wealth of experience and knowledge. They do not come to have "religion pumped into them," but rather to have faith drawn out of them and augmented in the process.
2.  Adults learn best when they can build on their past experience. They are willing to change when they can better understand from whence they are coming and to where they are going. Seeing faith as a journey propelled by the message and mission of Jesus Christ and sustained by the Holy Spirit adults can embrace the voyage, especially if they know they are not alone on the trip.
3.  Adults are motivated to participate when they have been part of planning the activity. A representative group of adults must be invited to plan adult catechetical activities. If one can get the various "movers and shakers" in the parish to help plan activities that meet the needs of the different groups the programs will succeed in terms of participation.
4.  Adults become active participants when they are physically comfortable and can socialize with others. There is nothing worse than holding an adult session for twenty-five people in a school cafeteria that seats three hundred and calls for the adults to climb over attached benches to sit at tables! Or an equal nightmare is having adults sit in a fourth-grade classroom—at desks designed for ten-year-olds!
5.  Adults are attracted to programs where they can be with their peers and learn freely. Overly structured programs will not be effective. Adult programs need to do the same thing as other catechetical programs: build community, proclaim the message in a way that is

insightful and motivational, lead people to prayer and empower
people to serve, to continue to build God's kingdom.

6. Adults appreciate a variety of learning experiences. Some like to
   read and will do so between sessions. Some like a lot of interaction
   and small group processes. Others like input and quiet time. Some
   like visual learning and will get a great deal from videos. Some like
   to participate by doing things, such as learning about effective
   liturgical environments and then creating them, or learning about
   the homeless and then doing something to change their plight.

7. Adults do well in situations where there are problems to be solved
   and tasks to be done. In this regard parent support groups are effective especially for pre-teen and adolescent parent groups. Adults,
   too, have intellectual curiosities about their faith. When theologies
   can be presented in a way that addresses their questions and felt
   needs, people will participate. If the programs are done well, people
   will come back for more theological formation.

8. Adults will continually participate in programs where they can see
   some immediate results. These can be in terms of skills or self-
   assessment. Knowledge of the adult development life cycle is a
   must for every adult catechist. Parents raising small children have
   different needs than parents raising adolescents and both of these
   groups have different needs from the "empty nesters" or senior citizens. Space does not permit a presentation of adult development
   here, but many resources, including the Whiteheads' books listed
   on page 29, are available for the catechist to use to understand adult
   formation cycles.

9. Adults react favorably when "religion" or "spirituality" helps them
   integrate their lives and when it is not something added on top of
   everything else. Adults are open to a catechesis which helps them
   answer their "real life questions" in a way that is related to their
   experience. They are receptive to liturgical studies or biblical studies, especially when they are done in such a way that adds insights
   and answers real questions.

10. Adults participate when the barriers to participation are eliminated.
    One of the major barriers is scheduling problems. Offering the
    same sessions at two different times is one way to help alleviate
    that problem. For parents, another obstacle is child care. Or again,
    parents feel they have to rush home from work to feed their family
    before they come out. Successful programs that include parents

provide a light supper and child care at the site of the meetings. Sometimes it is the senior citizens, "empty nesters" and high schoolers that can be called upon to help with child care. This takes a big burden off parents. Schedulers should realize that senior citizens often prefer afternoon rather than evening meetings. Cost and transportation can also be barriers to participation. Eliminating the barriers and planning excellent programs which meet the needs of the people insure greater participation.

> *What is the demographic make-up of your parish? What needs do you think each group has? How would you verify your assessment?*
> *What barriers does your parish have that are keeping your parish from attracting people to adult catechetical activities? How can these be eliminated?*
> *How would you recruit people to help you plan adult formation activities?*
> *From the list of principles given above, name the three which you think are most important. Why?*

## 5) Catechesis Integrates Community, Message, Service and Prayer

The goal of catechesis is to help people grow in faith. This is accomplished by building community, proclaiming the message, leading people to pray and motivating them to serve others (NCD 229). Jesus is a good example of someone who led people to be more faith-filled by integrating community, message, service and prayer. Jesus was a holistic catechist. When he catechized he did not separate the "content" from the "process" or the methodology. He preached and taught by answering people's real questions.

When asked "Who is my neighbor?" Jesus did not give an academic dissertation. He told a story "...a certain man was walking down to Jericho..."(Luke 10:30–37). By using stories, dialogue and discussion, Jesus got people to answer some questions for themselves. In one sense Jesus sensed that "the answers" were already in the hearts and minds of the people to whom he proclaimed the message. Instead of being a "total answer man" he led people to answers by asking the right questions. This is the basic approach we take as catechists. We are called to help children, young people and adults answer the questions of the meaning and purpose of life by using story, scripture and tradition, and our own imaginations. Many of the scriptures are basically the written form of stories which were passed down orally for years and years. The stories were often told as a response to questions raised by children. The answers were vibrant imaginative vignettes which appealed to the imagination of the youngsters. The stories nurtured the seeds of faith in the children.

Community and the welfare of the community were important to Jesus. He saw faith rooted in the community. But in one sense he did not have to build community, it was already there. People from the same town knew each other and did many things as a community. Jesus affirmed them in this. When he knew people were tired and hungry, he had them rest, eat and visit with one another. He went to weddings and celebrated with the community. He shared meals in communal settings. Today, we often have to consciously build community among those we catechize as well as their parents.

Jesus as a catechist was a person of prayer. He prayed communally in the synagogue as all Jewish men did. He also prayed alone. Mark's gospel tells of him getting up early to pray. One has the idea that he was very busy and that the only time he could be alone for prayer was before anyone else was awake. As catechists we experience the same pressures as Jesus—everyone wanting a piece of our time. We are called to be persons of prayer; we are challenged as Jesus was to find time to pray.

Service was integral to Jesus' ministry. When he saw a need, particularly a person in need, he did everything in his power to make the person well or whole. We will be effective catechists if people see us as those who care for others and reach out to them. Besides witnessing to those in need, we are called to provide service opportunities to those we catechize. They need to be an integral part of our program.

In seeing Jesus as the model catechist, we view him as a person who considered where people were at before he began to enable them to grow in faith. He used various dialogical methods to reach people and help them discover the seeds of faith within themselves both individually and as a community.

In sum, Jesus was truly an artist in his approach. He took what he inherited, expanded it and breathed new life into it. Jesus integrated aspects of community, service and prayer as he proclaimed the message of salvation.

> *Examine the Gospel of Mark and cite the incident which you think best reflects Jesus as a holistic catechist.*
> *Explain why you think this is a good example.*

### 6) Multi-cultural Diversity in Effective Catechesis

Besides knowing the human growth characteristics of those whom you catechize it is also important to know their cultural and racial background. The effective catechist needs to be aware of gender issues as well. Each culture, race and gender contributes uniquely to society and the Church. If you find yourself in a situation where some people whom you catechize come from a different culture or race than your own, it is important to learn about their culture. Knowing the particular favorite saints, customs or holy days of the culture or race will add to your effectiveness. Beyond providing information about diversity, catechists are challenged to promote acceptance and appreciation of cultural, racial and gender diversity.

Christmas and Easter are often good times to have people share their cultural customs. Such sharing can be enriching for all in the session. If you are catechizing a group where most people have the same cultural and racial background, it is important for you to find ways to expand their horizons and introduce them to the various ways other cultures celebrate family and Church rituals. We are all part of a global society. With the Internet and many other new technologies, we can easily be in touch with people from around the world. Starting something like "Net-pals" may be a way to connect young people with their faith counterparts around the world.

The advantages of promoting diversity are multiple: those catechized begin to see things from different perspectives; they gain a greater openness to new ideas; and they learn that there can be more than one interpretation of an event or issue. This should increase creativity, flexibility and problem-solving skills.

Regarding gender diversity, research has shown that both men and women can be very effective leaders, though often they have different styles. As a catechist, it is important to encourage leadership in both sexes and empower to the degree possible all potential leadership qualities in those catechized.


## REFLECTION

Have the Bible enthroned with a lit candle next to it. Have paper and pencils for each participant.

*Presider:* God, Creator of the world, you gave us Jesus so that we might know of your love for us. Help us to appreciate Jesus' holistic approach to spreading the Good News. We ask this in the name of Jesus, our Lord and brother, through the power of the Holy Spirit.

*All:* Amen.

*Reader:* Proclaim Mark 1:14-35.

For reflection and sharing:

> *What things do I have in common with Jesus as seen in this reading?*
> *How did Jesus cope with pressure? How do I cope with pressure?*
> *What role did prayer play in the life of Jesus?*
> *How is my prayer life similar to that of Jesus? How is it different?*

Jesus proclaimed Good News to people. Have each person write a piece of "Good News" for a person in the group. Proclaim it publicly to the person. Give that person the written version of your "Good News." (Be sure all get a piece of "Good News" by drawing names or having each person gather in a circle and all give the "Good News" to the person to his/her right.)

*All:* Pray the Our Father.

*All:* Offer a sign of peace.

Sing an appropriate song.


## RESOURCES

Burghardt, Walter J., S.J. "Catechetics in the Early Church: Program and Psychology." *Living Light,* Autumn 1964, 100-108.

Hebblethwaite, Peter. *Pope John XXIII, Shepherd of the Modern World.* Garden City: Doubleday, 1985.

United States Catholic Conference. *Sharing the Light of Faith, National Catechetical Directory for Catholics in the United States.* Washington, DC: USCC, 1979.

United States Catholic Conference. *Catechism of the Catholic Church.* Washington, DC: USCC 1994.

Whitehead, Evelyn Eaton, and Whitehead, James D. *Christian Life Patterns.* New York: Doubleday, 1979.

Whitehead, Evelyn Eaton, and Whitehead, James D. *Seasons of Strength.* Garden City: Doubleday, 1984.

**QUMRAN**

THE FIRST SETTLEMENT ON THE SITE WAS
IN THE 8TH CENTURY B.C.E, AT THE TIME
OF THE KINGDOM OF JUDEA.
MEMBERS OF THE DEAD SEA SCROLLS
SECT SETTLED HERE DURING THE REIGN
OF JOHN HYRCANUS I, AT THE END OF
THE 2ND CENTURY B.C.E.
DURING THE PERIOD OF KING HEROD (37
B.C.E. - 4 B.C.E.) THE PLACE WAS ABANDONED,
BUT WAS LATER RESETTLED BY ADHERENTS
OF THE SAME SECT.
THE COMMUNITY TOOK CARE OF THE NEEDS
OF ITS MEMBERS, WHO LED A KIND OF COLLECT-
IVE WAY OF LIFE. MOST SCHOLARS IDENTIFY
THEM AS THE ESSENES, THE SECT FREQUENTLY
MENTIONED IN CONTEMPORARY AND LATER
SOURCES.
D 'RING THE WARS OF THE JEWS AGAINST
THE ROMANS (66-70 C.E.), THE PLACE WAS
CONQUERED BY THE ROMANS, AND LEFT DESERTED.

**"Yours are the heavens, yours the earth; you founded the world
and everything in it." (Ps 89:12)**

# 2
# Making Scripture Work for You

## UNDERSTANDING THE BIBLE

The Bible is the work of the Spirit working through many faith-filled and creative people. The Bible uses the imagination and the tools of many artists. Thus, the scriptures manifest both the creative power of God and the creative gifts of the inspired writers. To be an effective catechist who can paint a picture of the wonders of God for people today, one must be imbued with knowledge about the Bible and the Spirit found in the inspired writings.

The Bible is a wondrous sign of God's continual presence in human life. For catechists to be able to access the richness of the scriptures they need to be familiar with three important concepts related to the interpretation of scripture: the literal sense, the spiritual sense and the fundamentalist approach.

### 1) The Literal Sense

Sometimes people describe fundamentalists as those who interpret the Bible literally, but that is not what the Church means by interpreting the scriptures from the literal perspective. The literal interpretation of scripture in the Church refers to understanding what the authors wanted to convey and what God wanted to communicate to people (CCC 110-116). To be able to understand the meaning the authors of the various books had in mind, we need to know the words they chose but in the context of the culture and history of the times in which they lived, the kind (genre) of literature they were writing and the familiar expressions or idioms of the time.

### a) History and culture

In 1943 Pope Pius XII wrote an encyclical called *Divino Afflante Spiritu* which affirmed the scholarship of the prior fifty years and encouraged further biblical research on the Church. Since that time scripture scholars have given us many insights into the history and culture of various biblical times. Studies especially during these last fifty years have led the researchers to understand in more depth what was happening at the time certain books were written. For example, between 1947 and 1956, what has come to be known as the Dead Sea Scrolls were discovered in Israel. Some of the manuscripts date back to 225 B.C. They contain an ancient manuscript of the book of Isaiah and a wide range of other texts common to the Jewish community who lived in the area. Such discoveries allow scholars to better understand and appreciate the culture and history of the times in which the various parts of the Bible were either written or collected and edited.

While the Bible is bound as one book, it does not have one author, nor was it written at one time. The Old Testament, or First Testament, covers events which happened over a period close to two thousand years. Most of the Old Testament was written in Hebrew, but parts of it were composed in Aramaic and Greek. The New or Second Testament was written, for the most part, in the last half of the first century, and in Greek. None of us need to know Hebrew, Aramaic or Greek to appreciate the work of the researchers, because now much of the academic work has been summarized for us in English and is available in biblical commentaries or personal study editions of the Bible. It is important to refer to the commentaries before using the Bible to catechize.

### b) Literary forms

Besides looking at the history and culture of the Bible, scholars also have analyzed the Bible from a literary perspective. The Bible is like a mini-library. It contains poetry, short stories, myths (profound truths in story form), love songs, historical accounts, songs of praise and gratitude, laments, scoldings from the prophets, proverbs, letters, biographical sketches, sayings, and still other forms of writing. Most parts of the Bible were first shared orally. Before they were ever written down, stories were passed down from generation to generation, shared at meals and told around the campfire at night. Literary devices such as repetition, exaggeration, humor, allegory, comparisons and parables are found throughout the Bible. The authors of the various parts used whatever creative elements they could to get their points across and inspire others to believe in an all-caring God.

The Bible does not contain scientific studies or history in the strict sense of the word. This does not mean that the people mentioned in the Bible did not live or that the events described did not happen. There is historical evidence that Abraham, Moses, David, Solomon, the prophets, and others played a very important place in Jewish history. However, the purpose of the Bible is to nurture faith, not to give historically accurate details. It is to help people see God's presence in their everyday lives. It is to disclose the mystery of God in human life so that people of every age can recognize and respond to God's presence.

An example of the scholars' contribution can be found in how they have helped us understand the creation stories in the book of Genesis. Recall that there are two stories of creation. One begins in the first chapter of Genesis and goes until chapter 2, verse 4. It contains the familiar passages: "God said: Let the waters…come together…and God saw that it was good. God said: Let the earth produce vegetation…and God saw that it was good." Its seven-day pattern is intended to stress the duty of sabbath rest. The second story, which begins in Genesis 2:4, tells another story of creation, the story of the garden and Adam's and Eve's sin and expulsion. These are very different stories.

The scholars examined the literary forms of these and other stories and began to notice similarities and differences. They began to date works and to name certain styles and narrative patterns that they discovered throughout the first five books of the Bible. They referred to the origins of these patterns as "sources." One source they called the "Yahwist" because this source referred to God as Yahweh. This is the oldest written source for the scriptures and was probably written around 900 B.C. The Yahwist tradition is reflected in the second creation story (Genesis 2:5–25) in which God is seen walking in the garden, creating plants and animals and creating and talking to Adam and Eve. It reflects a God who is very much like a human person, admittedly a super-human one, a God who is very close to people.

The "newer" story, written perhaps in the sixth or seventh century before Christ, three or four hundred years after the oldest story, actually appears first in the book of Genesis (1-2:4). Here we see God's Word as powerful. God says…and it happens. This story comes from a source the scholars call "Priestly." One can imagine Genesis 1-2:4 being used in a liturgical litany. The cantor might sing, "And God said, 'let there be light.'" The congregation might respond, "and there was light." In sharp contrast to the Yahwist account, this story reflects God's transcendence—that is, God is above us, not walking in a garden with us. This was written at a time when the Israelites were enduring hard times and were living in exile. At this time the Israelites did not experience God as very close to them, even though they knew God was still their God and cared a lot about them.

Neither of these stories represents a scientific or historical account of creation. But both contain theological truths about creation—for instance, that God is responsible for all creation and that people are a very special part of God's creation. One story presents the transcendent side of God, where God is powerful and above us. The other reflects a God who is right here with us, walking and interacting with us. Both of these stories contain important truths found in Christian teaching about God. Both are true. Both are incomplete without the other.

Examine each story of creation: the older (Genesis 2:5–25) and the newer (Genesis 1–2:4).

> *What truths can you name in each story?*
> *Where do you find scientific inconsistencies, at least as we know them today?*
> *Can you describe any insights you have gotten from briefly looking at two different literary styles?*
> *What creative approaches can you suggest for helping those you catechize see the value in understanding how the scriptures were formed?*

### c) Words and expressions

In the study of literary styles and historical and cultural references related to the Bible, researchers have often found that words have different meanings today than they did at the time they were written. For instance, for people who know anything about baseball, the expression that five people died on base is not alarming (unless it happens to the team for whom you are cheering!). But people who have never heard of baseball might think that we play a game and leave people dying on base. Sports headlines provide endless examples of such non-literal use of words. Some of these same kinds of misunderstandings have occurred in our understanding of the Bible.

In Mark's gospel there is a reference to Jesus' "brothers" and "sisters" (Mark 6:3). Again scholarship has explained that in the Jewish vocabulary at the time of Jesus, the words *brothers* and *sisters* did not necessarily mean blood brothers and sisters, but could also include nephews, nieces and cousins. Indeed, there was no popular word for *cousin.* In another passage, where Jesus talks about it being easier for a camel to get through the eye of a needle than for a rich man to get into heaven (Mark 10:25), some scholars think that Jesus may have been referring to an old gate in Jerusalem which was called the "eye of a needle." This gate was just large enough for someone to walk through, but not to come through on a donkey or camel.

An example of misinterpretation that has shown up for centuries concerning sculpture is the word "horned" which was used to describe Moses when he came down the mountain. Because the term was misunderstood, great sculptors like Michelangelo in the sixteenth century and Mestrovic in the mid-twentieth created statues with Moses having horns growing out of his head. Today, because of the work of scripture scholars, we know that the author in Exodus was telling us that Moses came down the mountain with rays of light around his head, not horns!

Much more could be said about the literal interpretation of the scriptures. Biblical scholars are continually sharing their insights and their work with us. It is important for us as catechists to be informed about the intended meaning of the scriptures when they were written. In the *Catechism of the Catholic Church,* the Church cites St. Thomas Aquinas' reminder that all interpretations of scripture are based on the literal. That is, what the inspired authors intended to communicate in selecting those words (CCC 116).

### 2) The Spiritual Sense

Generally speaking, the spiritual sense of scripture can be understood, according to the Pontifical Biblical Commission, as interpreting the scriptures under the influence of the Holy Spirit in light of Jesus' death and resurrection (CCC 117). The *Catechism of the Catholic Church* uses the spiritual sense of scriptures throughout its four parts. The spiritual reading of scripture especially uses a method called typology. Typology interprets everything in light of some major event, such as the exodus or the paschal mystery. For example, the story of the crossing of the Red Sea in the Moses story may be structured like another event, and thus be seen as a sign or type of Christ's resurrection and ultimately Christian baptism. Similar patterns and elements form the "type." The manna from heaven found in Exodus is seen as a type or prefigurement of the Eucharist. The New Testament is seen as the fulfillment of the Hebrew Scriptures. Jesus fulfills what the prophets promised. For Christians, the spiritual interpretation of the scriptures is always seen in light of the resurrection. It is like saying, "now it makes sense," or "now I get it." Or, as the modern idiom puts it, it interprets meaning from "hindsight."

The moral sense is another aspect of spiritual interpretation of the Bible. By this we mean that what is written is there for our moral instruction. In liturgy we believe that God is speaking to us through the scripture readings. In other words the Word of God is alive and is speaking to us today as God spoke to people centuries ago.

> *Read and reflect on the readings for next Sunday's liturgy. Using a scriptural commentary or personal study edition of the Bible, learn something about the literal meaning of the texts. Choose several verses which strike you as particularly meaningful at this time in your life. Think about what God is saying to you today in the texts that were written many centuries ago. Use the following questions to aid your reflections:*
>> *What do I have in common with the first people who heard this text?*
>> *How am I different than those who first heard the passage?*
>> *What is God calling me to in the passage?*
>> *In what creative ways can I use the spiritual sense of scripture with those I catechize?*
>> *How can I help make the passages come alive for today's people?*
>> *How will I respond to God?*

### 3) Fundamentalist Interpretation

Fundamentalism began at the time of the Reformation. It had a new spurt of growth in 1895 in the United States at the American Biblical Congress. Its roots are Protestant, but it has influenced Catholics and has spread around the world. The fundamentalist interpretation of the Bible is not the way the Catholic Church explains the scriptures.

The fundamentalist approach sometimes excludes the scholars' research. It excludes any sense of history by ignoring the historical evolution of the text itself as well as the historical context of its original expression. In short, the fundamentalist approach does not look at the historical origins of the texts. Nor does it take into account the literary form used. It explains the meaning of passages only in terms of what the words literally mean today.

Fundamentalism, for example, portrays God creating the world in seven days of 24 hours, as we understand them. Fundamentalists believe that the flood in the Noah story actually covered the whole earth and that Noah and his family were the only human beings saved. Such an interpretative method does not allow for symbolic meanings of scriptural passages. It assumes that all details of the Bible are historically and scientifically accurate. In addition, fundamentalism does not take into account the development of the Gospel tradition. The *Catechism of the Catholic Church* (CCC 126) tells us that there were three stages in the formation of the Gospels: (1) the life and teaching of Jesus during his life on earth, (2) the oral tradition, in other words, the preaching of the Apostles after the Resurrection; that is what was passed down by word of mouth for twenty-five to thirty years before much was written; (3) the individual accounts which we call the Gospels, written by different people, for different communities over a period of thirty to forty years, each with a slightly different portrait of the life and ministry of Jesus. In *The Interpretation of the Bible in the Church,* the Pontifical Biblical Commission states that because fundamentalism fails "to take into account the historical character of biblical revelation, it makes itself incapable of accepting the full truth of the Incarnation itself. As regards relationships with God, fundamentalism seeks to escape any closeness of the divine and the human."

The Pontifical Biblical Commission summarizes the hazards of fundamentalism in a poignant way:

> "The fundamentalist approach is dangerous, for it is attractive to people who look to the Bible for ready answers to the problems of life. It can deceive these people, offering them interpretations that are pious but illusory, instead of telling them that the Bible does not necessarily contain an immediate answer to each and every problem. Without saying as much in so many words, fundamentalism actually invites

people to a kind of intellectual suicide. It injects into life a false certitude, for it unwittingly confuses the divine substance of the biblical message with what are in fact its human limitations" (quoted from *Origins,* January 6, 1994, p. 510).

Young people today are especially vulnerable to those who are committed to fundamentalism both on high school as well as college campuses. Catechists need to be aware of the dangers of fundamentalism and help those they catechize to be aware of them also.

*Examine the following passages.*
*Read a biblical commentary to get a better understanding of the literal sense which the Church promotes.*
*Think of how the passage might be interpreted from a spiritual sense.*
*How would a fundamentalist interpret the passage?*
*Use the following chart to guide your reflections.*
*Share the differences you find in these approaches.*

| Passage | Literal Sense | Spiritual Sense | Fundamentalist Approach |
|---|---|---|---|
| Genesis 6:5–7:23 | (Example) Similar to ancient Near Eastern story; different in that it portrays God as just, loving and caring. This is the theological truth of the story, which is not dependent on the flood which is said to have covered the whole earth. | (Example) God saves us through the water of Baptism. Even when things look bad, God is with us caring for us | (Example) We need to try and find out where the ark is so we know where the flood actually happened. |
| Compare Exodus 13:17–14:31 and Exodus 13:1–16 | | | |
| Matthew 13:36–43 | | | |

## BRIEF HISTORY OF THE ISRAELITES

It is impossible here to do justice to the history of the Israelite people. But highlighting some important events can be helpful for those involved in catechesis. The term Old Testament and the abbreviation B.C. were commonly used to describe the biblical writings before the time of Christ. Today two other expressions are also found to describe the same realities. Out of a sensitivity to the Jewish people, some scripture scholars now refer to the Old Testament as the First Testament and the New Testament as the Second Testament. Instead of using B.C. to describe the time before Christ they use B.C.E., which means "before the common era." "C.E." is used to describe what used to be called A.D., the time after Christ or the common era.

The following outline gives a brief history of Israel. It is based on *The New Jerome Bible Handbook.*

    I.    The Patriarchal period: 2000–1700 B.C.E.
        Abraham and Sarah
        Isaac and Jacob
        Joseph
        Twelve tribes of Israel

    II.    The Exodus and Movement to the Promised Land: 1300–1050 B.C.E.
        Moses
        Joshua
        Judges

    III.    Early Kings of Israel: 1020–587 B.C.E.
        Saul–1020 B.C.E.
        David—1000 B.C.E. Beginning of the building of the Temple
        Solomon—960 B.C.E. Temple is finished

    IV.    The Kingdom of Israel is divided into Judah and Israel, the Southern and the Northern Kingdom. The division occurs shortly after Solomon's rule.

| Judah | Israel |
| --- | --- |
| Fall of Jerusalem 587 B.C.E. | Fall of Samaria 721 B.C.E. |

    V.    The Exile 587–539 B.C.E.

   VI.   Persian era 539–333 B.C.E.

  VII.   The Greek era 333–63 B.C.E.
         Alexander the Great
         Maccabean revolt

 VIII.   Roman influence in Palestine 63–37 B.C.E.

   IX.   Herod the Great 37–4 B.C.E.

    X.   Herod Antipas 4 B.C.–39 C.E.

## THE BOOKS OF THE OLD TESTAMENT

Besides a thumbnail sketch of the history of Israel, it is also important to have a brief overview of the various parts of the Old Testament.

### 1) Pentateuch or Torah

The first five books of the Bible are called the Pentateuch or the Torah. They include the books of Genesis, Exodus, Leviticus, Numbers and Deuteronomy. *Torah* is the Hebrew word for instruction. The first five books of the Bible are very important especially to the Jewish people because they tell of the promises made to the patriarchs, the liberation out of Egypt, God's presence with the people in the wilderness, the revelation of the Law on Sinai and God's guidance into the promised land. The Pentateuch is significant because through its various literary forms it contains God's relationship to Israel, as especially seen in the Law; the covenant or promise God made with the people to be with them into the future; the way God wished to be worshipped (human sacrifice was not acceptable); the rebellious nature of people and the divine redemption; and the beginnings of the Judeo-Christian tradition.

> Read each passage below and reflect on it.
> Use a scripture commentary to learn more about the times in which it was written and its original meaning.
> What theological message or insight do you get from the passage?

| Passage | Theological Meaning/Insight |
|---|---|
| Example: Genesis 12:1–21 | God calls us to take risks and blesses us and supports us when we do. |
| Exodus 20:1–17 | |
| Leviticus 25:8–12 | |
| Numbers 6:24–27 | |
| Deuteronomy 22:1–4 | |

### 2) The Historical Books

The historical books are not history as we know it today, but these books have fragments of historical events which helped to form the people of ancient Israel. The historical books include (but are not limited to): Joshua, Judges, Ruth, Samuel, Kings, Chronicles, Ezra, Judith, and Maccabees. Joshua through Kings tells of the Israelites' existence in the promised land from Joshua to the exile. The other historical books reflect aspects of the time from the exile to the first century before Christ, ending with the Maccabean rebellion. These books render descriptions of the Hebrew people's relationship to God rather than exact political or social history. Not all have the same degree of historical content. Some, like Ruth or Judith, seem to be shaped by the moral message they teach. They all reinforced the rewards of fidelity to God's law and belief in God's saving presence.

> *Read the following passages.*
> *Reflect on them.*
> *Use a study edition of the Bible or a commentary to give you insights into the meaning of the passage.*
> *What are the passages telling you about God's relationship to the people?*

### 3) The Prophets

The prophetic books include but are not limited to the following: Isaiah, Jeremiah, Ezekiel, Daniel, Hosea, Joel, Amos, Malachi, Micah,

| Passage God's | Relationship to the People |
|---|---|
| 1 Samuel 10:1 | |
| 2 Samuel 22:1–4 | |
| Ruth 1:16–18 | |

Jonah and Lamentations. Prophetic literature is very important in our tradition. The primary thing that the prophets did was not to foretell the future but rather to interpret the mind and will of God to the people, always reminding them of the covenant God made through Moses and the people's call to be faithful to that covenant. The prophets' means of communication with God often involved dreams, visions, or mystical experiences. The messages include strong judgements and condemnations as well as promises of deliverance and prosperity.

*Read the following passages.*
*Get additional insights from reading a scripture commentary.*
*What is the prophet communicating to the people?*

| Passage | Message about God and God's Expectations to the People |
|---|---|
| Isaiah 1:18–20 | |
| Isaiah 40:1,35 | |
| Jeremiah 31:31–33 | |
| Hosea 11:1–4 | |

### 4) The Wisdom Books

The Wisdom literature in the Bible consists of the books of Job, Psalms, Proverbs, Ecclesiastes, the Canticle of Canticles, Wisdom and Sirach. Wisdom literature was common in the ancient world of Egypt and Mesopotamia. Its basic characteristic is that it deals with life and how to lead a good and prosperous life. To do that one must have an essential relationship to God which is based on "fear of the Lord." Wisdom literature is full of pithy sayings such as: pride goes before the fall (Proverbs 16:18); laziness is at the basis of poverty (Proverbs 10:4); and there is a time to be born and a time to die (Ecclesiastes 3:2). The book of Psalms is also part of Wisdom literature. Some of the psalms date back to King David, about the year 1000 B.C. The psalms were sung prayers often used in liturgical prayer settings.

> *Find three phrases in the Psalms that show that the psalmist was having a terrific day.*
> *Find three phrases in the Psalms that indicate the psalmist was having an awful day.*
> *What is the underlying significance of this?*
> *Examine the book of Proverbs and find three pithy statements with which you agree and three that you question.*
> *How would you rewrite the ones you question to better reflect your beliefs?*

The beauty and depth of the Old or First Testament takes a lifetime to pursue. These brief comments are meant to whet the reader's and catechist's appetite for more. See the list of resources at the end of this chapter to continue your journey into God's Word.

## INSPIRATION OF THE BIBLE

One basis for the fundamentalists' narrow interpretation of scripture is the fact that they do not accept the Catholic understanding of the Bible as the inspired Word of God. The Second Vatican Council reiterated the Church's teaching on the inspiration of the scriptures by saying:

> "Holy Mother Church, relying on the belief of the apostles, holds that the books of both the Old and New Testament in their entirety, ...are sacred... because, having been written under the inspiration of the Holy Spirit, they have God as their author and have been handed on as such to the Church herself" (DV 11; also quoted in CCC 105).

Having God as the author of the Bible does not mean that God dictated the words of scripture and that the human authors automatically wrote down everything that God decreed. This is the position that fundamentalism holds. What follows from that is that every word of scripture is absolutely true from all perspectives including scientific and historical accuracy. Rather, as we have said before, the scriptures were written in a very human way under the inspiration of the Holy Spirit. Therefore, they reflect the personality and education of the human author as well as the culture and experiences of the times. They contain basic theological truths. It should also be noted that the community was inspired to accept the scriptures as the Word of God in human form. The Church recognizes God's presence in the scriptures and believes that the scriptures have their origin in God and are foundational to Judaism and Christianity. The scriptures are given to us by God for our own salvation. The same Spirit of God hovers over us as we hear or read those words today.

The Church thus believes that the scriptures are not dead words, written centuries ago only for another era, but rather are "incarnate and living" (CCC 108). Under the inspiration of the Holy Spirit we are called to hear and embody the scriptures in our lives today. The Second Vatican Council indicates three criteria for interpretation of the Bible:

1. Be especially attentive "to the content and unity of the whole of Scripture."
2. Read the scripture within "the living Tradition of the whole Church."
3. Be attentive to the analogy of faith, that is, note the relationship of the truths of faith among themselves and within the whole plan of revelation and salvation (DV 12 and CCC 112–114).

## PROMOTING JUSTICE

The prophet Micah summarizes much of the Old or First Testament's call to justice when he says:

> "This is what Yahweh asks of you:
> only this, to act justly,
> to love tenderly,
> and to walk humbly with your God."
> Micah 6:8

One cannot effectively catechize from the scriptures without integrating the dimension of justice. No one is too young to be catechized on social justice issues. Such issues cannot be separated from the scriptures. They are at the heart of the Bible. Justice issues must be presented according to the age and ability of those participating in the catechetical programs. The kingdom of God is still being built and it calls for the participation of all. Contributing to soup kitchens or helping change the systems which created the need for soup kitchens are all aspects of catechetical social justice projects.

The first step in eliminating social injustice is to raise the consciousness that injustice exists. This can be done at all ages, but it must be done imaginatively so that it tugs at the heart as well as the mind. Secondly, raising consciousness is not enough. Indeed, sometimes all that does is make people feel guilty and helpless. If the plight of the poor is too overwhelming, people back away because they do not know where to begin. Catechists, parish leaders and community leaders must have specific ways people can contribute to building a more just society. Creative catechists and parish leaders provide many different kinds of opportunities. Some people may have time to spend helping others; others may have positions where they can influence public policy to be more just; others may have financial resources to contribute; still others may be the "prayers" in the community who support through intense prayer. Some may wish to work with others on justice issues. Others may feel called to work alone on a project. Some may want to protest abortion, while others may feel called to take pregnant teens into their homes and help them through difficult times.

One aspect of catechetical programs that parishes are often not effective in handling is building a more just society. The sad thing is that for many, justice has nothing to do with passing on the faith. However, our Catholic tradition tells us otherwise. Saints such as Francis of Assisi, Vincent de Paul and Louise de Marillac and many others saw the intimate connection between faith and justice. The Second Vatican Council has reemphasized the ancient obligation to work in this area. More and more opportunities to work for justice are available both for children and adults. Lastly, social justice workers need to see the connection between their efforts and their identity as Christians. This means that parishes need to be identified as seats of social justice, not just as "do-gooders" but as people who are operating out of a sense of what it means to be Church. This happens when justice efforts permeate all the ministries of the parish.

## PRACTICAL IMPLICATIONS

The Bible is a primary source for catechesis for all ages. Children as young as preschoolers can be initiated into a relationship with God through the scriptures. Senior citizens can come to new insights from biblical stories and renewed perspectives. However, it is important to use appropriate texts and to use them suitably for those catechized. Some guidelines include:

1. For preschool and primary children choose passages which do not require the child to know the culture and history of the times (literal sense) in order to appreciate the texts. Carefully use Old or First Testament stories which the child may think actually happened exactly as stated in the Bible (e.g. crossing the Red Sea, Adam and Eve story, Noah, etc.). These stories need too much explanation for the child, or the theology is too abstract for the child to comprehend. Use some verses of the psalms, especially those that sing praise and thanksgiving to God for all creation. For example, Psalm 8 can easily be used to get across the point of how wonderful God is.

2. Especially for preschool and primary children, avoid the images found in the Old or First Testament about God being a vengeful God, about God destroying the enemies of the Israelites. Again children need to have more developed intellectual capacities to understand these in the historical context. Catechists will want to avoid presenting God as a police officer who is there to punish little ones.

3. Use New or Second Testament stories such as the Good Samaritan (Luke 10:29–37) or Old Testament stories such as water in the desert (Exodus 17:2–7) to help children recognize what God expects of them. Use the story of the Good Shepherd (John 10:1–16 or Psalm 23) to remind children how much God loves them even when they do things that may be wrong. Use the infancy narratives at Christmas (Luke 2:4–20 and Matthew 2:1–12) even though, when the children are older, they can learn more about the literary style and the historical events which lead to their being written. The stories of the call of the apostles (Luke 5:1-11), some of the parables (Luke 8:4–8; Luke 13:18–19; Luke 13:20–21), the great commandment (Luke 10:27), can all be appropriate with young children. Note that not everything has to be explained to children. The scripture stories through the power of the Holy Spirit have a way of speaking to children. Sometimes all we need to do is proclaim them reverently and allow for

silence for children to think about the Word of God and ask appropriate questions.

4. Have the Bible or the Lectionary (the scripture readings organized for use in liturgy) enthroned in a prominent place where you catechize. A Lectionary for Masses with Children is a valuable resource. Next to the scriptures have a large candle in a candlestick. Light the candle in preparation for proclaiming the scriptures. The scriptures will have a primary place in communal prayer which should be part of all catechetical sessions. Your own reverence for the scriptures as a special book, the book of God's Word, will be absorbed by both children and adults. Younger children will need to have the Word proclaimed to them. With practice, older children can proclaim the Word for their peers.

5. From fifth grade on upward young people can begin to be exposed to the various literary forms, historical research, maps and other tools which will help them better appreciate scripture in the literal sense we have previously discussed. Before this time most of effective scripture interpretation will need to be based on the spiritual sense of God's Word. However, it is to the catechist's benefit to understand the literal sense by studying scripture commentaries or personal study editions of the Bible, whether the youngsters can understand that level of sophistication or not. The scriptures have so many levels of meaning that no one, not even scripture scholars, can say they totally understand them. One advantage of being a catechist is that we are constantly challenged to reflect on the Bible and come to deeper understandings of it.

6. Adolescents, besides being challenged to understand the history of the Israelites and the literary forms found in the First Testament, can and should be invited to identify with the heroes and heroines of scripture and the "feelings" of scripture. One successful catechist had the young people select verses from the psalms that reflected their own moods. The youngsters were thrilled to find out that it was OK to be in a funky mood, to be overcome with joy, to be depressed. After all, the people who walked before them and who were loved by God ages ago had the same moods, some of the same problems with relationships, and the like. As intellectually stimulating as it might be to understand some of the scholarship associated with scripture study, it is also critical to open up the spiritual sense of

scripture to our young people. This excites their imaginations and nurtures faith. This, too, is the work of the catechist-artist.

7. Most adults find it exciting to be exposed to rich scripture study that includes both the academic insights of scholars as well as the spiritual insights of the Church. For most adults it is important not just to take an academic approach but also to make the connections between scripture and everyday life, thus probing the spiritual meaning of the scriptures.

8. Some families have found it helpful to write their "family scriptures" beginning with their family tree, their rules, their prophets, their psalm/songs, their words of wisdom and their historical and spiritual journeys. They do this after reflecting on the biblical stories and readings.

To catechize means to echo God's Word. It is God's Word that is at the heart of catechesis.

## REFLECTION

Have the Bible enthroned. Light a candle before beginning the prayer service. Provide an individual taper for each participant. Individuals may wish to reflect on the reading from their own Bibles, after the reading is proclaimed in the community.

*Presider:* God, Creator of us all, you sent us Jesus Christ your living Word to be with us and to model how we are to live. Help us to appreciate the presence of your Word in our daily lives. We ask this through Christ our Lord.

*All:* Amen.

*Presider:* Introduce the reading by recalling that the story to be proclaimed is one of two creation stories to be found in Genesis. Evidence suggests that it is the younger of the two and might have been written around the year 600 B.C. The story may have been used as a litany at community prayer. Invite people to think about the image of God that comes to their mind as they listen to the story. What theological beliefs are at the heart of the reading?

*Reader:* Proclaim Genesis 1–2:4.

*After a period of silent reflection, discuss the questions suggested above and those which follow.*

*How does this reading help you to be a better catechist?*
*How does knowing something about the background of the reading (the literal sense) help you to appreciate it?*
*How can current environmental concerns be seen in light of the first chapter of Genesis?*
*What are some social outreach efforts which might flow from the story of creation?*
*How can you promote these with those whom you catechize?*
*What imaginative activities can you design for those you catechize to help them see God's presence in all of creation?*

*Presider:* God, our Creator, you have enriched us by sending your Word to live among us. Continue to enlighten us with the Word of God as we embrace the catechetical ministry. We ask this through Christ our Light who lives among us.

*All:* Amen.

*Presider:* Call each person forward. Light each taper from the large candle near the Bible. Present the lighted candle to the catechist saying, "The light shines in darkness and the darkness has not overcome it."

Have all stand in a circle around the Bible and sing an appropriate hymn.

## RESOURCES

Brown, Raymond E., Fitzmyer, Joseph A., and Murphy, Roland E. *The New Jerome Bible Handbook.* Collegeville, Minnesota: Liturgical Press, 1992.

Brown, Raymond, E., Fitzmyer, Joseph, A., and Murphy, Roland E. *The New Jerome Biblical Commentary.* Englewood Cliffs, New Jersey: Prentice-Hall, 1990.

Hiesberger, Jean Marie, general editor. *The Catholic Bible, Personal Study Edition.* NAB with Revised Psalms and Revised New Testament. New York: Oxford University Press, 1995.

**"I am the light of the world. Whoever follows me will not walk in darkness...."** (Jn 8:12)

# 3
# Exploring the Gospels

One of the roles catechists play is to proclaim the "Good News" that all people are loved and cherished by God and saved and redeemed by Jesus Christ. It takes an artistic brush stroke to be able to proclaim this effectively in today's world. The interpretation and rendering of the "Good News" in contemporary society is essential for effective catechesis. There is no one way to do this because the age of the people catechized, their experiences, their cultural background will dictate which colors and hues the catechist will use to bring meaning to the participants' life situations. The present chapter summarizes some important information and reflections about the Gospels, that catechists need to know and be engaged with before they create their "Good News" pallet.

## UNDERSTANDING THE GOSPELS

The Gospels are at the heart of catechesis. One cannot help another grow in faith without being steeped in the Gospels. The Gospels not only reflect what Jesus taught but also how he lived and how he expects us to live and act as a community. They portray Jesus' teachings, some events in his life, his relationship to God, his family, his disciples and the people who lived in his time. The word "Gospel" means "good news." It is the good news of Jesus that catechists proclaim.

The Gospels of Matthew, Mark and Luke are called the "synoptic" Gospels because they have many of the same stories and events. John's Gospel, which was the last to be written, is quite different from the synoptic Gospels. It does not have parables or exorcisms; it has fewer healing stories. John's Gospel is in some ways more abstract and symbolic than the synoptic Gospels; it is also more "typical," in the sense explained in the previous chapter.

It is important to realize that the Gospels are not strictly biographies of Jesus. No one followed Jesus around and recorded everything he said or did. For the most part, when Jesus walked the earth he was seen as a human being like others of his time. Momentarily he may have been seen as a great prophet or teacher, but he was not, for the most part, viewed as a celebrity or hero of his day. He was seen as an ordinary Jewish person. Some recognized that there was "more" to Jesus than met the eye (Mary, the woman with the hemorrhage, the folks at Cana); some found him to be insightful ("render to Caesar..."); some recognized him as a person of compassion (Zaccheus, Mary Magdalene, the apostles); some saw him as a great teacher (apostles, disciples, crowds); some saw him as a good friend (Lazarus, Martha and Mary); some saw him as a great storyteller.

Considering the time that Jesus lived on earth and recalling that there were no radios, newspapers, e-mail, televisions and World Wide Web, it is amazing that we know as much about Jesus as we do. The first Gospel was written between thirty and forty years after Jesus' death. During that time most of what was remembered about Jesus was passed on by word of mouth by those who knew Jesus or heard the preaching of the apostles. All of Paul's letters were written before the first Gospel was written. There is evidence to suggest that gradually people began to write down the sayings of Jesus so that they would not be forgotten. Paul's preaching was based primarily on what others had told him of Jesus. He had no first-hand knowledge of Jesus. The disciples conveyed the message about Jesus so forcefully and passionately that others, like St. Paul, through the work of the Spirit began to believe in Jesus and preach his message.

The fact that there are four Gospels, not one, is important for catechesis. Multiple Gospels help us to understand that the Spirit of God works through human people in different ways and develops diverse ways to express the key beliefs of the Christian people. Four Gospels mean that there was not just one memory, not just one way to express the experience of Jesus and what his life had meant. In fact, the Gospels are founded on the communal memory, experience and faith of four different communities which were drastically affected by Jesus, his mission, work and death-resurrection. Today we express faith in Jesus, his life, death and resurrection in different ways based on our experience of him and the Church. While diverse, there is still a great unity in the major tenants of the faith.

> *As a catechist, what value do you see in the fact that there are four Gospels?*
> *The Spirit of God is working through you as a catechist, empowering you to express key beliefs in Jesus Christ in such a way that helps others grow in faith. What challenges do you see in this task?*
> *How are you like the early disciples?*
> *What things are different about catechizing now, as opposed to being a catechist in the Early Church?*

## MARK'S GOSPEL

Each of the three Synoptic Gospels was written from a certain point of view, for a particular audience and at a specific time in history. According to modern scripture scholars, Mark's Gospel was the first to be written and is the shortest. Some think that the author was John Mark, a disciple of Peter and a cousin of Barnabas. Others propose that the author is an unknown Hellenistic Jewish Christian from Syria.

Mark's Gospel is vivid in detail and almost breathless in pace. It is a dramatic narrative, probably written for Gentiles in Rome after the persecutions of Nero about 64 C.E. During that time some Roman Christians had been martyred, others had abandoned the faith out of fear of persecution. Mark is determined to let the reader know in a compelling way that Jesus is the Son of God whom God sent to save humanity. Salvation took place, according to Mark, by Jesus serving God in building up the Kingdom and consequently giving up his life for others. This is the good news that appears in Mark 1:1.

> *To get a flavor for this Gospel, read Mark 1:16–35. Describe some of the events that must have left Jesus very tired.*
> *Why do you think Jesus had to get up early to pray?*
> *Describe one of your busy days.*
> *When do you manage to get a few quiet minutes to pray?*
> *In what ways are your busy days and Jesus' very much alike?*

Mark's Gospel often shows Jesus in conflict with his opponents and with the demons. Jesus challenged the powers of the world. His challenge against evil put him in conflict with many in his day. This conflict ultimately led to his death on the cross.

### 1) Messianic Secret

One of the theological threads found throughout Mark's Gospel concerns the question of who Jesus is. In Mark 8:29 the question is very direct. Mark has various people answer the question, but usually the people closest to Jesus are not the ones who know who he is. For Mark the answer is: Jesus is the Son of God and the Messiah. As a good storyteller, Mark, however, always has people silenced after they give the answer about who Jesus is. This adds suspense to drama. Mark's use of this literary technique is often called the "messianic secret." In other words, it is almost like someone "let the cat out of the bag" before Mark was ready, so they are told to keep quiet. But just to be sure the reader gets the point, Mark reveals the secret several times.

### 2) Healings and Exorcisms

Mark's Gospel is full of healings and exorcisms (the casting out of the devil or evil powers). It is important to understand such phenomena in the context of the first century. Much of what appeared to be evil was understood at the time of Jesus to be the work of the devil or demons. Many things which today we might attribute to psychological or physical health problems were seen as the work of the devil. Because Jesus came to free people from anything that was getting in the way of building the rule or kingdom of God, Jesus went to battle against the evil spirits. The evil spirits according to Mark realize that they are in conflict with "the Holy One of God" when they meet Jesus and know they are powerless before him. Typically, as a result of their encounter with Jesus, they leave the possessed person. The person is thus freed from inner compulsions or forces and "saved" to be a disciple.

Today in some ways we are just beginning to see the connection between "spirit" and "body" in our own lives. One can hardly pick up a piece of literature on health without some new discovery about the "spirit-mind-body" connection. Positive imaging is said to contribute to the cure or remission of cancer, the lowering of blood pressure, or relief from stress. As part of the healing process Jesus gives people a glimpse of what could be—a positive image of the rule or kingdom of God—and consequently whatever had infected their afflicted bodies is gone. This is not to dismiss healings or miracles, but rather to put them in a context with which we can identify. For Mark, Jesus is a power for good, one who does everything he can to alleviate conditions that are caused by fear, by the evil viruses of his time and by lack of vision. In such a context Jesus does miraculous deeds.

### 3) Discipleship

Discipleship is very important to Mark. Jesus calls the disciples in the first chapter of Mark's Gospel. The disciples often have a hard time knowing who Jesus is and what he is about. At the crucifixion, they ultimately abandon Jesus. For Mark, however, at least in the longer ending found in some manuscripts of the Gospel, there is a moment of reconciliation between Jesus and the disciples when the messenger at the tomb tells the women to go tell the disciples and Peter that Jesus has been raised from the dead and that he will see them in Jerusalem.

It is good to read Mark's Gospel in one sitting, without interruption. That way the drama is apparent. Think of it as divided into these parts: The desert: Mark 1:1–13; the Galilean ministry, 1:14–8:21; the journey to Jerusalem, 8:27—10:52; and the death-resurrection, 11:1–16:8. Use the map to follow Jesus' journey.

> *After reading Mark's Gospel, reflect on the following questions:*
> *What phrases best describe for you Mark's Gospel?*
> *As a catechist, how are you most like Mark?*

## MATTHEW'S GOSPEL

Although Matthew's Gospel is the first that appears in the Bible, it was not the first to be written. It was probably written between the years 70 C.E. and 90 C.E. and not by the Matthew who was an apostle, but by a Jewish Christian who had training as a rabbi (or at least was well trained by rabbis). The Gospel was written in Greek, probably in Antioch or Syria, for Jewish Christians. Matthew's goal was to keep connecting Jesus back to the Jewish law and tradition, so that the people could see that Jesus was the long awaited Messiah, the son of

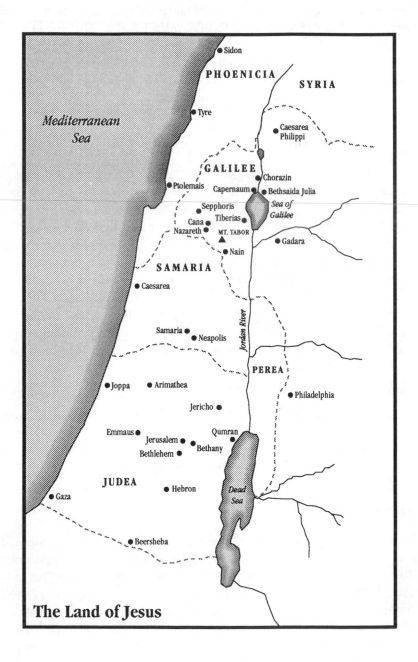

**The Land of Jesus**

David, the fulfillment of the First or Old Testament prophecies. While Mark wrote for the Gentiles and emphasized Jesus, actions (healings, exorcisms), Matthew wrote for Jewish Christians and focuses primarily on Jesus' teachings. Yet, while Matthew is writing for Jews, he is also telling them that Jesus came for all people. While Mark was the great dramatic storyteller, Matthew is the teacher, the catechist.

Matthew knew of Mark's Gospel. He includes about ninety percent of what is in Mark. But Matthew had another source too. Both Matthew and Luke seem to draw on an additional source which scripture scholars call "Q." The "Q" source takes its name from the German word Quelle which means "source." It was probably a collection of sayings and parables of Jesus which Mark either ignored or did not have access to. The theory of two sources for Matthew and Luke helps in the explanation of so many similarities, yet differences in the Gospels.

> *Explore the beginning of Matthew's and Mark's Gospels.*
> *Compare Mark 1:1–8 with Matthew 1:2–18 and 3:1–4.*
> *How are they different?*
> *How are they alike?*
> *Recalling the purposes of each Gospel, why do you think each writer started the way he did?*

If we had only Mark's Gospel, what would be missing from the passages noted above?

The first part of Matthew's Gospel gives us some clues about what Matthew is about. At the time of Matthew's writing, two struggles were challenging the early Jewish-Christian community. First, there were tensions between the Jewish and the Jewish-Christian communities. The Jews were beginning to accuse the Jewish-Christians of infidelity to God's law. Second, the Jewish-Christians were struggling with how to incorporate the newly converted Gentiles into the community. The fundamental question was, "Did the Gentiles have to become Jews before they could become Christians?" In fact the first council of the Church was centered on that question, with Peter and Paul on opposite sides of the issue. The ultimate answer to the question was, "No, one did not need to become a Jew before one could be a Christian" (Galatians 2:1–21; also see Acts 15).

The incorporation of the Gentiles into the Gospel of Matthew is seen as early as Chapter 2 with the visit of the Gentile Magi or astrologers and the flight into Egypt. The Gentile Magi come to worship

Jesus. This makes the "establishment" people very nervous, to the point of seeking to kill the one who appears to be a threat to their power. Jesus escapes his hostile homeland to the safety of Gentile Egypt. Even when it is secure enough to return to Israel, Joseph, Mary and Jesus do not go near the capital, Jerusalem, but rather to a safer Galilee, a Jewish territory where many Gentiles lived.

## JESUS AS TEACHER AND CATECHIST

Volumes have been written about what Jesus taught, but here only five major themes from Matthew will be suggested as a point of reference.

### 1) The Sermon on the Mount

The first serious teaching is found in what is called the Sermon on the Mount and the related passages which prepare for and follow it (Matthew 4:17–7:29). In these chapters, which are a collection of sayings of Jesus, Matthew gives the marvelous new insights of Jesus which build on the "Old Law," but go beyond it. The Beatitudes point to a new and transforming way of seeing life and acting. The old way is no longer sufficient. Jesus announces that God is interested in people being peacemakers, in promoting justice. Jesus brings meaning to those who suffer, to those who yearn for something more, to those who mourn because they can see that this world's goods and power will no longer satisfy their search for meaning and purpose in life. Life will not be business as usual. Now God demands that people love not only those who return their love, but those who appear as enemies too. The new life that Jesus is teaching about is not for the faint-hearted. And Matthew wants to be sure the readers see how radically new the message is.

> *Read Matthew 4:17–7:29 and reflect on the following questions.*
> *Imagine you are a first-century Jewish-Christian. What new insights would you have found in these teachings of Matthew?*
> *Select one passage that you think would be particularly appropriate for adults in your parish to reflect on. What new or renewed insights might they get from the passage? What new actions would be called forth by the passage?*

*Select one passage that you think would be particularly appropriate for those whom you catechize. Why did you choose this passage?*
*What new insights and actions might it bring forth?*
*How would you creatively engage the participants in the passage and its meaning?*

### 2) Teaching About Mission

Jesus' work was doing what God expected of him. It was a mission of healing, of compassion, of reaching out to others, of bringing hope to the destitute. In chapters 9:36–11:1, Jesus commissioned the apostles to preach the good news and to heal others of maladies that were keeping them from recognizing and furthering the kingdom of God. Jesus warned the apostles that their message at times would be rejected, and that the road would not be smooth. He also gave the apostles a safety net; if it does not work out, if people reject you, leave the town, shake the dust from your feet—but keep on going. In other words, it will not be easy, but do not give up. Discipleship is not for the tentative or hesitant.

To show how much he expected of discipleship from the apostles, Jesus taught them how they were to show their love for him. The ultimate sign of love was to take up one's cross and follow Jesus. Jesus was not promising comfort, not guaranteeing popularity, not promoting status, but rather challenging people to a mission where they would have God on their side and the building of God's Kingdom as their mission. Ultimate union with God was their destiny.

Jesus had the apostles and disciples in a training program initially. They could only herald the Kingdom and bring people to a spiritual wholeness. It was only after the death-resurrection that they were commissioned to teach, to catechize, because it was only then that they were more fully formed by the death-resurrection experience and more fully empowered by the Spirit to help bring others to faith.

### 3) Teaching Through Parables

The parables were a third focus of Jesus' teaching. Parables are like riddles, but not-easy-to-figure-out riddles. Parables often include various figures of speech. For instance, the parable of the mustard seed compares a tiny seed which grows into a big bush to the kingdom of God (Matthew 13:31–32). The parable of the women with the yeast gives insights into the power of the kingdom of God to transform as the yeast transforms the flour (Matthew 13:33). Parables are sayings or short stories that have many levels of meaning and no obvious right answer. The value in using parables in catechizing is that they open one's imagination to various interpretations, each being a valid way of looking at something. A parable for a child may have one level of meaning, while the same parable for an adult may have another meaning. Jesus chose to teach using parables because he always wanted to connect some new insight into something the people had experienced such as mustard seeds and leavened bread.

> Read Matthew 13:1–52 and reflect on the following questions.
> Using a parable is a very creative way to teach. What other techniques did Jesus use to catechize in Matthew 13?
> Why do you think they were effective?
> What role did experience play in Jesus' teaching or catechizing?
> Choose a parable that you think is particularly insightful today. Rewrite it using contemporary images and share it with another catechist or those whom you catechize. Have those you catechize, working in groups, write or act out their own contemporary parables.

### 4) Teaching In and About Community

Matthew shows concern for the Christian community that has already formed by the time he writes his Gospel. Leadership is clear in Matthew. In fact Matthew is the only Gospel to use the word "church." In Matthew 16:18, Jesus tells Peter that he is counting on him to lead his Church. For Jesus the Church was the community. In Matthew 18:1–35, Jesus gives insights into what kind of a community he expects his followers to form. The parable of the Lost Sheep and the Unforgiving Servant shows what the hallmarks of Jesus' community or Church will be. The signs of the Christian community will be two-fold: (1) reaching out to the alienated, the disenfranchised, the marginal; (2) a high quality of forgiveness of not just monetary debts but a forgiveness which comes from the heart.

### 5) Teaching About the Final Age and Judgment

The final teaching found in Matthew is seen in chapter 24:1–25, 46. Many images of the true disciple are found here, but they all point to the characteristics of the faithful follower of Jesus as the one who builds the kingdom or rule of God, of the one who reaches out and makes a difference, of the one who feeds the hungry, gives drink to the thirsty, clothes the naked, visits those in prison and genuinely searches out the ways of God.

## HEALING STORIES IN MATTHEW'S GOSPEL

One cannot leave Matthew without commenting on the healing stories (Matthew 8:1–9:35). Jesus' healing stories reflect three things: (1) Jesus is always ready to stand with the infirm, those who are suffering, those who are isolated; (2) Jesus demands that his disciples keep focused on the kingdom or rule of God which includes facing tearful, life-threatening experiences with mercy and compassion; (3) faith is indispensable to healing. People who believe that Jesus can transform and heal are the recipients of transformation and healing, whether they be Jew or Gentile.

*Matthew had five major strands in his reflection on the teaching of Jesus which were briefly described above. As you reflect on the way Matthew presented Jesus' teaching and your role as a catechist, what are the five major strands of the teaching of Jesus that you see yourself proclaiming?*

*Jesus always taught by examining the life experiences of those whom he taught and by helping people see God's presence in and through their life experience. What insights from this can we gain for our own catechetical ministry?*

*Not only did Jesus challenge us to see the revealing presence of God but also to respond to God's presence by actions which build the kingdom or rule of God. In what ways do we strive to do the same thing?*

*Reflect upon the three things we learn from Matthew's account of Jesus' healing stories. In what ways can we be healed today by Jesus and be healers in the name of Jesus to others?*

## LUKE'S GOSPEL

Luke is the only Gentile among the Gospel authors. He most likely was a disciple of Paul, and he was writing for the Greek community. Often called the "beloved physician," Luke was probably from a well educated Syrian family. Luke's Gospel was written between 70-90 C.E. Many scholars think it was written more precisely between 80-85 C.E. While Mark was the storyteller who presented Jesus as a man of action and Matthew presented Jesus as the great teacher who fulfilled the old law, Luke is more the historian, but not an historian by modern standards. Luke gives an orderly account of Jesus' ministry as a figure similar to the great prophet Elijah so that his audience can build their faith around the person of Jesus.

For Luke salvation is a wonderful surprise that is offered to all people. Luke holds Mary in high esteem and makes a case for her being the first disciple. While Mark features Jesus as the "hidden Messiah" who suffers and dies for us, and Matthew presents Jesus as the long-awaited Messiah, Luke highlights Jesus' humanity and prophetic profile. Luke and Matthew both have Jesus identifying with the down-trodden, the lowly, those in need of a sense of hope and identity.

Recall how Mark began with John the Baptist and Matthew began with a genealogy and infancy narrative that included the story of the three kings. Luke begins his Gospel with a statement of purpose and then retells the announcements for the birth of John the Baptist and Jesus. Luke takes great pains to fill in details such as the story of the annunciation and the visitation along with Mary's canticle and the canticle of Zechariah. Luke has Jesus' birth in a stable with Mary laying him in a manger. Shepherds come to see Jesus at the beckoning of the angels who announce his birth.

*Read Matthew 1:18–2:23 and Luke 1:5–2:52.*
*Compare the different stories. If we had only Matthew's Gospel what would we be missing in the first two chapters?*
*If we had only Luke's Gospel what would we be missing in the first two chapters?*
*What is the advantage of having both traditions?*

The opening chapters of Matthew and Luke are called the infancy narratives. They were probably the last parts of the Gospels to be written. They provide sound theological statements rather than historical detail or scientific fact. Luke begins his reflection on salvation as a joyous surprise by presenting two stories about how both Elizabeth and Mary were not expecting the great wonders that happened to them in their pregnancies. The canticles of Zechariah and Mary further point to the joy to be found in salvation. Thus, Luke's theological seeds are planted in the infancy narrative. The major titles of Jesus are introduced there: Son of David, Son of God, Messiah and Savior. The Spirit's primary role is seen in the annunciation story. The Magnificat proclaims the greatness of the lowly. The hint that all will not be glorious in Jesus' life is found in the presentation of Jesus in the temple.

### 1) Women

Luke mentions more women than any of the other evangelists. Women in the Jewish culture at the time of Jesus had few rights and generally were considered to be the property of their husbands. They were not deemed worthy to hear God's word or learn more about God's word as men were. Rabbis taught men about the law and the prophetic writings, and women were expected to learn from their husbands. Women were considered "lowly" by the Jewish culture of the time, even though they were in charge of the spirituality and prayers within the home. Jesus apparently wanted to break out of the cultural barriers and enhance the dignity of women. Luke, writing primarily for Greeks, highlights this as Greek society was more embracing of women than Jewish society at the time of Jesus. For instance, in the Acts of the Apostles (which Luke also wrote), we read of women owning their own businesses. This would be a rare experience in Jewish culture. Luke mentions thirteen women who are not mentioned in any other Gospel. He also includes five stories featuring women which are not included in the other Gospels: raising of the widow's son (Luke 7:11–17); forgiving the woman who anointed his feet (Luke 7:36–50); acknowledging Mary Magdalene, Joanna and Susanna who followed him in Galilee (Luke 8:1–3); visiting with Martha and Mary (Luke 10:38–42); and curing the lame woman (Luke 13:10–17).

### 2) Prayer

Luke's Gospel has more about Jesus at prayer than any other Gospel. Luke connects prayer and action by showing us how often Jesus prayed. He prayed at the Jordan River before he was baptized; he prayed in the desert and on the mountain. He prayed the "Our Father" with the apostles; he also prayed alone. He prayed in the upper room and in the garden, as well as from the cross. Jesus prayed with the disciples at Emmaus. Jesus' prayer life for Luke was paramount. By emphasizing it, Luke is telling his Greek community how vital prayer is to being a disciple of Jesus.

### 3) Discipleship

For Luke, disciples are those who follow Jesus' values and embody what he taught: empowering the lowly, living according to religious values, embracing service as a hallmark of greatness, using wealth for the good of the community, and being people of prayer. According to Luke, these were the expectations Jesus had for his disciples.

> *Reflecting on Luke's Gospel and your catechetical situation, which aspects of his Gospel do you think would be appropriate to highlight with the people you catechize?*
> *What is the greatest insight you received from your reflection on the three Gospels?*
> *How will this insight help you to be a more effective catechist?*

## LUKE AND THE ACTS OF THE APOSTLES

It is generally accepted that Luke wrote not only the Gospel but also the Acts of the Apostles. Acts was probably written between C.E. 80 and 90 in a community that knew Paul and his missionary endeavors. It was written to help Christians understand themselves and their early communities. Acts is divided into four distinct parts highlighted by the story of Paul's conversion, told several times. The first part (Acts 1:1–26) is the introduction to the beginning of the Church community and deals with the ascension and the coming together of the apostles and the inclusion of Matthias to take the place of Judas. The second part (Acts 2:1–5:42) presents the mission to Jerusalem, highlighting the

Pentecost event, the sermons of Peter and the early persecutions. The third part (Acts 6:1–15:35) looks at the mission beyond Jerusalem and further deals with persecutions as well as Paul's conversion and subsequent missionary efforts to the Gentile world. The last part (Acts 16:1–28:31) unfolds more of Paul's trip to Greece, Antioch and ultimately Rome.

The Acts of the Apostles reflects how the Spirit led the early Church beyond Jerusalem far into the Gentile world. It describes how the Church thrived despite internal and external conflicts. It shows how conflicts could be resolved and how courageous the young martyrs were, as they faced death steeped in the belief of Jesus Christ. Luke's Gospel themes pointing out the importance of prayer, the work of the Spirit, the presence of joy and hope and the importance of women, permeate the Acts of the Apostles.

## JOHN'S GOSPEL

John's Gospel was the last to be written. It was probably developed between 90 and 100 C.E. The Gospel is addressed to all Christians world-wide. Scholars are quite sure that the Gospel was not written by the beloved apostle John, but may have been written by one or several of John's disciples.

## JOHN AND THE SYNOPTICS

The Gospel of John is very different than those of Mark, Matthew and Luke. In a way it is more literary and more of a theological reflection than any of the synoptics.

Differences can be found in the following comparisons. The synoptics focus on the Kingdom of God, while John emphasizes Jesus' relationship to God, his Father. Note also that the writing style is very different. The synoptics have many parables and sayings of Jesus as well as moral mandates; John has no parables or sayings. John's most frequently repeated moral mandate is to simply "love one another." Whereas Matthew and Luke highlight Jesus' human origins, John focuses on his divine origins…the Word made Flesh. In Matthew, Mark and Luke, Jesus spends a great deal of time in Galilee and little in Jerusalem. In John, Jesus makes three trips to Jerusalem. In the synoptics the Last Supper is a Passover meal, while in John it is the day before

Passover. In the synoptics the disciples gradually become aware of who Jesus is. In John, they profess belief in the Messiah from the beginning. For Matthew, Mark and Luke the miracles speak for themselves and are not dwelt upon. In John they become the impetus for theological reflection and an explanation for various levels of meaning.

The richness in John's Gospel can be found in its four distinct parts.

## 1) Prologue (John 1:1–18)

John begins his Gospel with a wonderful hymn of praise which sets the tone for what is to follow. The familiar, "In the beginning was the Word…" is a sign of the theological and symbolic nature of the Gospel. Some believe that the origin of the poetry in the prologue is a hymn used by the Johannine community. The source of salvation is made clear from the beginning of John: salvation comes to those who accept the Word of God, Jesus Christ.

## 2) The Signs (John 1:19–12:50)

Signs are important in John's Gospel because they point to the "more" behind the sign or symbolic action. John calls people to see deeper levels of meaning than what they may get at first. It is in probing the "more" that one discovers the meaning of Jesus' life and especially his relationship to God. The literary quality of John's Gospel can be seen in the use not only of symbolic actions but also of metaphors. It is as if John were trying to use any imaginative way he could to spark faith in others. Some of the most poignant metaphors include the following: I am he (the Messiah) (John 4:26); I am the bread of life (John 6:51); I am the light of the world (John 8:12); I am the good shepherd (John 10:11); I am the resurrection and the life (John 11:25); I am the vine (John 15:1).

Space permits only a brief look at three stories in this section of John's Gospel. But each of these stories unfolds John's style and his way of probing for deeper meaning. The first is that of the Samaritan woman (John 4:1–30). For centuries, Jews went out of their way to avoid being tainted by Samaritans. But Jesus did not buy into such snobbery. Jesus asked the Samaritan woman for a drink at the well. This amazed her, but she obliged. Only through dialogue with Jesus did she realize that there was "more" here than met the eye. Jesus' dual role of confrontation and acceptance makes a disciple out of the Samaritan woman. She sees more in Jesus. She begins to understand that the water Jesus refers to is "living water," the water of the Spirit, and that she is being called to partake of it. Once the woman moves beyond the literal meaning of what Jesus is saying, she receives the grace of salvation and becomes a disciple, recruiting others to follow and believe in Jesus.

The second story is that of Jesus as living bread (John 6:25–40). Like the synoptics, John recounts a story about Jesus feeding the multitudes. However, the next day Jesus takes time to dialogue with the people to help them understand that there is much "more" to eating bread than filling human hunger needs. There is much more than being fed by the manna in the desert. In the dialogue found in John 6:22–69, Jesus helps people to see that he is living bread, the bread of life sent by his Father. Those who refused to see the symbolism in the dialogue, those who refused to believe that Jesus was sent by God, those who refused to accept Jesus' close identity to God, left Jesus' company. His teaching was too hard. They could not move beyond the literal sense of Jesus' message. They could not believe. Peter in answering for the Twelve expressed his commitment to Jesus by acknowledging that Jesus had the words of eternal life. In John's Gospel, Jesus is always promoting eternal life for those who believe in him and recognize the close identity between himself and his Father.

A third story which illustrates John's style is the story of the blind man who believes in Jesus (John 9:1–41). In the story, one of the first things Jesus does is dispel the notion that if a person has some sort of infirmity, that it must be the result of sin. Jesus proclaims that blindness was neither caused by the blind man's nor his parents' sins. Again, as is John's way, he gradually unfolds the faith dimension of the story so that the readers know that Jesus is talking about more than physical blindness. The man is first cured of physical blindness but then questioned by the Pharisees who are presented as spiritually blind. Slowly the healed blind person recognizes the spiritual dimension of Jesus and during his second encounter with him professes his faith in him. These three stories are good examples of the way John exposes the nature and power of Jesus, Jesus' relationship to God and that salvation comes to those who believe in Jesus' words and symbolic actions.

### 3) The Book of Glory (John 13:1–20:31)

In this section of the Gospel, John portrays a very different Jesus from the synoptics. Jesus is not the suffering servant who is unjustly beaten and tormented; rather, Jesus is a noble divine person who is very much in control. Jesus demonstrates the role service plays in the lives of Christians by washing the feet of the apostles. In his discourses (John 13:1–17:26), Jesus both reminisces about the past and gives assurances for the future. The imagery he uses is both profound, as he pledges to send the Advocate, and concrete, as in the portrait of the vine and the branches. The imagery is intimate: "you are my friends"; it is also challenging: "if the world despises you, know that it despised me also." The words chastise: "Philip, how long have you been with me and you do not know that the Father and I are one?," as well as promise: "Ask the Father in my name and he will give you what you seek."

In the arrest and crucifixion Jesus is very much in control. He is not praying for the cup to pass; he is not sweating blood; rather he is surrendering himself to the will of God as his divine protégé who brings eternal life to those who believe in him.

The resurrection narratives include the stories of Jesus' appearances to doubting Thomas (John 20:19–25), to the disciples with Thomas (John 20:26–31) and to the seven disciples who were fishing (21:1–14). The latter appearance is in the epilogue to the Gospel (John 21:1–25) and seems to be a later addition. It is an interesting addition because of how it portrays Jesus Christ's relationship to Peter. Remember Peter denied that he knew Jesus before the crucifixion. But Jesus saw more in Peter than Peter saw in himself. Jesus allowed Peter time and space to "recover" from his betrayal. Jesus saw the leadership qualities in Peter and wanted to affirm Peter's role in the newly established community. Jesus also wanted to affirm the fact that we need not be paralyzed by our transgressions, shortcomings or sins. He called for Peter's loyalty and faithfulness and showed that he had confidence in Peter before he commanded him to carry on the mission.

According to the study edition of the *New American Bible,* there are four things we learn from John's Gospel: (1) that Jesus is the Son of God and God is revealed in him in a way far greater than God has ever been revealed or will be revealed in the future; (2) salvation comes through belief in Jesus Christ; (3) Jesus' death reveals God's love for all people; and (4) mutual love and unity in the Church reflects the love of God.

> *If we did not have John's Gospel what insights about Jesus would we be missing?*
> *How does John's concept of discipleship differ from Matthew's or Luke's?*
> *Why do you think it is important to have four Gospels?*

## THE LETTERS, OR EPISTLES

The Acts, along with the letters of Paul, Peter, James, John, and Jude, give us a good idea of the Spirit's work in the early Church. This body of biblical literature is of immense value to the Church today. Space does not permit an exploration of these scriptural writings here, but all catechists should be familiar with them because they offer so many insights that can help us understand our roots as Christians today. The resources listed at the end of this chapter are valuable for those wishing to know more about the travels and letters of Paul and the other disciples.

## THE BOOK OF REVELATION *presents a gospel in apocalyptic language*

This last book in the New or Second Testament is very difficult to read and has a history of being misinterpreted over the ages. Many people take the book as a prediction of doom and become obsessed with the "end-time" themes. The millennium awakens certain "end-of-the-world" fears which some find rooted in the book of Revelation. While a thorough exploration of Revelation cannot be given here, it is important to note that this book falls into a literary group or genre, called "apocalyptic literature," which was popular in the Middle East for about two hundred years before and after the birth of Christ. It was the literature that reflected an oppressed people who, if they remained faithful to God, would be saved from destruction. The literature included visions, animals, numbers, cosmic catastrophes, all presented in poetic and symbolic descriptions. It is not intended to depict the final events of the world in a day-by-day sequence. (Cf. Jean-Pierre Prevost, *How to Read the Apocalypse,*

Crossroad, 1993.) It is of critical importance to be well versed in the origins of the book of Revelation, to have studied the commentaries and to have discussed the book with someone well versed in it before using it in catechesis.

## PROMOTING JUSTICE

Promoting justice is a constitutive element of the Gospels. Jesus came to build God's kingdom, not to promote superficial personal relationships. Doing catechesis means doing justice. The justice the Gospels call for can be looked at as building a more just and peaceful society, attending to the poor, being honest, following the spirit of the law, using common sense, taking time to pray and reflect on what is important in life, worshipping God through rituals of praise, thanksgiving and petition, loving one's neighbor as oneself, forgiving and accepting enemies, giving to the government the things that belong to it and so on. When the Gospels are proclaimed, justice is proclaimed. They cannot be separated. The Acts of the Apostles gives examples of the early Church performing acts of social justice. One of their primary efforts was directed to helping widows and orphans.

> *For each of the areas listed above, name social justice activities in which you and those you catechize (or your parish) could become involved.*
>
> *Doing social justice is often a matter of networking with others who are involved. In your local area with whom can you network?*
>
> *All social justice activities are not Church-sponsored. Check with your local ecumenical and civic community to see what opportunities are available.*
>
> *How is promoting good ecological practices a justice activity which builds God's kingdom?*
>
> *How and where can you get involved in such activities and get those whom you catechize involved?*
>
> *Why is it important to have various opportunities for people?*
>
> *Today there may not be a great need to take care of orphans, but where can you find widows or widowers? What can you do to bring joy to their lives?*

## PRACTICAL IMPLICATIONS

1. Certain Gospel stories are very appropriate for preschool and primary children. They include but are not limited to the following: the story of the good Samaritan, the good shepherd, the prodigal son, and many other stories. Processing the stories with the children to help them probe their meaning is critical to successful catechesis. Experiences of planting and caring for seeds, making bread and watching it rise, sharing bread, looking for a lost coin or other precious article, tasting salt, lighting a candle (carefully, under supervision) are all things children can do in a catechetical context that opens them up to some of the significant imagery in the New Testament. Always examine the moral implications of a story with the children. Try to draw these implications out of the children rather than "preaching it" to them. After a discussion, clarify and summarize the moral teaching.

2. Intermediate grade children can also do some of the things suggested above, especially if they have not done them before. Repeated exposure to the stories of the good Samaritan, good shepherd, and prodigal son with effective processing is important. These stories should get into the psyches of the youngsters so that the values and behaviors of the stories become second nature to them. The values of reaching out, asking for and offering forgiveness, admitting mistakes and sins, finding and being found are at the heart of good, solid, healthy Christian life. Children at this age want to know the "rules" of the Church. Clarify these from the scripture stories. Intermediate grade children can also be exposed to the parables and be asked to interpret them as well as write different endings. Children also like to dramatize scripture stories. They can begin to understand the "death-resurrection" experience of Jesus Christ by being helped to connect it to their own life experiences. Being rejected by a friend can be identified in some small way with the rejections Jesus experienced in his life.

3. Pre-adolescents and adolescents can become much more attuned to the literary forms in the Gospels, to the different purposes of the Gospels and to the journeys portrayed in the Gospels. They can be challenged to understand the infancy narratives and their purposes as well as to get "under the skin" of some of the Gospel heroes and heroines. They usually can be motivated to imagine what it must have been like to have been blustery, impulsive Peter, or doubting Thomas or "why am I in the kitchen?" Martha. They can also write or script

contemporary "scripture stories." Young people often enjoy studying maps of the biblical times and examining the archaeologists' tools and pictures of their findings. History buffs find it enriching to parallel the scripture "history" with the history of the world. Slides and videos of the Holy Land are also interesting to this age person. Most of all, young people need to be able to identify with the spirituality and values of the Gospels. They need to become attentive to the spiritual sense of the Gospels which continues to give life today.

4. Adults benefit from all kinds of exposure to scripture, from the sharing of academic insights that are rendered in non-technical language, to analysis of the different kinds of literature, to examining the different purposes of the Gospels, to studying Paul's travels and his theology, to a serious study of the book of Revelation. Adults, as well as children, need to have the Gospels spoken to them in a way that appeals to them and works for them today. The scriptures need to be interpreted not as something that was meaningful only two thousand years ago, but something that is life-giving today. Clarifying the moral dimensions of the scriptures through discussion is helpful to adults.

**REFLECTION**

Have the book of the Gospels enthroned with a burning candle next to it. Have some oil in a small bowl for anointing of hands. Have towels as needed. Provide for reflective music.

Begin with an appropriate opening song which is familiar.

*Presider:* God, our Creator, you have given us your son, Jesus Christ, to be our savior and a model for our lives. From the Gospels, we know of his life, his values and his selflessness. Send your Spirit upon us and enlighten us so that we may be more like Jesus Christ. We ask this in his name, our Lord Jesus Christ, who lives and reigns forever.

*All:* Amen.

*Reader:* Proclaim: Luke 9:1–6.

Pause for reflection using the following questions:

> *In what way is Jesus sending me forward today?*
> *How do I encounter rejection from those I catechize?*
> *How am I sustained when I feel like I am not making a difference?*

*What is Jesus saying to me now about the mission he has asked me to do?*

*How can I empower others to be involved in social justice activities which build the kingdom of God?*

*Presider:* Invite the participants to come forward and have their hands anointed for catechetical service. Reflective music can be playing in the background. Use the following or a similar phrase: "I anoint you to continue to be strong in echoing God's Word in your ministry of catechesis and social justice activities."

*All:* Amen.

Invite participants to offer general intercessions. The response can be, "Lord, hear our prayer."

*Presider:* God, our Creator, we come to you with the following requests:

*(Petitions and response.)*

*Presider:* Accept our petitions in the name of your son, Jesus Christ our Lord.

*All:* Amen.

All pray the Lord's Prayer.

Exchange a sign of peace.

Sing an appropriate closing hymn.

## RESOURCES

Brown, Raymond E., Fitzmyer, Joseph A., and Murphy, Roland E. *The New Jerome Bible Handbook.* Collegeville, Minnesota: Liturgical Press, 1992.

Brown, Raymond, E., Fitzmyer, Joseph, A., and Murphy, Roland E. *The New Jerome Biblical Commentary.* Englewood Cliffs, New Jersey: Prentice-Hall, 1990.

Hiesberger, Jean Marie, general editor. *The Catholic Bible, Personal Study Edition.* NAB with Revised Psalms and Revised New Testament. New York: Oxford University Press, 1995.

Prevost, Jean-Pierre. *How to Read the Apocalypse.* New York: Crossroad, 1993.

"Stories that instruct, renew and heal provide a vital nourishment
…that cannot be obtained in any
other way." (Clarissa Pinkola Estes)

# 4
# Story and Imagination

The artistic impulse of the catechist must explore two interwoven fabrics: story and imagination. In one sense these formed the backdrop for all of Jesus' catechetical work. They will become important for the catechetical formation we do also.

The role of the catechist is not just to give information about the Bible, the Church, sacraments, the commandments and the saints, but rather to use these treasures of the Church in an artistic way to assist both children and adults to grow in faith. Faith is rooted in God's revelation. The unfolding of revelation happens first in the religious imagination of those being catechized. Before they can believe there is a caring God who loves them unconditionally, people need to envision a loving God who knows them personally. Information is not enough. The famed Jesuit theologian, Karl Rahner, reminded us that the theological challenge today is not to "pump religion" into people but to draw it out of them. Portraying the treasures of the Church with the artistry of a skilled painter is what the catechist does over and over again, always adjusting the hues and shapes to the needs of those catechized.

As Catholics we are well known for our creeds, moral laws and catechisms, but not for our stories. Somehow, stories seem to take a back seat to the "real thing" found in belief formulas.

However, John Shea reminds us that storytelling is the "bedrock of human activity." Good stories draw us out of our own little worlds. They help us live temporarily in another world with all its trials and tribulations, to be returned to our own actuality with new insights and more energy to cope with our lives. From a catechetical perspective faith can be more effectively engendered by good stories than by memorizing truths about God, Jesus or the Church.

75

Without the experience of story, propositions about faith are dull and lifeless. Stories are the tool of the catechist as a brush is the tool of a painter. After being transformed by the story, one can reflect on the theological truths in the narrative and articulate their value. Stories demand an emotional response, an affective response. Stories require the use of imagination; faith requires the use of imagination. Listening to a good story and telling a good story are ways of establishing meaning, of linking us to others, of affirming our experience, and of supporting us through difficult times.

## THE VALUE OF STORIES

### 1) Stories Have Teaching Value

As noted in the previous chapter, Jesus often taught by using stories because stories engage the imagination and heart of a person. Jesus particularly used stories in ambiguous situations, when people were trying to trip him up. For instance, the story of the Good Samaritan was prompted by a question asked from a narrow perspective, "Who is my neighbor?" The inquirer was hoping to hear that his neighbor was the person who lived nearby. Instead, he heard a story about a person who was rejected by the self-righteous professional religious, and saved by a "non-official" religious foreigner who was held suspect by the local people.

Contemporary "good Samaritan" stories, when told well and processed appropriately, can be exceptionally effective in catechizing on the great commandments: love God above all things and love your neighbor as yourself. Searching for "good Samaritan" stories in contemporary magazines and newspapers, creating skits, writing parodies or illustrating "good Samaritan" stories are all ways to reinforce a major theological premise of the Church.

Stories about saints or contemporary heroes or heroines can help young people and adults to see how these holy people applied the teachings of Christ in their everyday lives. Such stories, if grounded in reality, help contemporary people interpret their own lives in the light of the joys and struggles of others.

Stories help clarify values. Older children can create their own stories which reflect contemporary moral dilemmas. Sharing these stories gives them an opportunity for feedback on how to solve the conflict both from their peers and catechists. In "acting out" the results of various decisions and their consequences, young people have an opportunity to make more mature moral decisions.

Stories often summarize major tenets of the faith. The story is told about an atheist who went to a rabbi and said that he would become a believer if the rabbi could teach him the meaning of the whole Torah as he stood on one foot. The rabbi became enraged and threw out the atheist. The atheist went to another rabbi with the same question. The second rabbi summarized the meaning of the Torah as, "What is hateful to you, do not do to your neighbor...This is the whole Torah. All the rest is a commentary." This short story gets directly to the point and illustrates the simplicity of God's message.

> *What do you see as a major advantage to using stories in catechesis?*
> *What are some of your favorite stories which you think would be appropriate for catechesis?*

### 2) Stories Clarify the Truth

Stories from literature and those found in the Bible can often help the listener avoid errors in the truth. Tolstoy's *Martin the Cobbler* and Van Dyke's *The Other Wise Man* are examples of stories that clarify the truths that God is with us and that when we do ordinary acts of care and concern for those in need, we are truly encountering God. Matthew's Gospel alludes to the same thing when people are rewarded for feeding the hungry, giving drink to the thirsty and clothing the naked. In all of the above cases the doers did not recognize the authenticity of their actions as truly ministering to Christ. The stories amplify the truth, put flesh and blood on a religious principle and thus motivate people to respond in like manner.

### 3) Stories Offer Opportunities to Laugh and Cry

One of the great values of stories is that they allow us to laugh at ourselves. They give us an opportunity to stand back and smile at how seriously we have taken ourselves and how wrong we might have been in the judgments we have made. Laughter is good because it helps us see the incongruity in life and in some sense it empowers us to stand in another's shoes.

Humorous stories can call forth "belly laughs" which are good for the body as well as the spirit. Some claim that the healing power of laughter has helped them overcome physical diseases.

For small children some of the first stories they like to tell are riddles where they know the answer and you do not. They see that riddles engage you. They have some power over you. In fact children like to tell riddles so much that once they get started it is hard to stop them, even though the quality of the riddles quickly diminishes. Some catechists have found it helpful to begin each session with a riddle to settle the children and get their attention.

Tears are often the result of hearing sad stories, of being involved in the tragedies of another's life. In entering the life of a suffering individual through story, often our own woes seem less poignant and begin to diminish. The person suffering a loss of a loved one might be consoled by the story of someone who lost both spouse and children in a disastrous accident. Listening to others, to their adversity, also prepares us to be able to deal with calamities when we encounter them in our own lives.

### 4) Stories Awaken Spiritual Awareness

Hope is a foundational virtue for one's spiritual life. Fairy tales engender a sense of hope, a perception that one can cope even in difficult times and that, ultimately, things will turn out for the best. Fairy tales also reward those who are good, those who care about others and those who believe that they have something to contribute to others. Fairy tales begin to help children answer the questions: What is the world really like? Who am I in relationship to the world? How can I live happily in the world? Fairy tales speak to children because they reflect a child's way of thinking as opposed to an adult's rational approach. Fairy tales are unambiguous about good and evil. There is very little to be found in fairy tales that is not strikingly good or evil. In fairy tales good overcomes evil. For example, in *The Three Little Pigs,* it is obvious that there is a happy ending and that the wolf gets what he deserves. Notice in the tale also, that the oldest pig is smart and hard working. Happiness is not a matter of luck, it calls for discipline and effort. Fairy tales such as Hansel and Gretel help children deal with the anxiety of separation. In this story each character plays an important and complementary role. Hansel puts out the pebbles which guided him and his sister home, but Gretel defeats the witch. Other tales, such as *Snow White* and *Beauty and the Beast,* can be similarly utilized.

Reading the stories is not enough. They must be processed, even with preschool children. The storyteller must give the children time to ponder the story. Asking questions such as the following can also help the child process the story: Which parts did you like the most? What was the scariest part? Do you wish the story ended differently? Retelling the story after a brief discussion can also be helpful. Having three or four classic fairy tales to tell over and over again for preschool and primary children can enhance their faith life by reinforcing in them a sense of hope. They learn that even when things do not go well, if they hang in there and try their hardest, things will turn out better in the end.

Older children, middle school and junior high age, can also benefit from fairy tales, not so much from hearing them over and over again, but from recalling them and noting how the stories have influenced their lives since they were intrigued by them. Using fairy tales to help young adults see that they can understand the complexities of life now more than when they were children gives them a sense of confidence in their own maturing process. Pre-adolescents and adolescents may still be able to get some insights from fairy tales. One young adolescent girl had an older brother whom she adored. But as time passed, she began to resent him for being too domineering. She recalled one of her favorite childhood fairy tales, Hansel and Gretel, and was struck by the fact that the boy Hansel was not totally responsible for the success depicted in the story. In fact, Gretel was the one who ultimately defeated the witch. Such a reflection enabled the young girl to feel more confident in herself and to separate herself in a healthy way from her brother. Her new insights helped diminish her resentment and opened lines of communication with her brother.

> *Examine some fairy tales and select some that you think might be appropriate for your catechetical sessions.*
> *How would you use them?*
> *Are there any connections between the fairy tales and some scripture stories?*
> *What discussion questions would you use to bring out their meaning?*
> *What might be some advantages and disadvantages to using fairy tales in a catechetical setting?*

Scripture is full of stories and images which nurture our faith lives. The Gospels help us to identify with the compassionate Mary in the story of Cana, the fearful Peter threatened by the turbulence of the sea, the hungry people who were searching for more than food, the busy apostles who were becoming impatient with the children, the forgiving father and the resentful son. Story upon story calls us to see our spiritual relationship to God through our relationship and commitments to each other. John Shea reminds us that the stories in scripture are memorable because they are similar enough to our own lives for us to identify with them, but different enough for us to see new possibilities and act upon them.

God's revelation is found in scripture stories. God's presence and attributes are only known through God's revelation of them. Sometimes the revelation was so mysterious that it could only be spoken of in mysterious images. Moses used a burning bush to tell of his experience of God. However, once Moses tells us that God spoke to him in a burning bush, he needed to remind us that the bush was different from other bushes because it was not consumed by the fire. Any image of God is always inadequate. For us to comprehend God's revelation, we need images, because that is how we humans learn. Once a person finds a helpful image, one always needs to add, "yes, but…." In other words no image is totally adequate. God is like a burning bush, but the bush truly does not consume itself. God is like a faithful mother, but God is even more faithful than the most faithful of parents. By using images we can identify with, God has given us a treasure to enrich our spiritual lives. The images and stories found in the Bible give us confidence that the God of Abraham, Moses and Jesus is our God today, because we experience things similar to what they experienced and we still are drawn to fire, water, oil, words and gestures of care and forgiveness.

Retelling the stories each year according to the liturgical cycle keeps fresh in our memories the roots of our values and identity. The stories continually energize us to build the reign of God on earth.

> *Recall some Bible stories and images which you think can be used to enrich the spiritual lives of those whom you catechize. How are the stories similar to the experiences of people today? How can the images provide enrichment for those who are journeying today?*

### 5) Stories Heal Wounds

Stories, particularly those from scripture, have the power to heal. As Catholics we believe that God is present in the Word proclaimed to the community. Words, especially those found in the Gospels, have great healing qualities. Stories which deal with forgiveness and healing are powerful. Healing in the Catholic tradition means not only physical healing but also spiritual healing. The healing of painful memories, the mending of broken promises, the grieving for what could have been, all are part of the healing process. We hear proclaimed from scripture: your faith has saved you; I have come to give you life and to give it more abundantly; he who eats the Living Bread will never die; unless the grain of wheat die it cannot produce new life. These words are filled with evidence that God heals through words, through stories, and that these healings are holistic.

> *Select your favorite healing story. What kind of healing is going on?*
> *How is faith connected to the story?*
> *How can the story be healing today?*

### 6) Stories Build Memory Banks

Many stories we have heard since we were children. At the time we understood them on one level, but because of the richness of the story we can uncover deeper meanings as we bring more of our experience to the story. For instance, we have heard the story of the Prodigal Son since we were six years old. We know it well. It is ingrained in our memories. However, not until we have had the difficult experience of practicing "tough love" with one of our obstinate teenagers do we understand the full impact of what must have been going on in the minds of the parents in the story. Sleepless nights, weeks, months and years have caused self-doubt in us. Did we make the right decision? Where is he now? Is he safe? Is he alive? The helpless, depressing feeling finally surrenders to joy and jubilation as the son returns unexpectedly, asks for forgiveness and says that he will abide by the "house rules." This story with different characters and different circumstances plays itself out in the lives of thousands of people every year. The original story is the one that sustains us, gives us a sense of hope, helps us connect with Christ and others who have gone before us.

Telling the stories of the tradition, unpacking them, retelling them is building up a treasure chest that people can draw from over a lifetime. There are so many levels of meaning in scripture stories that once they become part of one's psyche, they can be enriching over the years. Catechizing children is the beginning of the process of stimulating the imagination to grasp spiritual realities of life. Without imaginative inspiration, catechetical sessions will be dull and uninteresting. Children may forget "facts" about God and Jesus Christ, but they will not forget the stories and images that connect them to their spiritual heritage and enrich their lives. Once a spiritual imagination has been stimulated and developed, it is near impossible to "kill" it in later life.

As catechists our job is to help both children and adults to develop their religious imaginations. This is giving them a healing, connecting, value-laden gift for the rest of their lives. It is truly a preparation for eternity. Some believe that the level of happiness one will enjoy in heaven is based on the depth of development of one's imagination.

> *Name some Bible stories which you think could easily serve a person for a lifetime.*
> *What caused you to select these stories?*
> *How can you use them in your catechetical activities?*

### 7) Stories Unite Communities

Perhaps the power of stories is never more evident than when we examine stories found in the Native American traditions. The creation stories in these traditions are vibrant, respectful, and instructive. They are often told in a circle where a fire is built and a song is danced.

The creation stories of many traditions talk about Father Sky and Mother Earth and show the connectedness of all creation. A common thread of the Native American traditions is their imaginative ability to try to explain the mysteries of life. Some stories explain snow as the result of wind blowing grasses in the sky. Some explain how animals got their colors. Some explain long winters as the result of the bears stealing all the warmth from earth. Most are told around the campfire at night to help children understand the mysteries of life.

In many ways the Native American stories mirror the origin of our own story tradition. In our biblical tradition all the stories which we have

inherited were first told around the campfire at night. They were passed
on from one generation to the next and altered to pique the imagination of
each new generation of listeners. Gradually the stories were committed to
writing. The point of all the stories was to explain the mysteries of life and
most especially God's presence among the people. Stories of creation
from other traditions can be used effectively in catechizing. Older children can compare the Judeo-Christian stories with the Native American
stories. By analyzing their similarities and differences and the theological
constructs under both, children can come to a richer understanding of
their own tradition, while at the same time appreciating another tradition.

Stories formed the community. Stories were what held the group
together. Clarissa Pinkola Estes states that some people see communities based on blood ties, but the stronger gravitational field that holds a
group together are their stories, especially the common and simple
ones they share with one another.

Scripture stories are the written memory of the Church, but they
do not just reflect past events or past beliefs. They are proclaimed as a
living memory which continues today. Stories underline the great biblical truth that people learn about God through the events of their lives.
The biblical stories continue in our own lives; the beliefs are lived out
in our own joys and struggles to find meaning and purpose in life. The
stories shed light on the eternal questions: What is the meaning and
purpose of life? How can I know God? What contribution can I make to
build a better life for myself and others?

> *Read one of the following scripture stories and reflect upon
> how the story continues to be told in the lives of contemporary
> people like yourself:*
> *1 Samuel 3:2–11; Mark 2:1–12; Luke 9:10–13.*

The scripture stories are at the heart of Christianity. They teach
about events, values, struggles and salvation. They clarify the truth
about created, saved, incarnated human life. They provide opportunities
to vicariously experience the joys and sorrows of others and consequently to see one's own life from a new perspective. Stories nurture
spiritual life because they provide a construct for the Spirit to speak to
people in their everyday experience. Stories help heal wounds. They can
help restore relationships; they can touch our inner workings and release
the body's curative powers. Stories provide a wealth of memories that

can be tapped into at times of celebration, sadness and disorientation. Stories unite people. Nowhere was this more obvious than in the stories told about World War II or the Vietnam War. Stories are the sinew that hold the community's hopes and values together.

William Bausch summarizes the value of stories in the following ten points:

1. Stories introduce us to sacramental presences. They prompt us to look beyond our own experience.
2. Stories are always more important than facts. Stories engage the listener in an imaginative way to be part of the "truth."
3. Stories remain normative. Our faith is rooted in the biblical stories about God, Jesus and other people and events. The richness of the stories allows us to continually unpack the levels of meaning in the story.
4. Traditions evolve through stories. People are caught up in good stories and make them their own. The same story may generate different traditions based on the experience of people. The Christmas story(ies) is a good example of this.
5. Stories precede and produce the Church. Church is made up of people who believe the story, pass it on and live by it.
6. Stories imply censure. Not all stories told about biblical heroes and heroines have been passed down to us. Some were not "caught" by the community and, therefore, never become part of the tradition.
7. Stories produce theology. Theology is an attempt to reflect on the beliefs inherent in stories. Theology draws out meaning from stories.
8. Stories produce many theologies. The four Gospels give evidence to this. One person walked the earth, told us about God, lived, died and was raised to new life. Four traditions arose from the one story, based on the experience of different communities.
9. Stories produce ritual and sacrament. Our sacraments are the result of people ritualizing stories.
10. Stories are history. History is a bridge from which we come to understand the meaning of stories.

## THE USE OF STORIES

The use of stories in catechesis depends upon the creativity of the catechist. There are six steps to take in deciding on which stories to use in a catechetical session.

1. Examine the topic of catechesis and decide what is really important to you about the topic. We teach best through our own passion. If the topic is baptism, for instance, think about what you consider to be vital aspects of the topic. Is it the use of water as a life-giving force? Is it becoming a member of a larger caring community? Is it the candle and the white garment which point to a new relationship to Christ and the body of Christ? Or a combination of the above? Recall baptisms you have attended and your feelings about them. Think about how they are celebrated in your parish.

2. Examine the same topic from the viewpoint of the people to be catechized. Recall their age, their intellectual abilities, their cultural backgrounds, the scope and sequence of the curriculum, the spiritual maturity and experience of those catechized.

3. Combine your passion on the subject and the needs and circumstances of those catechized to decide your emphasis for the session.

4. Decide on strategies you will use to make the topic effectively engaging. Will you use stories? Will you use audio-visuals? Will you use manipulative materials? Will you use art projects? How will you involve the justice dimension?

5. What stories do you know that relate to the topic? Stories from your own experience? Stories from children's literature? Stories from other cultures? Stories that others in the parish can tell? What process will you use to help those whom you catechize to interpret the story and link it to their experience?

6. What scriptural stories will you use? How do these relate to other stories? What process will you use to open up the meaning of the story and connect it to the experience of those whom you catechize?

> *Use the questions stated above to begin preparation for your next catechetical session.*
> *What resources will you use?*
> *What will the interactive process be?*
> *How can you promote the creativity of the participants?*

## PROMOTING JUSTICE

Stories provide wonderful opportunities to promote justice and to encourage moral development. Stories in which someone has suffered an injustice affect people who hear them, often motivating them to work to eliminate the unfair situation. These stories can involve racial discrimination, unfair employment practices, exploitation of the poor in this and other countries, the raping of the earth out of greed and lack of concern for future generations, inhumane prison conditions, pollution, violence, hunger, homelessness, sexual abuse, lying, cheating, stealing, killing, drunkenness and many other evils of today.

Inviting people who have been experiencing injustice to catechetical sessions and having them tell their own stories is very effective. After hearing the story, those catechized should have an opportunity to interact with the storyteller. Building human relationships is the beginning of healing and creating positive change. Bonding with someone who is different than we are helps us walk in the shoes of another and experience to some degree their plight.

Role playing often flows from the use of story and imagination. This methodology allows participants to know in an experiential way and to a limited degree what others suffer. This experience often encourages the role player to be an advocate for others and to be more sensitive to the situation in which others live. All these experiences can help create a more just society, both locally, nationally and globally.

Storytelling can be used to promote an understanding of the Ten Commandments as well as the commandments of Jesus. Such efforts aid children and adolescents especially to integrate the Church's moral teachings into their own lives.

## PRACTICAL IMPLICATIONS

Effective storytellers take the following into consideration in their catechetical methodology.

1. Select age appropriate stories. This is especially important when working with younger children. They need vibrant action stories that hook their imaginations. Older children need stories with which they can identify. They can deal with more complexity than younger children, but they want their stories to have something "real" about them. Older children can use fables and fairy tales for analysis but not as stories that appeal to the realism of their lives. Adolescents are drawn into stories about heroes and heroines with whom they can identify. Adults need stories which address the complexities of their

lives. Remember that stories can be viewed as well as read. Videos are effective ways to communicate stories.

2. Select stories whose length relates to the attention span of those whom you catechize. Younger children have very short attention spans and stories should be able to be told in five minutes or less. Middle-grade children are capable of having stories told or read to them in segments. One successful catechist of fifth-grade children saved the last ten minutes of each session to read a chapter of a book. The book was about an adolescent dealing with everyday problems. Its subtlety and connectedness to the anticipated life of the children hooked them each week and they looked forward to the next chapter of the story. A classic, *A Tree for Peter,* by Kate Seredy, is the kind of book that will hold fourth-, fifth- and sixth-graders' attention chapter by chapter. Adolescents relate to all kinds of stories from different perspectives. They can examine literature for younger people to discern the values inherent in it; they can grapple with complex plots in young adult literature. Adults appreciate poignant stories which relate to their struggles and give them courage to face them.

3. Prepare well the stories that you will tell, read or view. If you plan to read a story in class, read it beforehand several times, so that you are not overly dependent on reading it word for word. If you are telling a story, be sure to do it with a lot of expression, pausing appropriately to ask a pertinent question or solicit a comment from the hearers. If you are viewing a story, be familiar with the needed equipment.

4. Use a lot of eye contact when telling and reading a story. This engages the hearers and keeps them involved.

5. Begin a storytelling process with an opening question which will engage the memory and imagination of the hearers. Comments and questions such as: "Have you ever"…or, "Remember when you were"… or, "Pretend that you are"… are ways to involve the people in the storytelling process.

6. Discuss the meaning of the story by using thought provoking questions. Some might include: "What do you think Mary was thinking about when she…?" "Why was it hard for Pedro to…?" "What dilemma was Lisa facing when…?"

7. Help the listeners interiorize the story by engaging them in some activity related to the story. Doing skits, discussing the story, creating different endings, performing dances, developing art projects and singing appropriate songs are all ways to help participants make

the story part of their lives. Using discussion and creating alternative decisions are ways to involve adults in the process.

8. Develop the justice component of the story and relate it to the moral teaching of the Church.

9. Use contemporary news stories to analyze the values inherent in them, to discuss the underlying "causes" of the story, to encourage participants to identify with the hero or heroine of the story, to write different endings of the story and to suggest how those catechized might have acted if they were part of the story.

Choose a storytelling activity and creatively develop it according to the ideas suggested above.

## REFLECTION

Have the Bible enthroned. Light a candle before beginning the prayer service. For each participant, have seeds prepared in small packets as well as soil and small pots. Have a bowl with water and a branch to sprinkle the planted seeds.

*Presider:* God, Creator of us all, you sent us Jesus Christ to tell us stories that would convince us of your love for us. The stories Jesus told remind us that you are all merciful, all forgiving and full of compassion. Enable us to retell the stories in such a way as to awaken the faith of those we catechize. Help us to connect their stories to the scriptural stories so that they too may know of your presence in their lives. We ask this through Christ our Lord.

*All:* Amen.

*Reader:* Proclaim Matthew 13:1–9, 18–23

For reflection and sharing:

> *Notice that Jesus prefers to teach where people are, outside near the sea, not in an academic setting. The crowd must have been rural people because Jesus chose to use an image with which the farmers would have been very familiar.*
> *What images do you use with which those you catechize can easily identify?*
> *The common refrain, "to those who have ears to hear," is an invitation to reflect on the meaning of the story. Just as we invite our hearers to examine the meaning of a story, so did Jesus.*

*Who do you think the sower represents? What does the seed represent?*

*Some scripture commentaries refer to the sower as God or Jesus or a messenger of God, and suggest that the seed is God's kingdom or God's revelation. If these are the symbols used in the story, how would you interpret the four different environments into which the seed falls. What other interpretations might you give the story?*

*What insights do you have from the story which you can use in your catechetical ministry?*

*Presider:* God, our Creator, you have enriched us with your Word, continue to enlighten us as we embrace our catechetical ministry. We ask this through Christ our Lord.

*All:* Amen.

*Presider:* Call each person forward, present them with seeds, soil and pots saying: "Receive the seeds of God's revelation. Plant them, water them and care for them as you till the soil and nurture the faith of those whom you catechize."

When all have their seeds, sprinkle them with water while saying: "God, we ask you to bless our efforts to make your stories and your Word better known to all. We ask your blessing in the name of Jesus, our Lord.

*All:* Amen.


## RESOURCES

Bausch, William J. *Storytelling: Imagination and Faith.* Mystic, Connecticut: Twenty-Third Publications, 1984.

Estes, Clarissa Pinkola. *The Gift of Story.* New York: Ballantine Books, 1993.

Van Laan, Nancy. *In a Circle Long Ago: A Treasury of Native Lore from North America.* New York: Alfred A. Knopf, 1995.

Whitehead, James D. and Whitehead, Evelyn Eaton. *Shadows of the Heart.* New York: Crossroad, 1994.

"I have come that you might have life and that more abundantly."
(Adapted, Jn 10:10)

# 5
# The Church

The Church is like a mosaic, with all its small parts contributing to the whole. As catechists we work with people who have some experience of Church but rarely see the whole or the "big picture." Our task is to enhance people's concept of Church by engaging them in its many facets and helping them appreciate its history, its presence and what it is called to become. This is an artistic endeavor!

Pope Paul VI stated that the Church is a mystery. "It is a reality imbued with the hidden presence of God." The unfolding mystery continues to energize those who belong to the Church and those who serve in the Church as its ministers.

Catechesis is one of the primary ministries of the Church. It is a ministry of the Word. For this reason it is imperative that catechists have a sound understanding of what or who the Church is, even its nature as mystery. The Gospels describe Jesus as a person with a mission and a message. He shared his mission and message with his family, his apostles, disciples and friends. Jesus preached, taught, made life better for people, celebrated, made friends and captured people's imaginations about who they could be. He experienced disappointment, failure, success, anger, happiness, sadness, loyalty, disloyalty and all other emotions. He walked the earth two thousand years ago and because of the friends he made and the people he influenced, who would not let his memory die, we can claim to belong to his Church.

Matthew's Gospel is the only one that uses the word "church" and he uses it only once. Matthew identifies the Church with those who hear the message about God's kingdom and promote it to the ends of the earth. Mark emphasizes Jesus' relationship to his disciples with whom he gradually revealed the secrets of his kingdom. Luke, in the

91

Acts of the Apostles, portrays the early Church as growing in self-awareness as to what it meant to belong to the community of the Lord and walk in the steps of the Lord. To be a member of this early community one had to repent from sin, believe in Jesus Christ, be baptized and receive the Holy Spirit. John sees the early community of Jesus Christ as a community of love guided by the Spirit and based on the "Word made Flesh." The one thing all these descriptions have in common is that the Church is a community of disciples who try to live the mission and ministry of Jesus Christ.

The earliest meaning of the word "church" was the family of the Lord or the assembly of the Lord. It did not refer to a church building, but rather a community who believed what Jesus Christ believed and strived to live as he lived. If one were to ask Jesus what he envisioned for the Church, he would probably answer by using some of the dynamic imagery found in the Gospels used to describe the kingdom or reign of God. The images of the tiny seed that becomes a large bush (Matthew 13:31–32), or the yeast that enlivens a whole batch of flour (Matthew 13:33), or the sacrifices described to obtain the treasure or pearl (Matthew 13:44–47), would undoubtedly be among the images Jesus would use. These images tell us that the Church is dynamic; it continually grows; it is not rigid; it finds its source in the life, death and resurrection of Jesus Christ and is continually nourished by the Spirit.

While the kingdom of God and the Church are not the same, the Church is a principle agent of the kingdom of God, a sign and sacrament of the kingdom in human history. The kingdom of God is the result of God's creative power, yet it relies on the Church to further its development and realization. The New Testament speaks of the tension between the kingdom that is present and the kingdom that is to come. The reality of salvation is present, but its full potential is still being unfolded. There is still more to come!

## BRIEF HISTORY OF THE CHURCH

Nothing more than a thumbnail sketch of Church history can be presented here. What is important about Church history is to realize that the Church has changed over the centuries and these changes have been prompted by the changes and demands in society. The issues of the fourth and fifth centuries are mostly not our issues. But we are called to take the "answers" of the earlier Church and expand on them where needed so as to contribute to the continual unfolding of the Spirit in our lives today.

## 1) The Apostolic and Early Church

Pentecost is often called the birthday of the Church. According to scripture, Pentecost is the day the apostles and disciples felt the power of the Holy Spirit and spoke the message of Jesus Christ with courage, thus gaining many new followers. One could say that, indirectly, Jesus laid the foundation for the Church. In that sense, the Church was born the day Jesus started choosing his apostles, for the values found in the early Church were those that Jesus shared with the apostles and his followers during the formation time when he was with them. Peter was given a leadership position in the early Church. But he never seemed to exercise it alone. He is seen to consult and even to follow the directives of the others (Acts 8:14). He teams up with John and is not a lone ranger (Acts 3:1–11 and 4:1–22).

Although founded on the rock of Peter, the Church soon grew in diverse ways. It spread throughout much of the Greco-Roman world. As it did, it adapted to contemporary social, political and cultural ways. It adapted organizational structures that were present in the political world of the Roman Empire and ultimately was headquartered at the empire's center, Rome. Despite its diversity there were constants that ran through the faith of the early Church: faith in the life, death and resurrection of Jesus Christ; the practice of baptism and eating at the table of the Lord; the teaching and preaching of the apostles; the practice of sharing, caring and loving one another; and the expectation that the final coming of the Lord was about to happen.

The early Church was not free from conflict both within and outside of it. As Paul preached beyond Palestine to the Gentiles (the people of Antioch, Athens and Rome) there was resistance to adherence to the Jewish rituals such as circumcision and the Jewish dietary laws. If people were receiving the Good News of Jesus Christ, why did they first have to become Jewish? Some of the apostles and disciples felt that the Jewish rituals were important to the initiation of new believers. This tension led to the first council of the Church in Jerusalem (Acts 15:1–21). At this meeting Paul and Barnabas spoke convincingly from the Gentile point of view. After hearing all sides Peter spoke in favor of suspending the Jewish law for the Gentiles.

The first three centuries of the Church also produced many martyrs who gave up their lives for their belief in Jesus Christ. People such as Peter, Paul, Ignatius of Antioch, Cecilia, Agnes, Clement and Stephen are but a few names of the early martyrs.

> *In what ways is the early Church like the Church of today? How is it different?*
>
> *Who are some of today's martyrs? For what did they die?*
>
> *How would you describe the leadership in the apostolic Church? How does it compare with the leadership of your local parish?*

### 2) Constantine and the Early Councils

The Church continued to grow despite the controversies it attracted. In 312, the Emperor Constantine was converted to Christianity. As a result he suppressed pagan religious practices and in 323 officially approved Christianity as the religion of the empire. This meant that the Church would no longer be subject to persecution and would be considered the privileged religion.

However, heresies were being fought within the Church. The nature of God, the divinity of Christ, the meaning of redemption and the divinity of the Holy Spirit were among the most heated arguments of the day. The Council of Nicea (325) declared that Christ and the Father were both divine. The Nicene Creed which is prayed at Sunday liturgy is a result of that Council. The Council of Constantinople (381) affirmed the humanity of Jesus as well as the divinity of the Holy Spirit, and the equality of the Father, Son and Holy Spirit. The Council of Ephesus (431) and the Council of Chalcedon (451) dealt with the nature and person of Jesus. The later Council attested that Jesus was one person with a divine and human nature. In other words, Jesus is truly God and truly a human being. These doctrinal councils all dealt with the questions of the day and they were solved by bishops representing various parts of the Church, even though the Councils were called by the reigning Emperors. These years brought the Church great bishops and theologians such as St. John Chrysostom, St. Ambrose and St. Augustine.

### 3) Charlemagne

The sixth, seventh and eighth centuries were the dark ages for the Western Church and Europe. Barbarian invasions left much of Europe in chaos. The Church, through its monasteries, preserved what it could of civilization as well as Christianity. Between the fall of Rome in 476 and the crowning of Charlemagne in 800, the Church became responsible for commerce, agriculture, civic functions as well as the spiritual development of the people. The Church filled a power vacuum. In many ways the Church and civilized society became synonymous. This is hard for us to understand given our history of the separation of Church and State. When Charlemagne rose as a political leader, one of his challenges was to have the Church give over political power to him so that the Church could be about the spiritual growth of people. This seemingly happened when Charlemagne was crowned king of the Holy Roman Empire by Pope Leo III in what is Germany today. But what looked like a harmonious relationship soon became conflictual as both the Church and the government competed for political power. These conflicts continued for centuries.

Charlemagne had a great love of learning, a bent for the arts and architecture and a knack for "smart farming." By working often with monks in monasteries, he used his natural talents and interests to further civilization. Charlemagne promoted Romanesque architecture. The fortress quality of the style served the Church well. The thick walls and narrow windows provided safe harbor for citizens seeking refuge from attack from warring armies. The upper story of the churches also provided a safe place to store grain.

However, the Church continued to be entangled in political struggles. It tried throughout Europe to influence who would rule various countries. The civic governments in turn tried to influence who would be bishops and popes. As late as 1903 the emperor of Austria tried to influence the election of Pope Pius X.

Through a series of complex political developments a breach occurred between the Church of Constantinople and the Church of Rome. The excommunication of the patriarch of Constantinople (1054), the Fourth Crusade and the sacking of Constantinople by Western knights in 1203 led to what is now called the schism. Efforts are being made today to heal the rift between the two traditions, which is one of the great tragedies of Christianity.

*What were the advantages of the Church getting involved in the work of civil society?*
*What were the disadvantages?*

### 4) Gothic Architecture, Franciscans, Dominicans, and the Crusades

The architecture of Church buildings changed in the middle of the twelfth century. Fortress-like edifices (Romanesque architecture) were not needed as the Church was no longer under siege from the barbarians. The outside world was not as hostile. Towns and cities were beginning to flourish. New theological understandings, due to a large extent to the work of the Benedictine monks, called people to a more transcendent view of life. Devotion to Mary flourished. The great Gothic cathedrals were being designed and built. These cathedrals were light and airy with large, stained glass-windows depicting scenes from the life of Mary and Jesus. Light played an important role in these churches. The assemblies were drawn up to the divine light, to the Spirit of God, as the dappled light shown through the windows. The theology of St. Bernard was played out in the cathedrals. The cathedrals became teaching tools for the uneducated. Those who could not read could learn the mysteries of their faith by looking at the windows and statues which decorated the outside of the buildings. The decorations included scenes from the scriptures as well as the signs of the zodiac, the seven liberal arts and the works of the months. All these elements of life were seen as relating to faith. The great cathedrals of St. Denis, Chartes, Notre Dame, Laon, Rouen, Reims, all pointed to a renewed emphasis of faith focusing on the transcendence of God.

During this same time two new religious orders were founded. Since the middle of the sixth century, St. Benedict's influence and his monastic rule were the prevailing influences on religious life. In the thirteenth century, St. Francis Assisi and St. Dominic de Guzman founded orders that would greatly influence the Church. St. Francis's charism focused on simplicity, poverty, the care for people and nature. All this was part of Francis's way of following in the footsteps of Jesus. St. Dominic's charism was that of preaching. The Dominicans became known as the order of preachers, with a special emphasis on teaching and preaching the truth. The Dominicans worked in the universities in Europe and had a great influence on the theological thinking of the day.

The order produced such scholars and saints as St. Albert the Great, St. Thomas Aquinas and St. Catherine of Siena. The theology of Thomas Aquinas was a major theological influence in the Church up to the Second Vatican Council. His theology is still significant today.

The Crusades reflect a sad part of Church history which began in 1096 and ended about 1270. Although they were called "holy wars," they were neither holy nor just. The ultimate goal of these wars was to "kill the infidel and reclaim the Holy Land." From the beginning there were some motivational leaders, but the "holy wars" were ill-conceived. The Crusades involved peasants, children and princes. Thousands of Jews, Muslim and other Christians were killed in the process and in the name of Christianity.

> *What were the great things that happened in the Church of this period?*
> *Why do you think these were positive contributions?*
> *What do you think could have caused the Crusades?*
> *Does anything in the twentieth century remind you of the Crusades?*
> *How can we be sure a "crusade mentality" does not bring havoc on the Church and the world today?*

### 5) The Reformation

The fourteenth and fifteenth centuries were not illustrious ones for the Church. Conflicts between the civil society and the Church continued. At one point three different people claimed to be the pope! Forgiveness and salvation were being "sold" in the form of indulgences. Martin Luther was a Catholic priest who became scandalized by some of the corruption in the Church. Selling indulgences without sufficient interior conversion pushed him over the edge and in 1517 he nailed "95 theses" on the door of the Church at Wittenburg in Germany. Luther had many legitimate complaints against the Church. There was a lot of corruption and abuse going on. The scriptural roots were being neglected in favor of a piety that was not founded on sound tradition. Luther's ideas spread fast due in large part to the invention of the printing press. He translated the Bible into German, wrote a catechism and composed hymns. He resisted all efforts by Rome for reconciliation.

His influence was so great that much of Germany followed him and split with the Church of Rome.

Although the sixteenth-century protests against the Church began with Luther they quickly spread. Two other movements developed. One originated with a Swiss priest named Zwingli and another with a French lawyer we call John Calvin. Many of the Puritans who settled on the eastern shores of the United States were influenced by Calvin. Both Calvin and Luther did not believe they were starting a new religion; they believed they were reforming Christianity. John Knox picked up Calvin's ideas and in Scotland began what would become Presbyterianism. He helped form the Church of Scotland. When Henry VIII, the King of England, proclaimed his break with the Papacy, the writings of Luther had already reached the country and were received and appreciated by some, thus paving the way for other Protestant theologians to influence England. All the reformers put a great emphasis on scripture and held a somewhat negative attitude toward human nature. The Church never recovered from this splintering. Among the groups themselves there was no agreement, and no group was in agreement with Rome.

### 6) The Counter-Reformation and the Council of Trent

The Council of Trent (1545-63) was a major force in the Counter-Reformation. It reaffirmed traditional Catholic teaching, including the place of scripture along with tradition, the seven sacraments, the authority of the hierarchy and the importance of human actions in the work of salvation. The Church emphasized the value of what the reformers challenged: devotion to Mary, eucharistic devotion, the priesthood and the hierarchy.

Many religious orders subsequently were founded. The Jesuits are perhaps the most well known. They were founded by Ignatius of Loyola and put themselves at the service of the pope. Their greatest contributions are their educational endeavors and their missionary labors. The Jesuits began to spread confidence in a Church that had been wounded by the Reformation. The *Spiritual Exercises* developed by Ignatius provided a discipline and framework for spiritual renewal in the Church.

The Baroque period in the world of art accompanied the Church's recovery from the Reformation. This period of opulence reflected a

Church which seemed triumphant. However, the scars of the Reformation continued to be a blemish on a divided Christianity. As long as everyone was not at the table of the Lord together, there was a blight that could not be ignored.

> *What responsibility do you think the Catholic Church bore in relationship to the Reformation? In what ways can healing the breach take place in your local area?*
> *What good came out of the Reformation?*

### 7) The Church in the United States

The Catholic Church in the United States began in a very different way than the European Church. From the beginning, when the United States was founded, there was always a separation between Church and State. Catholics were despised in many parts of the country; they were tolerated in other parts, but always held in some suspicion. As late as the 1960s, when John F. Kennedy, a Catholic, was running for president, there were those who feared that if he were to be elected, the pope would be running the country. Nevertheless, as time went on the Catholic immigrants held their own and came to be recognized as contributing citizens of the country. At present, Catholics in the United States are in many corporate and governmental leadership positions. While anti-Catholicism creeps in occasionally, it is not pervasive. Catholics have learned to live in a pluralistic society and are gaining more confidence in learning how to be Catholic and influence public policy and culture to reflect Christian values.

### 8) The Second Vatican Council

The First Vatican Council was held in 1869 following a time when the papacy had lost political control over the Papal States. The issue of papal infallibility was the primary issue which took over the Council. It was a controversial issue but it passed the Council. The work that the Council intended to focus on, the nature of the Church and the role of the bishops and the pope, did not take place until the Second Vatican Council which began in 1962 and ended in 1965. The Second Vatican Council brought about substantial changes in the Church and in the Church's understanding of itself. Four major documents called "constitutions" were issued, along with nine decrees and three declarations. The *Constitution on the Sacred Liturgy* had the most tangible effect on Catholics. As a result of the document many reforms happened in liturgy. The liturgy could use the "mother tongue." The faithful came to new realizations that as they gathered for liturgy they became the body of Christ; they were not merely present to watch but to do the work of the liturgy. They were called upon to participate in many ways from being readers and cantors to bringing up the gifts and helping distribute communion. As a result of this document, all the rites of the sacraments were revised. Much of the renewal incorporated understandings from the early Church which had been lost in the intervening years.

The *Dogmatic Constitution on the Church* set forth as clearly as possible the nature and purpose of the Church. Much of the imagery used to describe the Church is very pastoral: pilgrim people, a sheepfold, a field, "our Mother," a temple, a spouse, the body of Christ, the people of God. The document spoke of the close relationships with other Christian denominations as well as associations with other religions, especially the Jews and Muslims.

The Church calls all its members to the fullness of holiness no matter what their state in life is, be it ordained, religious or lay. Within the Church there are different roles and functions. As an organization the Church is hierarchial. It has the offices of bishops who are united with the pope and who govern their particular dioceses. Bishops are assisted by priests and deacons. Many religious and lay people also fill important roles in the Church. All the roles and offices in the Church are those designed to serve the whole body of Christ.

Another important document of the Second Vatican Council is the *Dogmatic Constitution on Divine Revelation.* The first draft of this document was sent back to committee by the pope because apparently it did not include any new insights or any of the benefits of modern research. The document which was promulgated in 1965 calls for the whole world to hear the call to salvation especially through the sacred scriptures. The document sees the Church as the authentic interpreter of the word of God. In this document Catholics are encouraged to read the Bible and to reflect on it frequently. This is important because after the Reformation the Protestants became people of the Bible and Catholics tended not to be well versed in the scriptures.

The last major work of the Council was the *Pastoral Constitution on the Church in the Modern World.* This work deals with the relationship of the Church to the people in the world in all their hopes and struggles. Whereas the first document on the Church looks inward, this one looks outward, taking on the "joy and hope, the grief and anguish of the people of our time, especially of those who are poor or afflicted in any way" (GS 1). The document sets out to analyze the "signs of the times" and interpret them through the lens of the Gospel in ways that are meaningful to contemporary people (GS 4). The *Constitution* examines the dignity of the human person, the role of the human community, the Church's role in modern issues and the urgent problems facing both the Church and the world.

The Second Vatican Council is often called the Council for Ecumenism. Four documents relate to the Church's relationship to others. The "Decree on Ecumenism" presents Catholic guidelines for the response to and promotion of Christian unity. This decree has been followed up with further principles and guidelines. It is obvious from these efforts that the "soul" of the Church wishes to heal the breaches of nearly five hundred years of broken relationships. However, it takes time to mend such divisions. The "Decree on the Catholic Eastern Churches" affirms the rites of the liturgies of the Eastern Churches as part of the Catholic Church. It calls on the Eastern Churches to work with Rome to promote unity with the Separated Eastern Churches. The third document, the "Declaration on the Relationship of the Church to Non-Christian Religions," affirms what is true and holy in Hinduism, Buddhism and Islam. The document recalls the bond between Christians and Jews, fosters mutual understanding and respect and deplores all forms of anti-Semitism. Finally, the "Declaration on Religious Liberty" declares that the human person has a right to religious freedom and that any kind of coercion that inhibits this freedom is forbidden.

Volumes have been written about the Second Vatican Council and its influence on the Church today. The above sketch merely touches the tip of the iceberg, but hopefully will entice the reader to pursue a serious study of the Council documents.

> *Looking back over this very brief sketch of Church history, name three periods which you think were the most significant in terms of the Church today. Explain why you chose what you did. In what ways has the Second Vatican Council influenced your thinking, believing and acting? How has it influenced your parish?*

## ONE, HOLY, CATHOLIC AND APOSTOLIC

These words, "one, holy, Catholic and apostolic," are referred to as the marks of the Church. They find their origin in the Nicene Creed. Originally they were used to define the Church against heretical sects. For centuries they were used to "prove" that the Catholic Church was the one, true Church. Today the marks of the Church can be used as descriptors of what the Church is to become. These attributes are founded on the very nature of the Church as the People of God and the Body of Christ empowered by the Spirit.

The Church is *one* because it believes in and finds its source in one God (CCC 813). Today the Church does not enjoy the unity that it would like, based on the oneness of God. The disunity among Christians is a wound that needs to be healed for the oneness of the Church to be radiant. In striving for oneness, the People of God implore the Holy Spirit to bring about unity in all of Christendom.

The Church is *holy* because Christ is holy (CCC 823). This does not mean that its members individually or as a community are without sin. It means that the source of holiness is found in Christ and that, as the body of Christ in the world today, the Church strives to become more holy. The Church's holiness is inseparable from that of Jesus. One does not find holiness by leaving the world but by working in the world as Jesus did to bring about the kingdom of God.

The Church is *catholic*. The word catholic has several meanings. It can mean "on the whole," or "universal." The attribute was first used by Ignatius of Antioch to mean that the local church had power and authenticity only to the degree that it identified with the universal Church and its spiritual leader. The Church, then, is catholic because it is open to everyone and because it is founded on Christ who brought salvation to everyone (CCC 830, 831).

The Church is *apostolic* because it was founded on the apostles and continues to teach and do the things the apostles did (CCC 857). The apostles not only were witnesses to Jesus' works and teachings but they were also sent forward by him and empowered by the Spirit to do his work. The apostles insured that the message and ministry of Jesus stayed alive and was spread to the far ends of the known world at that time. The Church originated with the apostles and there has been a continuation of their mission and ministry down to the present time.

While all these attributes of the Church are inherent in the Church today, they are not always lived out in a way that truly exemplifies them. Yes, the Church is one because it is founded on one God who continues to give it life; but its oneness is blemished by disunity. It continually strives for "more oneness," especially for Christian unity. The Church is holy, because its founder, Jesus Christ, is all-holy; but the Church is also not without blemish; it is not all-holy. It endeavors to become more holy, more like its founder. The Church is catholic because Jesus Christ, by his life, death and resurrection, made salvation possible to all humanity. However, the Church still needs to remove from its trappings those things which keep it from being universally effective in promoting the kingdom of God in today's world. The Church is apostolic because it follows the traditions of the apostles, but it needs to be more imbued with the Spirit and the simplicity of the apostolic times. The marks of the Church point to what is present and what is to come.

> *Which of the marks of the Church do you see as "true" but not "fully true" at this time in history?*
> *How do the marks of the Church define Christianity as different from other religions?*
> *How can we catechize about the marks of the Church without promoting a "we are better than everybody else" mentality?*

## THE MAGISTERIUM

By the magisterium of the Church we mean the exercise of the teaching authority of the Catholic hierarchy. The word is derived from a Latin word, *magister,* which means the one in authority, the one who has mastered some skills or body of knowledge, the "teacher." In the Church the term magisterium specifically refers to the teaching authority of the pope and the bishops. They share in the authority that Jesus Christ gave to the apostles and have the authority to make judgements regarding matters of faith and how the faith is lived out (LG 25). The bishops are not above the word of God. They listen to God's word and interpret it with the help of the Holy Spirit (DV 10). The magisterium exercises its authority in two ways: ordinary and extraordinary.

### 1) Ordinary teaching

The ordinary exercise of the magisterium is the customary teaching of the pope and in some cases the pope and the bishops. The pope's encyclicals are examples of this kind of teaching. The documents of Vatican II are other examples of the ordinary teaching of the magisterium. They are the authoritative teaching of the Church and they must be respected with a willingness to accept the teaching and the truth of the teaching. The ordinary teachings of the magisterium must be taken seriously. Honest efforts must be made to accept the teaching of the magisterium when it exercises its ordinary teaching authority.

### 2) Extraordinary Teaching

The magisterium teaches in an extraordinary manner when it teaches infallibly. The Second Vatican Council describes infallibility as a "charism of the Church" (LG 25). It is based on the belief of the living presence of the Holy Spirit in the Church. The *Constitution on the Church* first speaks about infallibility as the "sense of the faithful" concerning matters of *belief.* It states that when something is believed by the Church as a whole (bishops and the people in the pews), it does not contain error (LG 12). In other words, when there is common agreement on a matter of faith and morals, this belief is infallible.

Infallibility was proclaimed at the First Vatican Council in 1870. At that time it was limited to the teaching authority of the pope and stated that he cannot make an error when teaching about faith and morals when he speaks *ex cathedra,* which literally means "from the chair." It refers to the highest level of papal authority.

The Second Vatican Council further described the extraordinary or solemn teaching of the Church. It states that infallible teachings can come from the pope or the pope acting with the college of bishops, especially united in a Council (LG 25). This solemn teaching authority of the Church is exercised when a doctrine is defined by an ecumenical council, or by a pope speaking *ex cathedra.* Infallible teachings relate to revelation and settle a question of faith definitively so that it cannot be rescinded. Infallible teachings are defined in such a way that the intention of the magisterium is clear—all the faithful are to adhere to the doctrine and the doctrine is free from error. The effect of infallibility is two fold: first, all the faithful must give assent to the dogma; second, the faithful are guaranteed that what they are expected to accept is free from error based on the presence of the Holy Spirit. Seldom has the exercise of infallibility been used by the magisterium. The only commonly acknowledged use of infallibility since Vatican I was in the declaration of the Assumption of Mary, in 1950.

### 3) Dogmas and Doctrines

All dogmas and doctrines come out of the lived experience of the Church in the light of revelation. Sometimes these words, "dogmas and doctrines," are used interchangeably, but catechists should note that there are differences in the meaning of the words as they are used today. A dogma is a definitive teaching of the Church. Dogmas must meet certain conditions: they must be rooted in scripture or the post-biblical tradition of the Church and they must be considered part of revelation; they must be presented by the Church as a divinely revealed article of faith; and lastly they must be solemnly declared by the magisterium.

All dogmas are doctrines, but all doctrines are not dogmas. Not all the major beliefs of the Church have been declared dogmas. For instance, there is no dogma on grace or the Mystical Body of Christ, yet these are universally held beliefs.

A doctrine is an official teaching of the Church. Doctrines can be altered as new understandings, new conceptual frameworks, or as new cultural insights avail themselves. A good example of this is found in the Middle Ages where the Church taught that making money by lending money, in other words, collecting interest on money lent, was wrong or sinful. Later the Church came to new understandings of the role of banking in the life of villages and towns and dropped its objection to the practice. In more recent times the "Declaration on Religious Freedom" from the Second Vatican Council pointed to an expanded understanding of the issue of religious freedom, which differed from a document, promulgated in 1864, called the Syllabus of Errors. The document on religious freedom was one of the most highly debated at the Council and at the heart of the issue was whether doctrines could change by being further developed.

> *Without making distinctions between dogmas and doctrines, name some teachings of the magisterium of the Church which you find very insightful and helpful.*

*Name some teaching which you find perplexing. What resources do you need to come to a greater understanding of these teachings?*
*What advantage is there in making the distinction between the ordinary teaching of the magisterium and infallible teaching?*

## WHAT ARE THE MOST IMPORTANT BELIEFS OF THE CATHOLIC CHURCH?

One of the problems catechists face is knowing what are the most important points to cover. Sometimes this issue is called the hierarchy of truths. *Sharing the Light of Faith* deals with this question in Chapter 5 where it describes essential elements of the faith, such as the mystery of God, creation, Jesus Christ, the Holy Spirit, the Church, the sacraments, grace, the moral life, Mary and the saints, and death, judgment and eternity. Among these essential elements some are more important than others even though distinctions of significance are not delineated in the document.

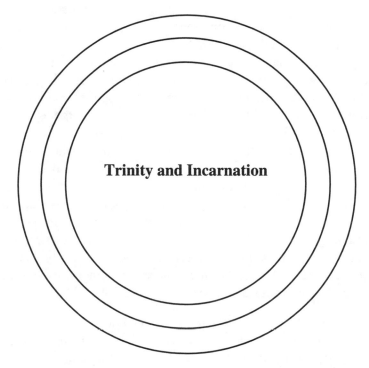

**Trinity and Incarnation**

The *Catechism of the Catholic Church* does not deal with the hierarchy of truths as such, but it does name two central beliefs. The first of these is the Trinity. It proclaims that the "Trinity is the central mystery of Christian faith," "the most fundamental and essential teaching in the 'hierarchy of truths'" (CCC 234). The second truth emphasized in the *Catechism* is the Incarnation. "Belief in the true Incarnation of the Son of God is the distinctive sign of Christian faith" (CCC 463). Perhaps the question about importance should not be asked using the image of hierarchy, which suggests a long list with a number one truth and then a last number which indicates least important. Michael Himes, priest and theologian, suggests using circles with core beliefs in the center, secondary beliefs in the innermost ring, etc. This image seems richer than a long, linear list of truths.

Envision for a moment a set of core beliefs in the center of a core circle. Himes imagines an inner or core circle with the names of two truths in it: the Trinity and the Incarnation. Feature all the other beliefs of the Catholic Church flowing from these like spokes in a wheel of concentric circles. What does that tell us about what we believe? By having the Trinity and the Incarnation in the inner circle we believe that God is a mystery that can never fully be understood. The death-resurrection mystery of Jesus Christ is linked to both Trinity and Incarnation.

Traditionally the dogma of the Trinity states that God is one God in three divine persons, the Father, the Son and the Holy Spirit. God the Son is totally divine and totally human. To describe this we say that Jesus Christ is one person with two natures, a divine and a human nature. Then when we try to explain it we say, "It's a mystery!"

Perhaps, instead of trying to explain the Trinity, it is much more worthwhile to tell what happens because of the Trinity. As a result of having a triune God we have God's self-communication to the world in creation, in Jesus Christ and in the Spirit. What does it mean to have God's self-communication? Basically it means that we as the human race are graced by God's presence in our innermost lives. Our God shares divine life with us. Our God shares divine energy with us. Our God is a dynamic God. Our God sent Jesus to bring the Good News that we are a loved, cherished, redeemed people. By his life, death, resurrection and the sending of the Spirit, Jesus makes it easier for us to understand how much we are loved, how much we share in God's life and how much support we have to continue his mission on earth. God's self-communication through Jesus basically tells us what great people we are and what great things we can do. By sending the Spirit, Jesus assures us that we are not alone and that the Spirit lives with us prodding, cajoling, giving us insights and courage to continue to build the kingdom so that others too may know the Good News of the divinity in their own lives. These two truths are so rich that their meaning is continually unfolding and being experienced in the Church today.

While it is not feasible here to name possible truths, beliefs, doctrines, and so forth for all the other circles, I would like to suggest two possibilities for the next circle: church and sacraments.

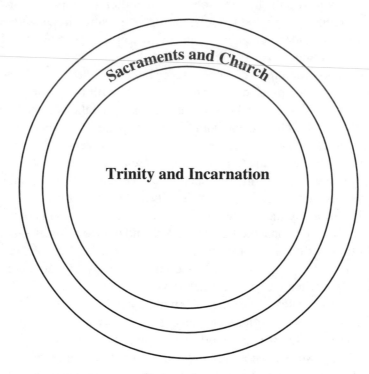

Neither the sacraments nor the Church can be separated from the Trinity and the Incarnation. The Church is the sacrament, or sign, of Christ. The seven sacraments are further signs of both the Church and Christ in the world today. Both the Church and the sacraments flow from the Trinity and the Incarnation. Other beliefs can be added to the concentric circles. The Church has never defined a precise hierarchy of truths. In one sense all truths of the Church are connected to the Trinity and Incarnation. In any area of the world or in any particular individual life certain truths are relied upon or emphasized at specific times based on the experience and needs of the people. The catechist must use all the skills of an artist to make the relationships between various aspects of the beliefs and life of the Church meaningful and appropriate for those catechized.

> *What core beliefs would you put in the center of your circle?*
> *Why did your choose these?*
> *How do they relate to other beliefs?*
> *How are they life-giving? In what ways do they influence you as a catechist?*
> *How would you design ways to engage those you catechize to articulate their core beliefs?*
> *In what ways can they be stretched to see a bigger picture of who the Church is?*

## PROMOTING JUSTICE

Promoting justice is integral to the mission of the Church. Social justice has its origins in both the First and Second or Old and New Testaments as has been noted above. Catholic social teachings have been developed in encyclicals, council documents and synods, especially in the last hundred years. The documents deal with political, economic, and social concerns. They address such issues as labor rights, peace, human dignity, religious freedom, the economy, world order, poverty, violence, the rights of all human beings, the environment concerns, solidarity and a fundamental option for the poor. All the documents are based on the Church's teaching on human dignity. Human dignity is founded on the biblical concept that all people are created in the image and likeness of God. Once human dignity is established, then the link is made to human rights. Rights and responsibilities flow from one's being created in the image of God and from one's being a member of the community. From human dignity to human rights and responsibilities come the emphasis on the social nature of the person. This ultimately involves the person's relationship to the civic, local, national and global communities, where concepts of the common good, public order and the principle of subsidiarity fall into place.

*What are the social issues in your local community?*
*How do they relate to human dignity, human rights and the rights of the community?*
*As a catechist how can you involve those you catechize in social issues in your community?*
*How would you help them see the relationship between social action, the scriptures and Church teaching?*
*In what ways can you promote the concept of solidarity with people in the United States and around the world who are suffering injustice?*
*Choose to study one papal or Council document involving justice such as* Church in the Modern World, Justice in the World *or* Pacem in Terris *(Peace on Earth). Examine it to see how the principles dealing with human dignity, human rights and the rights of the community are addressed.*
*How can you apply these principles with those you catechize?*

## PRACTICAL IMPLICATIONS

1. There are many images for the kingdom of God. Some are located in the New Testament. Have those you catechize discover in the Gospels three or four images of the kingdom of God and discover how they relate to the Church.

2. Have those you catechize do a timeline related to Church history. Have them highlight their favorite period. If you are catechizing middle school or older children have them do more research about the times of a particular period in Church history. Invite them to do creative projects related to the period they are studying, such as: imagine they are a reporter and interview people; develop a play based on the time period; pretend they are a saint who lived during the period; in what would they be involved?

3. Avery Dulles, a Jesuit theologian, wrote a book called *Models of the Church.* In the book he describes five models or ways of looking at the Church. Simply put, they are church as institution, church as mystical communion or community, church as sacrament, church as herald of good news and church as servant. To understand different aspects of the Church it is helpful to look at these models independently, but to get an adequate picture one needs to examine all aspects as being part of the Church. If you are catechizing adults,

invite them to explore the models. Have them make five columns, each headed by the name of one of the models. In pairs have the participants brainstorm all the things they think fit under each heading. Have each set of two share their list with another set of two people. Invite them to combine their lists into one where there is no overlap. Then have a group of eight do the same thing. Compare the descriptors. Note the richness of the Church. Be sure to point out that no model is adequate in itself, because the Church is a combination of institution, community, sacrament, herald and servant.

4. With younger children stress the community aspect of the Church. They are so concrete in their thinking that they will usually only identify the Church with a building. Help them to get to know various members of the Church, from volunteers, to the pastor, to members of the parish council. Have them do "service" projects for others, such as learning songs to sing at a visit to a nursing home or making decorative placemats for those living in a retirement community. By showing them through experience that the Church is both a community and a servant community you will enhance their understanding of the Church.

5. Have older children imagine they are various Church officials such as the pope and bishops. Have them imagine what problems they would face. Invite them to problem-solve and see the consequence of their solutions for a universal church.

6. The revelation of the Trinity and the Incarnation, while at the center of all Christian belief, can be viewed very abstractly because they are so profound and in some ways unexplainable. The role of catechesis is to interpret these truths in such a way that they become alive for those catechized. While they can never be fully understood and appreciated, the Trinity and the Incarnation can be the focus of catechesis based on the spiritual, emotional, intellectual, experiential, and social readiness of those catechized. A note of caution: in catechizing on these beliefs all things cannot be emphasized at once. Some aspects of the truth can be the focus at one time, other aspects at another time. Connecting the various aspects of the belief is important but often cannot happen at the same time a particular aspect of the truth is the point of focus. As a rule of thumb, the greater the maturity of those catechized, the more comprehensive the approach can be. Some examples follow about ways to catechize about the Trinity and the Incarnation.

a) God's gift of creation and an appreciation for it can be the
focus of catechesis across the ages. This can be done experien-
tially, for example, having young children explore the park for
the most beautiful fall leaves or signs of spring. Flowing from
this could come prayers of praise and thanksgiving to God the
creator of all things. Middle school and high school youngsters
could do a more sophisticated version of the same thing. They
might use cameras to film some beautiful aspects of creation,
including people, as well as some images of the pollution of
creation. They could make a documentary video about such
things. Part of the outgrowth of the project should certainly be
a recognition of God as the author of creation, of creation as a
gift from God, but also people's responsibility to care for creation and not exploit it. All this can be tied to biblical
metaphors about the beauty of creation, the Church's teaching
on environmental concerns, as well as specific actions which
the group can take to raise consciousness about the dangers to
the environment caused by greed, ignorance and exploitation.
These were addressed in Pope John Paul II's January 1, 1990
address.

This same idea can be explored with adults, not so much by having them do the research, but by presenting what is already available in
a very visual and provocative way. The challenge to the adults might be
how they can help change systems which contribute to environmental
destruction. All of the above examples emphasize one part of the Trinity: God's self-communication through creation and people's dependence on creation for human life. One of the benefits we experience
from a triune God is God's grace as present in God's creation.

b) God's greatest gift to us is Jesus Christ. Various aspects of
Jesus' life or images of Jesus are appropriate depending upon
the age and experience of those catechized. Young children can
identify with Jesus as their brother, who is also God's son.
Therefore, we are all children of God. This can be expanded by
exploring biblical stories such as Jesus' loving children or
phrases that describe Jesus as a caring person who did not want
people to be hungry. The greatest thing a catechist can do is
excite children's religious imagination. Once a person is
"hooked on" Jesus he or she is much more open to exploring
theological explanations about the mystery of Jesus and his

relationship to the Creator-God and the Spirit-God. Young children can be exposed to the three essential aspects of the Trinity, but they should not be confused by complex theological explanations which have no meaning for them.

Older children and adolescents benefit from knowing Jesus as a compassionate friend who knows them through and through and loves them even when they are not their best self. Friendship is so important to young people at this age that if they can know and believe that they have a friend in Jesus who is faithful to them through thick and thin, they will have experienced a powerful aspect of the Trinity. Biblical passages such as Jesus' love for Peter and Jesus' recognition of his leadership qualities, even though Peter made mistakes, can be a powerful sign of Jesus' love for adolescents today. Jesus' recognition of women as friends and missionaries—especially in a culture that treated woman as subservient—can be a persuasive statement with which many young people can identify. The Martha and Mary story as well as the story of the woman at the well are good biblical examples of this. Flowing from the concept that Jesus remains faithful to all people as their compassionate friend, adolescents can begin to see that Jesus works through other people, their friends, their teachers and other caring adults to help them realize that they are loved and cherished, even on days when they do not feel it. They can begin to understand the great mystery of the Incarnation, which is that God enters our human history and invites us to be one with the Trinity. This is the profound mystery which is continually manifested in our own history—sometimes as if it were happening for the first time.

There are so many aspects of Jesus' life with which adults can identify. As parents they can connect with Jesus' patience working with the apostles and disciples—waiting for them to catch on! They can associate Jesus' need to be alone for some time to pray with their own desire for a few minutes of peace and quiet to regroup, to reflect, to pray. They can identify with Jesus' compassion as they deal with the needs of their spouse and children. Adults of all ages can recognize the death-resurrection mystery of Jesus Christ in their own struggles, in the painful "deaths" of losing a job, of working with a terminally ill child, parent or spouse, of suffering a separation or divorce, of denying the need to be part of a recovery program and of suffering serious illness. The successful catechist needs to be able to help people see the interconnectedness between their real struggles and joys and the death-resurrection mystery of Jesus, otherwise they cannot tap into the wonderful treasure that is ours. We believe in a triune God and an Incarnate Word, who entered human history, lived and made many friends and a few enemies, told stories that piqued people's imagination and ultimately their faith, suffered, died and was raised to new and eternal life, making it possible for us to do the same. As a result of believing in our triune, Incarnate God, we are guaranteed that we are showered with the graces of a relationship with the divine from the moment we were being "knit in our mother's womb" (Psalm 39) into our eternal life.

    c) God lives in us today through the power of the Holy Spirit—the Spirit Jesus promised us until the end of time. As catechists we need to help people cultivate a sensitivity to the Spirit. The Spirit is with us, but if we are not conscious of the Spirit's presence, we miss opportunities to gain confidence in our ability to continue to build God's kingdom; we miss chances to make connections with the scriptural heroes and heroines and be strengthened by knowing the similarities between our common struggles. One of the effective ways to help people grow more aware of the Spirit's presence is through using scripturally-based prayer, where some time is devoted to quiet reflection on what God's Spirit is calling our hearts to do in relationship to making a difference in the world. This is not a "Spirit and me only" conversation, but a communal conversation where shared insights are used to discern the action of the Spirit in the community. Such prayer is effective for all ages, with more sophisticated approaches being used with young adults and adults.

It is important in catechesis to build on human experience because that is where God's presence is continually manifested. Revelation happened to human beings in their everyday lives. The art of catechesis must include the naming of the experience of God's manifestation in images and metaphors and doctrines that are part of the Church's life. Failure to do this consistently may be a weakness in catechetical ministry since the Second Vatican Council. Because young people cannot name their experience of God with the vocabulary and images that have been traditionally used by the Church, there is the impression that they do not "know" anything about the Church. The naming in connection with the tradition, but not being enslaved by the words and images of the past, is important because it connects us to the larger Church, informs and forms us, and gives us confidence that we are part of something bigger than ourselves, the communion of saints. A review and articulation of the Church's teaching related to the catechetical session is not only appropriate but necessary. Words like, "today we talked about one important aspect of the Trinity," or, "Today we saw how great our lives are because of the Incarnation," or, "Remember what the meaning of Incarnation is…" are simple ways to reinforce key doctrines of our faith. They must be reinforced often in order for them to be integrated into the lives of those we catechize. However, without the touching imaginative experiences which must proceed the articulation of doctrine, all we are doing is pumping information into people and not touching their hearts and minds in tandem. The latter is what "hooks" people on the Trinity and the Incarnation.

The ideas stated above are meant to "prime the pump" of each catechist's creativity. The point of attempting to share a few suggestions is that unless we believe that God continually manifests the triune presence in people's lives today, we are just passing on dry doctrine which is not going to excite anybody's faith-growth. As a matter of fact, it may do harm and inhibit God's gift of faith from taking form. Not only must we believe this ourselves but we must discover the art of passing on the faith in a way that will enhance the faith of those we catechize to be "living, conscious and active." To be able to know that the manifestations of God's presence are truly of God, we need the Church in its wisdom and in its treasure to help us make the connections with the past, to gain insights into the present and to be energized to face the future with hope. Catechists are faced with these challenges and need to be creative in approaching them to be successful. Catechesis is truly an art.

## REFLECTION

Have a Bible enthroned. Light a candle before the prayer service. Have a bowl of water and a leafy branch to sprinkle the assembly and copies of the Apostles' or Nicene Creed for each participant.

Sing an appropriate opening hymn.

*Leader:* God, our Creator, our Redeemer and our Sustainer, we come in utter humility as we think about what you have done for us and what you have empowered us to do for others. Encourage us especially in difficult times not to lose heart as we strive to continue to build your kingdom here on earth. We ask this through Jesus Christ, our Lord, our brother, friend and redeemer and through his risen Spirit present with us today.

*All:* Amen.

*Reader:* Proclaim John 14: 15–16, 18–20.

Pause for reflection using the following questions:

> *When and how am I aware of the Spirit's presence in my life?*
> *How do I cultivate a sensitivity to the Spirit's presence in my life?*
> *When I catechize how do I help others become aware of God's presence?*

If time allows invite the group to share reflections.

*Leader:* We are invited by our baptisms to continually grow in our understanding and awareness of our shared life with the triune God. As you are blessed with the waters of baptism, recall your baptismal commitment, perhaps made for you by your parents and godparents, to continually grow in faith by participating in the life of the Christian community. (Have someone carry the bowl of water and sprinkle the assembly with water.)

As a sign of our baptismal commitment let us pray the Creed together. (Use either the Apostles or the Nicene creed.)

*Leader:* Let us share a sign of peace with each other.

*All:* Pray the Lord's Prayer.

Close with a hymn familiar to the group.


## RESOURCES

Dulles, Avery, S.J. *Models of the Church.* New York: Doubleday, 1974.

Dulles, Avery, S.J. *A Church to Believe In.* New York: Crossroad, 1982.

Marthaler, Berard L., O.F.M. Conv. *The Creed.* Mystic, Connecticut: Twenty-Third Publications, 1987.

Sullivan, Francis A., S.J. "Magisterium," in The *New Dictionary of Theology,* Komonchak, Joseph; Collins, Mary; and Lane, Dermot, eds. Wilmington, Delaware: Michael Glazier, 1989.

Sullivan, Francis A., S.J. *Magisterium, Teaching Authority in the Catholic Church.* New York: Paulist Press, 1984.

# 6
# Prayer and Ritual

Imagination is at the heart of all artistic endeavors; it is also at the center of prayer and ritual. These twin processes of prayer and ritual are significant pillars in the catechetical efforts because each of them have the potential to unfold many levels of meaning and create a sense of bondedness with Jesus Christ and the Christian community. Catechists are challenged to provide many and varied experiences of ritual prayer which employ the rich symbols of the Christian heritage.

Prayer is the lifting of one's heart and mind to God (CCC 2559). It is a conscious effort to be in communion with God, to open oneself to a shared life with God (CCC 2565). Prayer is a way of having both a personal and communal relationship with God. Prayer connects people to God in a way that enriches their lives. For the Christian, prayer is Trinitarian. It involves a relationship to the Father, our creator, to the Son, our redeemer and to the Holy Spirit, our sanctifier and sustainer whose presence makes prayer possible.

Prayer requires the engagement of the whole person; scripture tells us that it is the heart that prays. The heart is the hidden center that only the Spirit of God can fathom. It is the place where we choose life or death. It is the place where we encounter God in a most intimate way (CCC 2563).

The word "prayer" means to make a request, to petition, to communicate with God. It implies that as human beings we stand in need before God and are dependent on God. Needs are not always seen as requests; sometimes they are portrayed as affirmations of awe and praise or thanksgiving. Some of the Hebrew scriptures use the word meaning "to bow down" as a word for prayer. At the heart of prayer is the acknowledgement that we are dependent and reliant on God.

"I am the bread of life...." (Jn 6:35)

## JESUS' PRAYER

Jesus was a person of prayer. Before beginning his public life Jesus spent time away from everyone praying in the desert. When occupied with teaching and preaching Jesus escaped the crowds to pray (Luke 5:16). Mark's Gospel talks of Jesus being very busy, but getting up early to pray (Mark 1:35). Jesus always prayed before he did significant things. He prayed before choosing the apostles (Luke 6:12). He prayed after feeding the crowds (John 6:15). He prayed in gratitude (John 11:41). Jesus prayed as death was looming (John 12:27–28, Luke 23:34, Mark 15:34, Luke 23:46). Both in the long narrative before his death in John's Gospel and in Matthew's Gospel we are reminded that Jesus and the Spirit are with us when we are gathered in prayer (Matthew 18:20; John 14:18–31). It is important to note that for Jesus prayer was a vital element of his life. There was no such thing as not having time to pray. The relationship between Jesus and his Father was so close that prayer and communication were integral to life, not apart from it. It is important to realize that Jesus did not belong to a religious order that had structured times to pray. He was a person who was committed to doing God's will and growing in understanding his relationship to God. His example and insights can help us know what is expected of us in terms of prayer and our relationship to God (CCC 2599–2606).

> *When do you pray? When is it easiest for you to pray?*
> *Some find it easiest to pray early in the morning; others like to pray while driving to or from work. Some people take time at noon to pray for ten minutes; others pray before bedtime. When a person prays is not as important as praying itself. Sometimes we find ourselves "praying on the fly," which is adequate in a pinch, but such prayer is not sufficient build a prayer life. Read and reflect on Mark 1:14–35. List all the things Jesus did in one day. How did he manage to pray? When is it possible for you to plan to pray?*

## THE LORD'S PRAYER

Jesus taught us to pray by example and by giving us the Lord's Prayer (CCC 2761–2865). The Lord's Prayer expresses two different kinds of relationships: those possible between God and ourselves and the relationships we are to have among ourselves. First of all, Jesus uses the word *Abba* for God. This word shows that Jesus had a very familiar relationship with God, a relationship that was intimate, loving and life giving. *Abba* was a word that would mean Dad, Daddy, or Pop in our language. It was full of reverence but not overly formal. It indicated a wholesome loving relationship of a son to his dad. This is the kind of relationship that is possible between ourselves and God. The fact that we call God "our Father" implies that we all have a relationship to one another as brothers and sisters, because we all share the one Father.

The first three parts of the Lord's Prayer point to our responsibilities to God. First, we are called to praise God: "hallowed be your name"; second, we are called to build up God's kingdom: "your kingdom come"; and, lastly, we are called to do God's will: "your will be done on earth as it is in heaven."

After we recognize our responsibilities to God we turn and say, "but we need your help in order to fulfill these responsibilities." We ask God to feed us, forgive us and protect us from temptation so we can praise him, contribute to the kingdom and do God's will. Notice that we ask to be forgiven by God while at the same time promising to forgive those who hurt or harm us.

In many ways the Lord's Prayer contains the heart of the Christian message. Some have called it the "summary of the whole gospel" (CCC 2761). It directs our attention to praise God, to look beyond ourselves and put effort into God's kingdom on earth, to recognize our dependence on God's will, to petition God for what we need, to forgive others and not to be overwhelmed by temptation.

> *The Lord's Prayer is so familiar that sometimes we forget how profound it is. Pray the prayer slowly and reflectively. Think of Jesus' use of the word* Abba *or Dad for the word Father. Use the following questions for reflection:*
>> *What words would you use to praise God other than those used in the Lord's Prayer?*
>> *What do you do to build God's kingdom or reign?*
>> *How do you know that you are doing God's will?*
>> *In what ways does God feed you?*
>> *How does God forgive you?*
>> *How do you forgive others? When is this most difficult?*
>> *Recall a time when you were led from temptation. How did*

*God work through circumstances to help you? Were you aware that you were being tempted?*
*What is your favorite phrase in the Lord's Prayer? Why did you choose it?*

## BASIC FORMS OF PRAYER

*The Catechism of the Catholic Church* names five basic forms of prayer: blessing, petition, intercession, thanksgiving and praise (CCC 2644). The *prayer of blessing* has two parts, our prayer ascends to God and God in turn blesses us (Psalm 16:7; Psalm 18:47). Prayers of blessing and adoration primarily acknowledge our dependence on the greatness of God who gives life and all good gifts (CCC 2626–28).

The *prayer of petition* acknowledges our dependence on God. It acknowledges that we need forgiveness and many other things to help shape the kingdom of God (Psalm 85:1–5; Psalm 130). All of our needs can become petitions to our all-loving God (CCC 2629–33).

The *prayer of intercession* is a form of prayer of petition which acknowledges who the intercessor is. As Christians we often pray to God through the intercession of "Our Lord Jesus Christ" (CCC 2634). Our liturgical prayers are good examples of intercessory prayers.

The *prayer of thanksgiving's* greatest form is the Eucharist. Eucharist means to give thanks. In the eucharistic prayer we thank God for all of creation, for creating us, for sending Jesus Christ, for his death-resurrection and the sending of the Spirit (CCC 2637–38). In a ministry setting, St. Paul sets a good example by continually thanking God for all of his collaborators in the ministry. (Romans, 1:8; 1 Corinthians 1:4–7; Philippians 1:3–4). Many of the psalms also give both praise and thanks for the wonderful things God has done (Psalm 65:1–5).

The *prayer of praise* glorifies God because God is God. It does not thank God for what God does, but it celebrates God for being God. In the book of Psalms we hear many phrases of praising God. There we hear people clapping with joy in praise of God (Psalms 47:2; 8:2; 22:23; 66:1–2).

The Magnificat is another prayer that includes both praise and thanksgiving. It is found in Luke 1:46–55 and is based on a Song of Hannah found in 1 Samuel 2:1–10. In Mary's prayer she sings praises for God's greatness and salvific mercy. She emphasizes her unworthiness and how much God does for the lowly, those who acknowledge their dependence on God. While scripture scholars may have varying opinions on who the lowly are in the prayer, they all agree that admitting need is a condition for receiving God's grace. God has no time for arrogant attitudes. For Luke, affiliation with "the poor of God" does not come from race or class, but rather as a response to those who share possessions, ask for and give forgiveness to enemies. Many of the themes which Luke will develop in his gospel are found in the Magnificat. The Magnificat is an important prayer of the Church and is used daily in the Liturgy of the Hours.

> *Reflect on the kinds of prayer described above. Pray using some of the biblical citations. In your own words describe what the Church is praying for when it blesses, petitions, offers intercessory prayers, thanks and praises God. Use the prayers of the nearest Sunday liturgy to find examples of the various kinds of intercessory prayer. The chart on the next page will help you organize your thoughts.*
> *Take some quiet time and pray your favorite passage. Why is the passage appealing to you at this time in your life?*
> *How does it appeal to your imagination?*
> *How can the passage you chose or another one be used in an engaging creative catechetical session?*

## METHODS OF PRAYER

Besides various kinds of prayer there are also different prayer traditions within the Church. These are communal prayer, meditative prayer and ritual prayer. These methods of prayer are often found in combination with each other.

### 1) Communal

The greatest form of *communal prayer* is the Eucharistic liturgy. It, along with all the sacraments, will be discussed in the next chapters. Communal prayer is conducted as a group, a body, a community. Prayer in catechetical settings where the group prays together is an example of communal prayer. Such prayer often includes:

a) an opening song
b) an intercessory prayer
c) a reading from scripture
d) time for reflection
e) general intercessions
f) a ritual and a closing prayer such as the Lord's Prayer

| Kind of prayer | Source | In your own words, what are we praying for? |
| --- | --- | --- |
| Blessing/adoration | | |
| Petition | | |
| Intercessory prayer | | |
| Thanksgiving | | |
| Praise | | |
| Combination of several kinds of prayer such as the Magnificat | | |

Communal prayer is very important for the Church because from the beginning God worked with us as a people. God never called individuals for their own sakes, but rather God called individuals to lead the community, the people of God. In an era where there is an emphasis on individualism and subsequently a "me-and-Jesus" mentality, it is important to stress the communal nature of our relationship to God. Well constructed communal prayer which makes good use of ritual and scripture is a fine preparation for the celebration of the Eucharist.

Communal prayer has both vocal and reflective pieces. The vocal part can include a sung hymn, a sung response to a reading or sung intercessions and acclamations. A cantor can lead the singing. Recitation can also be part of communal prayer. Reciting psalms, intercessions and prayers are all part of communal prayer. Gestures such as making the sign of the cross, holding hands, standing, sitting, doing movements expressing reverence and respect and prayerful dancing are all parts of communal prayer.

Reflecting and sharing are also part of communal prayer. After listening to the scripture and reflecting on it in silence, sharing thoughts and insights with the community is very appropriate. Sometimes art projects are good responses to scripture stories, especially if they link the story with the person's experience.

### 2) Meditation

*Meditation* is a form of individual prayer which may take place alone or in a group. Meditation involves the mind, imagination and the will. There are certain processes that some find helpful in meditation. St. Ignatius, St. Sulpice, St. Theresa of Avila and St. John of the Cross are well known for insights into forms of mental prayer.

### 3) Guided Meditation

Guided meditation comes out of an Ignatian spirituality. It is a way of praying using one's religious imagination and scripture. The following steps are helpful in doing a guided meditation.

1. Select a gospel story involving Jesus, such as Jesus calling his followers.
2. Quiet the participants using a centering technique, such as playing soft music and asking them to pray quietly to themselves, "Jesus, I love you; help me know you better," or some such prayer.
3. Invite the participants to close their eyes. The soft music can continue playing in the background.
4. Describe the scene: What is going on? Who is there? What kind of a day is it? Use your own imagination as you do this.
5. Get the participants into the scene. Small children can imagine that they are holding Jesus' hand as he walks along. Older children or adults can be one of the characters, or be an invisible shadow, or a

reporter. Young children can do this process for three or four minutes. It is good to do it often with them. Middle school children, adolescents or adults can usually focus on a guided meditation for fifteen to twenty minutes. If these are structured well, the middle school children may ask to do guided meditations once or twice a week. What seems to appeal to them is an intimate connection to the heroes and heroines of scripture.

6. Read the passage from scripture pausing appropriately to ask questions such as: "What is it like to walk next to Jesus? Does he notice you? What does he say to you? What is it like to be called to follow Jesus? What fears do you have? What excites you about the prospect? How will you tell your parents or your friends about the encounter? What are other people saying at the scene?" Be sure the questions are constructed to fit the scene. Allow sufficient time between questions and the continuation of the story for the participants to imagine their presence at the scene and imagine what is happening. The pray-ers should keep their eyes closed for the whole meditation.

7. Gradually have the participants leave their imagined world. On occasion have them share either verbally or artistically their experiences of encountering Jesus in this prayer form.

8. Ask the participants what they will do differently or how they feel toward Jesus because of this experience. If you chose the story of the calling of the followers of Jesus, ask how Jesus is calling them today to be his followers.

The value of guided meditation is that it allows the participants to affectively connect to Jesus and to the other people in the scripture. The experience builds their religious imagination which is where faith is rooted. Well-crafted guided meditations truly enhance spirituality and help make Jesus real to people.

> *Examine your future catechetical sessions. Find one that would lend itself to guided meditation. Use the steps outlined above to prepare for a guided meditation with the children or adults you catechize.*

In recent years there has been a renewal in attention paid to meditation. Use of a short three-to-five-word prayer such as "Blessed be God," or "Grant us peace, O Lord," or "Have mercy on me," are used to quiet one's inner self and prepare one's mind to be open to the infusion of God's Spirit. Short prayers are rooted in Eastern Christian spirituality and help one to pray in a simplified mode. Prayers also can be wordless, listening and appreciating God's presence. Contemplation is the word that is sometimes used to describe the highest form of meditation. It is considered a pure gift, infused by God to let one "taste" the goodness of God, to commune with the love of God. Sometimes it is described as a simple focus on God's presence. The experience is one of stillness. It calls for one to be very receptive to God, rather than being in active pursuit of an experience of the divine.

### 4) The Rosary

As a prayer form the *rosary* combines the sense of short prayers with meditation on the mysteries of Jesus and Mary. The rosary evolved over the centuries. Its characteristics were used by the Brahmans in India as well as by Buddhists and Muslims, who strung knots or beads together for prayer. The rosary took on a specific meaning and became popular in Christianity in the twelfth century, especially among those who could not read the psalms of the Divine Office (CCC 2678). The rosary became both a prayer tool and a catechetical tool. The mysteries of the rosary (Joyful, Sorrowful and Glorious) contained the major events in the life of Jesus and Mary and the foundation for Christian faith. As one came to know the mysteries one could meditate on them. At the same time, one was being freed from distraction by praying fifty short "Hail Marys." Today Christians continue to pray the rosary as a way of communing with Jesus and Mary through the mysteries of their lives.

### 5) Spiritual Journaling

A popular way of focusing on prayer and aspects of our elusive lives is journaling. Spiritual journaling is writing about one's insights and feelings. Many journals are free flowing where people simply record ideas that come to them without analysis. Other journaling techniques are more formal and call for following certain steps, coming to some conclusions. Journals are also used to document one's dreams. Still other techniques call for being in dialogue with people from the past. These may be relatives who have died, or saints or heroes or heroines who have walked before us. Being in dialogue with Jesus is also appropriate. This dialogue technique calls for the author to write for the various characters in the scene.

Journaling is often introduced as part of the catechetical process. It enables adults and young people to get in touch with some of their thoughts which they may not want to share or may not know how to share with others. Journaling can be a fine spiritual tool, if used well. Most people need some training in using journaling. The training can include examples of journaling that share feelings as well as questions. People need to know that all feelings, even negative ones, can be written in their journals and all questions can be asked, even angry ones. All ages should know that their journals are private and are usually not shared with others. Some successful catechists have set up individual meetings to discuss any parts of the young people's journals which they wish to share with them. If this is to happen, the youngsters should know about it before they begin their journals. If a catechist for some reason intends to use journals for sharing or grading, all should know this from the beginning.

> *Begin a journal yourself. Start by reading and reflecting on a scripture passage that you have always appreciated. Journal about what you like about the passage, what parts are perplexing, what parts are challenging, etc.*
>
> *Reflect on your role as a catechist. Write about some of the results you would like to have in your ministry. After each session, write about your feelings about the session and the reactions of the young people. If you are disappointed, note that. If some things went well, write about that. Regular journaling can be helpful not only to you as catechist, but also to you as one on a spiritual journey.*

### 6) The Labyrinth as a Spiritual Tool

The labyrinth is an ancient meditative tool. It basically is a metaphor for a spiritual journey. This walking meditation opens the soul much like a short prayer might and helps one to get in touch with many aspects of one's spiritual journey. A labyrinth is not a maze. It is not a place to get trapped. It is a spiritual journey in which one goes to the center and out to the world again refreshed and more connected to where one has come and where one is to go. Walking the labyrinth leads one to develop greater awareness of one's spiritual journey and to be energized for continuing the journey. Walking the labyrinth can channel one's spiritual restlessness. A famous labyrinth is found at Chartres Cathedral which dates back to the twelfth century. Replicas of that labyrinth can now be found across the United States. They are growing in popularity because of the work and dedication of Lauren Artress at San Francisco's Grace Cathedral.

### 7) Ritual Prayer

Ritual prayer is a structured activity. All the sacraments are structured activities celebrating the death-resurrection of the Lord. Ritual activity is part of all communal prayer. Rituals use stories, symbolic actions, gestures, sounds, smells and objects to form communities, to express beliefs and mysteries and to give meaning to life. Rituals transform people and give them new meaning. Water poured over one's head in the name of the Father, Son and Spirit initiates a person into the mystery of the death-resurrection of Christ as lived out in a community. This ritual activity is multi-dimensional. Rituals should not be limited to formal sacramental activity. In fact, if ritual actions were used more pervasively in communal prayer in catechetical sessions, those catechized would be more attuned, attentive and appreciative of the symbolic actions in sacramental celebrations.

#### a) Rituals help us be aware of the transcendent

Rituals are important to human activity, especially as humanity tries to "touch" the transcendent as well as express its experience of the divine—that there is more to life than meets the eye. According to the Jesuit theologian Teilhard de Chardin, by reason of creation and even more the Incarnation, the transcendent exists in each of us. This "touch" of the divine inherently desires to grow and permeate the fabric of our being. Because we are sensual beings we yearn to "put our finger on" the transcendent, the spiritual, the God-like of our existence. Rituals help us to do that. Rituals draw us deeper into the sensual so that we can bond with the spiritual. Rituals help us to take life in slow motion so that we can see the spiritual, the God-life in our everyday existence.

Ritual actions mirror the transcendent. They are concurrently touchable and elusive, present and fleeting, understandable and mysterious, personal and impersonal. The lighting of a candle before proclaiming the scriptures signals the mysterious, the fleeting, the elusive, the Spirit's presence, while at the same time reflecting a concrete, easily understood action. The lighting of a candle during a storm when all the electricity is out does not have the same meaning as lighting a candle before the scriptures are proclaimed, even though the action is identical.

### b) Symbolic actions unfold meaning

The symbolism in the ritual action at prayer draws us into various levels of meaning. One can perceive the action of the Spirit in the words proclaimed; one can feel influenced in one's heart by the power of the Spirit; one can be aware that there is something more here than meets the eye, even though one may not be able to articulate what the "something" is; one can benefit directly from the words proclaimed by gaining insights into the problems of one's life. In other words, the flaming candle has helped open the person's heart and mind to the presence of God speaking directly to the person.

### c) Communal prayer is the starting point for ritual

In catechetical settings communal prayer is an ideal place to situate ritual prayer. The actions can be varied. Some may include lighting a candle before proclaiming the Word of God, presenting a candle lighted from the paschal candle, blessing oneself or the community with water, breaking bread together, anointing of hands with oil, incensing the Bible and the community, sharing from the same cup, and the like. All these rituals are based on symbolic actions used in the sacraments. When used in communal prayer they should not be confused with sacramental actions, nor should similar words be used in the ritual actions.

Other ritual actions can be incorporated into communal prayer. For instance, if one is studying God's creation, signs of God's creation (flowers, leaves, etc.) could be collected as part of the session and then distributed as part of the prayer. As one blesses God for all creation, the person may be invited to come forward and take a sign of God's creation home. If one is studying the body of Christ from the perspective that St. Paul (1 Corinthians 12:12–31) teaches, one may have a large outline of a body shaped like a jigsaw puzzle and have the young people write their names and talents (as well as those of their families and friends) on the body. The puzzle can then be cut up and distributed to the participants. At prayer, after the proclamation of the scriptures and reflection on them, the young people can be invited to come forward to put the "puzzle" back together. This experience helps them have a tangible experience of how all contribute to the body of Christ by using their talents to build the kingdom of God.

### 8) Music as Prayer

Music cannot be separated from prayer. Historically music has always been linked cross-culturally to a sense of the divine, of the sacred. In the Judeo-Christian tradition music has been associated with major faith experiences. Miriam contributed to the celebration of the Exodus with her tambourine. David played his lyre or harp and created tunes by which he spoke to God. The Psalms, some of which are attributed to David, express almost every human emotion. There are songs of joy and exultation as well as songs of depression and lamentation. Music from the earliest of times has been both a way of praying and a way of enhancing prayer. Music is both mysterious and concrete. Its effect on individuals and communities is both predictable and variable. Its ability to help people "touch" the transcendent has never been questioned.

Nowhere are the transcendent possibilities of music felt more than in the revised sacramental rituals of Vatican II. There music plays an important role not just in helping the assembly relate to the transcendent, but also in enabling the assembly to fully participate in the action of the Eucharist. Music helps form the body of Christ as people gather to form the assembly; music is the medium whereby people celebrate the gospel, recognize the holiness of God's presence, recall the death-resurrection mystery, and celebrate the holiness of all creation, of all people who have been part of it, of all leaders and of all we still have to accomplish to build the reign of God.

Our catechetical efforts need to help those we work with appreciate and perform their musical gifts for the honor and glory of God. Doing this in communal prayer in our catechetical sessions is critical to the catechetical process of leading people to pray. When catechizing use the parish repertoire of responses, psalms, acclamations and alleluias to the extent possible.

## DOES PRAYER REALLY "WORK"?

Questions about the efficacy of prayer are not new questions, but ones that every generation asks. Does prayer make a difference? Does prayer change God's mind? Why should we pray? If we pray enough will we get what we ask for? All these questions deal with prayers of petition and imply a temperamental God who is counting prayers and saying "yes" when there are "enough" and "no" when we are a few short.

Faith helps us believe that God hears our prayers. Jesus tells us that God knows what we need before we ask for it (Matthew 6:8). No one seems to question whether prayers of praise or thanksgiving are heard. It is those petitions that get the scrutiny. Space does not allow all the complexities of the subject to be explored here. However, it should be noted that God is a personal God who cares deeply for each of us. God also has given us freedom to choose to be good, holy people who reflect the life and values of Jesus Christ. God sees the "big picture." We see the world and our lives from our limited perspective. Prayer is a very powerful tool. When we pray for one another, powerful energy is exchanged. When we pray for one another, spiritual bonding takes place between ourselves and God. When we pray to be empowered by the Spirit, especially to accept difficult things, we believe that God hears our prayer because Jesus has promised that we will not be tried beyond what we can endure with God's grace.

Father John Wright, a Jesuit priest, gives us insights about the efficacy of prayer in the following:

> "When we respond to God's invitation to ask for what we need, symbolic activity deepens the personal relationship of trust and dependence on him. Whatever else we ask for in prayer, one fundamental request underlies all others: that we may grow in our relationship to God as sons and daughters, and as brothers and sisters of one another and of Jesus Christ. It is in this sense that the prayer of petition is always answered."

As we are empowering people to pray, it is helpful to pray prayers of praise and thanksgiving. This empowers the pray-er to be more conscious of the presence of a loving, creating and caring God in his or her life. Once awareness of this relationship is solid, then prayers of petitions can be understood as enhancing a relationship rather than as simply requesting favors. Also, doing prayers of petition as intercessory prayers through the name of Jesus Christ roots the pray-er in the death-resurrection mystery. Introducing prayers of petition in a way that acknowledges communal needs enhances the pray-er's vision of the needs of the community and does not let the person get stuck on his or her own personal needs. (CCC 2735–41)

## PROMOTING JUSTICE

Prayer and working for justice are intimately linked. It is difficult to imagine a person or a community that is united with God through prayer but not concerned about the injustice that pervades the globe. In a document from the 1971 Synod, *Justice in the World,* we are reminded that the works of justice are a "constitutive dimension of preaching the Gospel." The need to strive to work for justice is based on the dignity of the human person.

> "In Catholic teaching the concept of human dignity implies not only that the person is the steward of creation and cooperates with the creator to perfect it, but that the rest of creation, in its material, social, technological, and economic aspects, should be at the service of the person. Human dignity is secure only when the spiritual, psychological, emotional, and bodily integrity of the person is respected as a fundamental value" (NCD 156).

Prayer can inspire and sustain those working for justice. Prayer can give a social justice consciousness because the Spirit working through prayer can help people see differently. Passages from the scripture, such as "let justice roll like a river" (Amos 5:24–27) and "as long as you did it to the least of my brethren, you did it to me" (Matthew 25:40) point to a new vision and new insights for people. These are but two examples of how justice pervades the scriptures. Praying with the scriptures is praying for justice.

Besides a new or renewed consciousness prayer can be about social justice issues. Cloistered religious men and woman pray for justice and effect it without ever leaving their monasteries. Prayer can bring about justice by supporting those working for it, by changing the awareness of those who cause injustice or allow it to continue and "giving them a new heart," and by empowering those affected by it to be courageous and not to lose heart. Prayer can also create a sense of solidarity with the poor and the victims of injustice. Through prayer we can walk with those suffering so they do not feel alienated, isolated or abandoned.

Because it is the same Spirit that is called upon by those who produce injustice and by those who are the victims of it, praying to the Spirit to enlighten those who perhaps unwittingly make life miserable for others can be helpful. St. Paul is a good example of someone who was promoting injustice by persecuting the Christians. Through the work of the risen Spirit of the Lord, he saw what havoc he was doing to the Christians, experienced a change of heart and became a staunch and loyal follower of Jesus Christ. This was not the result of what people were doing for justice, but rather it was the work of the Spirit in the life of Paul. That same spirit is available to us today. That same Spirit can bring about conversions to top executives, governmental and Church officials who are promoting injustice, perhaps unknowingly.

Prayer inspires a vision of justice, sustains the workers who strive for local, national and global justice and works through the Spirit to bring about conversions to justice by those who may be unaware of the evil effects of their actions.

## PRACTICAL IMPLICATIONS

As catechists our role is to open the many riches of prayer to those whom we catechize. Some of the ways of doing this follow:

1. Involve the participants in planning communal prayer. Depending upon their age and abilities all can help prepare for prayer. Sometimes this means preparing the environment for prayer, sometimes the readings, the rituals and the music.
2. Regularly engage participants in various kinds of communal prayer: blessings, petitions, intercessory prayer, praise and thanksgiving.
3. Be sure all prayer involves the use of religious imagination. It is in our imagination that we first encounter God. It is in our imagination that our spiritual lives grow and are nourished. Note that the use of imagination is not anti-intellectual. It is the way Jesus taught people

to pray. To have a dialogue with God one has to image some aspects of God and how these relate to us as real human beings.

4. Be sure communal prayer involves ritual actions and is not only word-centered.

5. Even in communal prayer be sure there is some time for quiet reflection so that the Spirit may engage the pray-er in communion with God.

6. Teach participants to meditate. Guided meditations may be a helpful way to get started in this endeavor.

7. Be sure prayer involves as many of the senses as possible. How can the senses of smell, taste, touch, seeing and hearing be involved?

8. Acknowledge that prayer is a gift of the Spirit. We can prepare the soil but God gives the "increase."

9. Be sure prayer includes the promotion of justice and the conversion of those who may be causing injustice on a local, national and global realm.

## REFLECTION

Have the Bible enthroned. Have a candle, matches, incense and a bowl to burn incense available.

Gather the praying community with a well-known hymn.

*Presider:* God, our Creator, you have given us the example of your son Jesus Christ as the person who taught us to pray. We know that Jesus prays with us as we praise your name, as we bless your creation and as we thank you for your gifts and your everlasting presence. We ask you to continue to walk with us as we build your reign on earth. We ask this in the name of Jesus Christ our Lord and brother.

*All:* Amen.

Light the candle near the Bible.

Allow for a moment of silence.

Incense the Bible and the community gathered for prayer.

*Reader:* Proclaim Matthew 6:9–13.

Incense the Bible and the community again.

Encourage people to select one phrase of the Lord's Prayer on which to mediate.

Allow ten or fifteen minutes for quiet reflection.

Invite personal sharing of their meditation.

Ask people to think about whom and what they wish to pray for in the general intercessions.

*Presider:* Eternal God, you have called us together to be your people, to spread your "Good News," to praise and thank you. We come to you now asking your continued blessing on those whom we care for:

Invite general intercessions. Response: "Lord, hear our prayer," or a sung response known by the group.

Group Intercessions

*Conclusion:* Eternal God, hear our prayers in and through your Son, our Lord, Jesus Christ.

*All:* Amen.

*All:* Pray the Lord's Prayer.

Sing a closing hymn known to the group.

## RESOURCES

Brueggemann, Walter. *Hope Within History.* Atlanta: John Knox Press, 1987.

Brueggemann, Walter. *The Prophetic Imagination.* Philadelphia: Fortress, 1985.

Fischer, Balthasar. *Signs, Words and Gestures.* Collegeville, Minnesota: Pueblo, 1992.

United States Catholic Conference. *Sharing the Light of Faith,* Chapter 7. Washington DC: USCC, 1977.

"No one has greater love than this, to lay down one's life for one's friends." (Jn 15:13)

# 7
# Sacraments as Symbolic Actions

The sacramental life of the Church is a multi-faceted sculpture. It reflects symbols of the divinity touching humanity. It mirrors what all of humanity can become. It points to the emerging consciousness of what is possible for communities of people to do. As a child once said when viewing the unfinished Michelangelo statues of the apostles in Florence, Italy: "Look, Mom, there is a man trying to come out of the stone." The catechist needs to chisel away at dead concepts so that fresh insights of the Spirit emerge; the catechist must polish what might appear dull and unattractive so that it can be viewed as important and energizing; the catechist is to draw people out of their rigid stances so that they can fathom the graciousness of God in themselves and in the body of Christ.

## THE POWER OF THE SACRAMENTS

Sacraments celebrate and intensify in individuals and in the community the death-resurrection mystery of Jesus Christ. Sacraments are touchstones to meaning. They embody the best in human existence and human activity that transpires to help people connect to others and interpret their existence in relationship to the divine. Sacraments are imbued with mystery, some of which can be seen, touched, smelled, tasted and heard.

We have inherited the sacraments from our Jewish roots. Our forefathers and mothers taught us how to bless, impose hands, anoint with oil, break bread and share wine, repent through the waters of baptism, kiss, greet and share a sacred meal. The Jewish people learned the power and value of ritual actions from other peoples with whom they were rubbing elbows as they were being formed by God to be a people. The Israelites often appropriated the ritual celebrations of other tribes and transformed them into celebrations of what God had done for them. In one sense, symbolic actions have existed that point to the transcendent and to the power of human relationships since human beings first roamed the earth.

Ritual celebrations are truly rooted in what it means to be human. We like to use things and actions to truly communicate who we are. Our interwoven bodily and spiritual nature is what drives us to make meaning, to communicate, ritualize and celebrate who we are and who we are called to be. As human beings we make and use signs to say who we are. We express who we are and who we yearn to be by using signs and symbols.

Our minds are symbolic minds. They are constantly searching for the "more" in life, for what has not yet been discovered, for what may still be ambiguous, for what has not yet been realized or experienced in human life. The mind constantly searches for connections, for meaning.

## SYMBOLIC ACTIVITY

The language of the artist is symbol. A symbol is not a sign that points to something else, like a label which says what is in the can, or a traffic sign that gives direction. A symbol manifests something that is clearly present. It makes what is hidden more apparent. The symbol allows what is symbolized to be truly present. For instance, a rose given to someone who is deeply loved makes the love apparent. It points to something that is present. It does not substitute for the love; it does not invent the love; yet the rose may intensify the love. It visibly symbolizes or expresses the love that is present and promotes the growth of that love.

Symbolic activity cannot say all that is present, just as the sculptor cannot express everything that is in the stone, nor in his or her heart. Symbolic activity is a limited expression that points to the heart of what is symbolized, but it does not exhaust what is symbolized. The rose cited above is not the "whole love reality" between the persons. When the rose dies, the love does not die. While symbolic actions are limited expressions of reality, they nonetheless are powerful expressive demonstrations of the reality. The symbolic activity of giving a rose not only expresses what is present, it can increase the love between the two.

Symbolic actions are not limited to rational explanations. As a matter of fact their power lies in their ability to use the imagination to touch the emotive and deeper values of human life. Human smiles, tears, hugs, kisses are moving symbolic actions. They touch the human psyche. Symbolic actions reveal meaning; they become our teachers. There is a certain readiness needed to understand symbols. This readiness is attained through human experience from the time we are small children. Gift-giving, birthday celebrations, holidays and holy days are all occasions when we are exposed to symbolic actions, stories and rituals which give us glimpses of the fact that there is "more to life than meets the eye." The experience of losing a tooth is offset by the visit from the tooth fairy. All these events point to the mystery of life and the human connectedness of all people. They are all celebrated symbolically. Broadening one's capacity to participate in symbolic activities involves increasing one's capacity to live a deeply human life. These daily ritual observances prepare us to celebrate the symbolic actions which honor our relationship to one another and to the divine.

Symbolic actions are transformative. Just as a magnificent sculpture gives us new insights into something we thought we knew and understood, so do symbolic actions. The transforming effect of symbolic actions can be both negative and positive.

A negative example of the power of symbols and actions can be seen in how the Third Reich totally changed a nation. The values underlying the symbolic actions were inhumane, but they were transformative. Decades later the symbol of a divided world, a communist and a non-communist one, would crumble and transform a country. The dismantling of the Berlin Wall became a symbolic action that transformed a divided Germany and Europe into a unified one.

> *List some symbolic actions which have been meaningful and transformative in your life. How did these come about? What was the underlying meaning they expressed?*
> *How do you feel you can involve others in a catechetical setting to experience symbols?*

## SACRAMENTAL ACTIONS

The *Constitution on the Sacred Liturgy* reminds us that the purpose of sacraments is three-fold: to sanctify people, to build up the body of Christ, and to worship God (SC 59). Sacramental actions are symbolic expressions which nourish, strengthen and express faith (SC 59). They declare who we are and who we are becoming as members of the body of Christ. Each sacrament celebrates the paschal mystery of Christ in the community. Sacraments are tri-focused. They recall God's presence in the past and thank God for that; they bring to mind God's presence in the here and now and praise God for that; and they express hope and confidence that God will continue to be with us in the future. The convergence of three time periods in one celebrative event points to the fact that when we participate in the sacraments, we enter God's time zone. We do not see God directly, but rather we experience God as reflected in creation, in people, in oil, bread, wine and water. In sacramental actions we experience the mystery of God and connect it to the mystery of God found in our everyday lives. In sacraments we are invited to deeper commitments, to discover immeasurable meaning. Sacraments, like all artistic movements, do not lead us to fullness but to the on-going search for God, for the "more" in life.

Sacraments are efficacious when they evoke and share human experience and when they evoke and share an experience of the mystery of God. The dynamic of this intermingling of the human and the divine points to the fact that no matter how dismal our lives might seem, God is with us, God is our friend. Wars, floods, fires, divorce, unemployment, cancer will not change this reality. The celebration of sacraments is a constant reminder that God is in our daily lives supporting and nurturing us. The sacraments are signs of shared hope in God's commitment to us and in our commitment to God and to God's reign on earth.

## WHAT IS GRACE? graciousness of God

Traditionally we were taught that sacraments "automatically" give us sanctifying grace. The image left in many of our minds was that when "we went to Mass, we got filled with grace." While it is true "that sacraments do indeed impart grace" the emphasis has shifted from what the individual gets to the quality of one's relationship with God and one's neighbor (SC 59). Today the images and insights about grace have changed due in great part to the work of a Jesuit theologian, Karl Rahner, and the Second Vatican Council. While the Council did not give a treatise on grace, many of its documents reflect a shift in emphasis. One insight was the fact that God is not limited to where and how grace was "distributed." The second was that in real life there is no sep-aration between grace and nature. They are logically different but by reason of creation and the Incarnation they are not distinct. Rahner pro-motes an understanding of human nature that is oriented to God. God has gifted all of humanity with grace. This grace is seen in an infinite longing for God inside each one of us. Admittedly this longing is dim, at times unspecified and always in need of nourishment, but it is part of each human being. We have moved from looking at grace as a thing, to grace as a gift and a relationship with God, a sharing in God's life (CCC 1997). This is first experienced in our yearning beyond ourselves for the "more" in life. At first we cannot define it as a yearning for God, but through effective catechesis and life experiences we can connect the yearning with God.

> *Reflect on your own life. Where and when have you been most aware of the presence of God?*
> *Where and when have you been aware of the yearning for the "more"?*
> *What are the advantages of thinking about grace as a relation-ship with God, as a free gift from God, as opposed to "some-thing we get" when we participate in sacraments?*
> *Where have you seen God's grace present in people's lives?*
> *What concrete ways can you catechize about grace?*

## GRACE AS RELATIONSHIP

When we think about grace it may be helpful to keep four things in mind. First, that grace is God's self-communication to us in our daily lives. Rahner says when we laugh, cry, stand up for what is right, hope against hope, refuse to be embittered by the stupidity of life—this is where grace occurs. Second, grace is oriented toward everyday situa-tions. It is experienced, of course, in sacramental activities, but it is not limited to that. Just as the giving of the rose as a gesture of love is indica-tive of the love relationship, it does not exhaust that love relationship. Third, grace is primarily an event, a relationship, not a thing. It is the infi-nite mystery of God revealing and communicating with us throughout all of history. Grace was the power that allowed us to tear down the Berlin Wall. Grace was the event that allowed the discovery of the Salk vaccine. Grace sustains people dying from cancer. Fourth, grace is always present before it is consciously recognized. As T. S. Eliot wrote: "We had the experience, but we missed the meaning." Reflecting on life's experiences helps us to "get it," as it were, and recognize God in retrospect. Hopefully this attunes us to the presence of God and helps us to be more responsive every day. The world and the people in the world are dappled by God's grace. Sacraments help us recognize this gift; we celebrate it in slow motion in sacramental events so that we may respond to our relationship with God and others in daily events.

## THE SEVEN SACRAMENTS

In the Roman Catholic Church there are seven specific sacramental celebrations (CCC 1113). These have developed over time. Each of these celebrations is a celebration of the death-resurrection mystery of Jesus Christ. Each provides us with an opportunity to commemorate the death-resurrection of Jesus Christ and in so doing to worship God, to become more conscious of our relationship with God and to deepen that relationship and our relationships with others in a communal context. The celebration of the sacraments is part of the liturgical life of the Church. The liturgy is the work of the Church. It is what the Church is all about. Liturgy is the source and summit of the Church's life. Liturgy is the celebration of the ongoing process of redemption in and of the world. Liturgy makes God's work in the world and in history explicit. It speaks not only of the wonders of God in the universe but also of humanity's brokenness and sinfulness. Rooted at the heart of liturgy is Jesus Christ who emptied himself and was raised by God so that all of us could have new life and hope in what at times appears to be a cruel and hopeless world.

### 1) Sacraments of Initiation

The sacraments of initiation are baptism, confirmation and Eucharist (1212). In the early Church these sacraments were the way adults were brought into the Church. Receiving the sacraments was the culmination of a long preparatory process of initiation. Gradually over the centuries infant baptism became the norm for entry into the Church and the Rite of Christian Initiation of Adults (RCIA) fell into disuse. With the liturgical reforms which followed Vatican II, the

RCIA was restored and is being implemented throughout the world. Infant baptism continues to be the way children born of Catholic parents are initiated into the Church.

The RCIA is a process divided into four time periods and three liturgical rites which are designated as steps. The first period is the precatechumenate where inquiry and evangelization happen. During this time the inquirer begins exploring with the local Catholic community the possibility of becoming a member and learning what that kind of commitment entails. When there is sufficient evidence of initial understanding and a beginning commitment to a new way of life the person is invited to be part of the second period of initiation. At this point the person takes the first step toward initiation and becomes a catechumen.

The second period consists of the formation of the catechumen. This is primarily accomplished through reflection on the Liturgy of the Word and regular participation in the liturgy. The catechumens are invited to participate with the community at Sunday worship, but are dismissed after the Liturgy of the Word to spend more time contemplating the scriptures and their meaning to the life of the community. This period of initiation lasts at least one liturgical year. When those responsible for the catechumen's progress feel that the person is ready, he or she is invited to participate in the Rite of Election. This is the second ritual step in the initiation process and usually happens on the First Sunday of Lent. During this rite the Church ratifies the catechumen's readiness for the sacraments of initiation and the catechumen expresses his or her desire to receive them. At this point, the person moves on to the next stage, that of purification and enlightenment. During this Lenten time also, the elect's intentions are publicly scrutinized and they are exorcised on the third, fourth and fifth Sundays. They are presented formally with the Creed and the Lord's Prayer.

At the end of the third period the third ritual step occurs: the celebration of baptism, confirmation and Eucharist occurs which normally takes place at the Easter vigil. The fullest expression of baptism is through immersion. There the symbolic action of entering the death-resurrection mystery of Christ is wonderfully visible. Baptism is followed by anointing with chrism, a sign of being a member of the priestly, prophetic and kingly body of Christ. The clothing of the white robe is a sign of entry into the new creation made possible by the death-resurrection of the Lord. The presentation of a lighted candle exemplifies being enlightened by Christ, the light of the world. The sacrament of baptism is a radical sacrament of conversion. Through baptism all sin is forgiven as the person embarks on a true journey of new life with a community who believes in the Lord Jesus Christ. Confirmation follows the baptism rituals. During confirmation the person is anointed with oil and the presider prays that the seven gifts of the Spirit guide the person on their new Christian journey. The newly initiated person participates fully in the Eucharist from hence forward. By being nurtured by the blessed bread and wine, which is the body and blood of Christ, and by working to build the kingdom of God the person participates fully in the Christian community. (Eucharist, the source and summit of Christian life, will be described more fully in the next chapter.)

The fourth period in the initiation process is called the mystagogia, which says that the initiation process does not end with sacramental initiation but moves forward with further steps to incorporate the person into the community. Often this is a time for unpacking the experience of the sacramental rituals to probe their meaning more deeply. Catechesis is part of this period, as well as more involvement in the social justice activities of the community.

> *What has been your experience of the RCIA process in your parish?*
> *What do you think are the advantages of this approach as opposed to being individually instructed by a priest on Church teachings and then being baptized in a non-communal setting?*
> *What do you think is the greatest strength of the RCIA process of initiation?*
> *What are the advantages of having infants baptized during parish Sunday eucharistic liturgies?*
> *What do you think the Church is telling us by these liturgical changes?*

## 2) Confirmation Celebrated Apart from the RCIA Process

It is impossible here to outline a full history of the sacrament of confirmation. For now it is sufficient to say that in the Middle Ages infant baptism became common and in the Western Church confirmation became separated from the baptism of infants. However, in the Eastern Christian traditions infant baptism and confirmation remained intact. In the 1200s, Thomas Aquinas made a case for separating the two sacraments. In his *Summa Theologiae,* Aquinas distinguished baptism from confirmation saying that baptism was the sacrament of birth into the Church, while confirmation was the sacrament of Christian growth and maturity and therefore should be celebrated at a later date.

Today there is a movement to restore confirmation to its original order. This means that confirmation would be experienced after baptism and before first communion. However, pastoral practice in the United States is varied. In some places confirmation is received prior to first communion. In other places confirmation is celebrated in the upper elementary school years. Finally, there is a more recent practice, which dates back to the late 1960s and early 1970s, to confirm in senior high school. This custom highlights Aquinas' thinking that young people in the later years of high school were "mature" enough to make a commitment to their faith. From a pastoral point of view there is no agreement on the best way or time to celebrate confirmation once it is removed from baptism. Liturgically speaking, there are problems in separating it from baptism, because confirmation is seen as an integral part of the initiation process. From a catechetical viewpoint some would say there are problems "overloading kids with sacraments" when they are seven or eight years old. Thus the practice is varied and only time will tell if there will ever be a common understanding of confirmation and a common age by which children or young people will experience confirmation.

> *What are the pastoral and liturgical problems you see in separating confirmation from the rites of initiation into the Church?*
> *How would you solve these problems?*
> *How are they addressed in your parish?*
> *Is this satisfactory from your point of view?*

### 3) The Sacrament of Penance, or Reconciliation

God's grace permeates all of life. The recognition of this is a lifetime goal. Before we can talk about the sacrament of forgiveness, we need to attend to a basic assumption. Similar assumptions apply in different ways to all sacraments. Before we ask for forgiveness from God through the Church, we need to ask forgiveness of those whom we have offended by our sins or transgressions. If we have offended a spouse, child, co-worker or neighbor by a selfish act or insensitivity, we need to express our regret to the person or persons involved and show some sign of the sincerity of our sorrow. The sacrament of penance is given to us to build up the community to better reflect the presence of the Lord Jesus Christ. Penance does not "work like magic." We do not run to confession to be forgiven by God and forget about those we have harmed, but rather, we seek forgiveness from the people we have harmed, and then, after realizing that this is also an offense against God, we seek God's forgiveness through the Church community. In some difficult situations it may be impossible to be forgiven by those whom we have offended. After we have sought forgiveness in whatever way that is appropriate, it is fitting to approach the sacrament of penance. Sometimes our sins are communal in nature. We pass unjust policies at work; we exploit people; we pollute the environment out of greed or carelessness. Where it may be impossible to approach a person to ask for forgiveness, the reparation for such sins may be communal in nature. In other words, we must be ready to work hard to eliminate the injustice that resulted from our decisions.

We sometimes mistakenly think that the sacrament of penance is the primary sacrament of forgiveness. However, as has been pointed out above, the "first and chief" sacrament of forgiveness is baptism (CCC 977). In baptism there is a radical conversion to the ways of Jesus Christ. The Eucharist is also an important sacrament of forgiveness. Eucharist celebrates the death-resurrection event of Jesus Christ—the very event by which we all receive salvation. Jesus declares at the Last Supper that his body and blood, his life, has been given so that sins may be forgiven (CCC 1846).

### a) Brief overview

The sacrament of penance has an interesting history which is too lengthy and complex to go through here, but highlighting a few historical movements will be helpful. Because the normal way to experience forgiveness for sins was through the Eucharist, there was not a separate ritual for sinners in the first several hundred years of the Church. However, at some point in the third century it appeared that some public sins like murder, apostasy (the denial of one's faith) and adultery were so public and grave that the community expected the sinner to do repentance for his or her sin before being readmitted to the eucharistic table. The people prayed for the sinner that he or she would be truly repentant and rejoin the community at Eucharist. This penance was very public.

The person was made to wear clothes that indicated his or her sinfulness. This also served as a public demonstration that he or she was sorry for the grave offense. Sometimes this went on for years and was hard for people to endure. There was also the assumption that grave sin would only happen once in a lifetime. You could commit one awful public sin in your lifetime, but that was all. For some people serious public sins were not limited to a one-time event. This led to "deathbed" confessions as people tried to avoid the long, arduous public penance and did not want to take a chance on publicly sinning again.

In the sixth century Irish monks began to give spiritual direction. For the confession of transgressions, certain penances were prescribed. This was a very private affair and no one knew one's sins except one's confessor. During this time a new concept was implemented. It was like an economic exchange. If you could not do the prescribed penance, you could substitute and do something else. You could "tap" into the good works of another and apply their "merit" for your sin. This began the infamous practice of "indulgences," which later haunted the Church. The practice of "private confession" which we have experienced has its roots back in the Celtic monasteries of the sixth century. Going to confession often began with the practice of private confession and reached its climax in the seventeenth century at the Council of Trent. In all of this the emphasis was on one's personal relationship to God, whereas one's relationship to the community or the community's relationship to God were seldom addressed.

### b) Second Vatican Council

The new rites for penance were established in 1974. Three rites are permitted by the document. The first one is what we know as individual confession; the second is the communal celebration including individual confession and absolution; and the third rite is for general confession. The latter is designed to be used in circumstances such as a battlefield where people are preparing for war and there are not enough confessors to hear individual confessions. All are absolved by one priest without individual confession. There are other circumstances where this rite is permitted, but its use is discouraged in normal parish life.

All the rites assume certain understandings of sin and conversion. All the rites—including the first one—attend to the communal aspects of sin. They see sin as not just an offense against God but also as a blemish on the community. The community is hurt by the sins of individuals.

All the rites promote the forgiveness of both grave sin and transgressions as part of a person's ongoing process of conversion. The word used for this in the scriptures is metanoia. The images used are those of the father receiving back the lost son, Christ finding the lost sheep and the great banquet of God's Church for the repentant sinner.

The liturgical celebration of this sacrament always begins with the liturgy of the Word. It is in the context of God's life-giving Word that sins are forgiven. This is followed by the confession of sins to a priest. The gestures and words used for absolving sins have three essential parts which reflect the theology of sin and forgiveness noted above. The first is the imposition of hands over the penitent. This symbolic action touches our inner spirit so that we feel God's presence in this forgiving moment. This gesture tangibly nudges us to be aware of the Holy Spirit. The words of absolution remind us that God is a God of mercy and through the death-resurrection mystery Jesus Christ has reconciled us to God and the world and sent the Holy Spirit for the forgiveness of sins. The words of absolution remind us that we are forgiven through the ministry of the Church and that we are absolved from our sins in the name of the Father, Son and Spirit. The words of absolution are accompanied by tracing the sign of the cross over the penitent. The words and symbolic actions along with the penance we agree to carry out unites us in a new fullness to the Christian community.

> *How would you describe the impact of the symbolic actions used in the sacrament of penance?*
> *In the restored order, the liturgy of the Word is an integral part of the sacrament; how does this increase the effectiveness of the sacrament?*
> *What role do you think forgiving those we have offended before approaching the sacrament plays in the effectiveness of the sacrament?*
> *What are some things we can do to "repair" the effects of our social sins?*
> *What harm has been caused by the social sins of consumerism, racism and sexism?*
> *How can the harm caused by these sins be repaired?*
> *How can we make people aware of the evil of social sins?*
> *How can we help people become aware of how they are contributing to social sins?*

*What do you think are the advantages of Rite II of the sacrament of penance (communal celebration of penance)?*

### 4) Anointing of the Sick

From the middle ages until the Second Vatican Council this sacrament was known as Extreme Unction, or the last anointing. It was understood to be the "last sacrament" one received before dying. As a result of the Second Vatican Council, in 1972 the rite was restored to its earliest meaning: the way of strengthening those whose health was hindered by illness or old age. This change in perspective has made the sacrament much more of a hopeful experience and not one associated only with being at death's door.

#### a) Brief history of anointing

The anointing of the sick has its roots in Jewish religious practice. The use of oil, the imposition of hands and prayers for the sick were very much part of the culture that Jesus experienced. The Christians did not devise new symbolic actions but rather gave new meaning to those that were common. Early on, the emphasis of the ritual was on the bishop blessing the oil. Then the connection was made that just as ordinary Christians would bring home communion for the sick after the Sunday Eucharist, so too they would bring back blessed oil for use with the sick. The bishop and priests often visited the sick and they may have been the ministers of the sacrament when they visited. However, lay people were probably the ordinary ministers.

As noted above, when the sacrament of penance became a "once-in-a-lifetime event," often on one's death bed, the sacrament of the sick became part of the "last rites" which were administered by the priest along with penance and viaticum (the final reception of communion before death). Because one needed to be a Christian in good standing in order to be anointed, the priest first heard the dying person's confession, then gave communion and anointed the person.

#### b) Celebration of the anointing of the sick

Except in cases of emergency, the restored rite assumes that pastoral care of the sick person has taken place. In other words, someone from the community has visited the person, attended to family needs, prayed with the person and been genuinely concerned about the sick person and the family. As stated before, all the sacraments assume that there has been human interaction related to the purpose of the sacrament before the sacrament is celebrated.

Sickness often isolates a person. One great benefit to the communal anointing of the sick is that it tangibly assists the ill person to realize that he or she is an important member of a community, not someone separated from the community. The laying on of hands helps the person realize that he or she is the focus of the Church's prayer. The liturgy of the Word, song and symbolic actions all communicate that sickness is part of the human condition and that one does not suffer alone. Except in emergencies, the rite is celebrated communally, often within the context of a eucharistic celebration. Anointing may be given repeatedly with the same illness or celebrated with different illnesses. It is not a once-in-a-lifetime sacrament.

The sacramental actions include, as mentioned above, the laying on of hands, which concretely helps the sick person realize that he or she is not alone in suffering, and the anointing with oil on the forehead and the hands with prayers that ask the Lord in his love and mercy to help the person and free them from sin and raise them to new health.

> *What advantages do you see to having the anointing of the sick celebrated in a communal setting?*
> *In what ways has changing the name of the sacrament from Extreme Unction back to its original name, the Anointing of the Sick, shed new light on the meaning of the sacrament?*
> *How would you help children understand the meaning of the sacrament?*

### 5) Sacraments of Vocational Commitments: Holy Orders and Marriage

Holy orders and marriage are two sacraments which celebrate vocational lifetime commitments. Holy orders confers the ministry of diaconate, priesthood and episcopacy. These are all ministries of service to the community. Like all the others, this sacrament has had a long and complex history. While it has its roots in the ministry of Jesus Christ, it is important to realize that Jesus did not ordain priests or bishops or deacons. Jesus called twelve apostles and many disciples to carry on his work and his mission to build God's kingdom. Together they exercised a collective leadership in establishing and guiding the early Church.

Sometime between the end of the first century and the beginning of the third century, three roles began to be distinguished. The first was that of overseer or bishop whose job was to lead the local community and to connect to the larger community of churches; the second was that of presbyter or priest who started out being an advisor to the bishop, but eventually ended up serving as the leader of a local community. The last was that of deacon. Deacons were ministers of charity and liturgical assistants to the bishop. Another development in the early Church was the gradual use of the Old Testament notion of priesthood applied to the bishops and presbyters who ministered in the name of Jesus Christ.

The medieval period clarified a hierarchial structure in the Church with bishops, priests and deacons in the clerical state and religious, laity and catechumens in the lay hierarchy. When the catechumenate fell into disuse, the laity was generally perceived to take on a passive role and to be the recipients of the actions of the clergy. Some of the hierarchial structures and practices contributed to the problems which gave rise to the Reformation. The Council of Trent basically confirmed the *status quo* and did little to contribute to a comprehensive theology of holy orders.

The Second Vatican Council did much to provide a more thorough understanding of the sacrament of holy orders. First of all, the Council stated that all the baptized are called to the fullness of grace and holiness. In other words, one's role in the Church, whether it be as a lay person or a bishop, is not a cause for holiness. All baptized people can live in the fullness of God's grace and share in the full relationship to God. Second, the council fathers stated that by reason of baptism all share in the mission and worship of the Church; all share in the common priesthood of Jesus Christ. There is, however, an essential difference between the priesthood of the faithful and the priesthood of the ordained. The Second Vatican Council speaks of the distinction but does not directly develop the relationship.

The Second Vatican Council defines the role of bishop as the one who preaches and teaches, the one who sanctifies and governs. The priest has a three-fold ministry: minister of God's Word; minister of sacraments and pastoral guide of the community. The deacon shares the ministry of the Word and liturgy with the priest, but the deacon is also seen as a minister of charity. All three roles are seen as ministries of service to the community.

In one sense those ordained have the responsibility of embodying the values of the community and being the symbol bearers for the community. They call the community to realize and respond to God's presence there. They continually challenge the community to build the kingdom of God. They learn from the community and take a leadership role in the community. They make sure the story is not forgotten; they make sure the rituals continually speak to the community's life experience. They do not do any of this alone; they do all of it with the community. They do not have power over the community; they share the power of God's spirit with the community.

Ordination to the priesthood happens during the celebration of the Eucharist. Two ritual actions and a prayer of consecration are integral to ordination. The bishop and all priests present, in silence, lay their hands on the head of the candidate. The bishop prays a prayer of consecration which acknowledges God's providence. The prayer requests God, in the person of the Holy Spirit, to grant the dignity of the priesthood on the person being ordained. The ordained is then clothed with a chasuble and stole and his hands are anointed by the bishop. At the preparation of the gifts, the bishop gives the new priest the bread and wine saying that they are the gifts of the people. He counsels the priest to imitate the paschal mystery which he is about to celebrate.

> *How has the Second Vatican Council enriched our understanding of the sacrament of orders?*
> *In what ways do you see bishops, priests and deacons serving the needs of the Church?*
> *How is the priesthood of the laity different from that of the clergy?*

### 6) The Sacrament of Matrimony

The sacramentality of marriage is hinted at in the story of the marriage feast at Cana. There Jesus does all he can to contribute to the celebration which he must have seen as holy. St. Augustine in the fourth century held that marriage was a sacrament between two Christians. Thomas Aquinas held that "marriage in the Lord" is a sacrament. Since the thirteenth century, marriage has been officially recognized as one of the seven sacraments. It is described in the revised Code of Canon Law as a covenant by which a man and woman establish a partnership which is geared to the happiness, holiness and well-being of the couple and the procreation and nurturing of children. In the Western tradition the spouses, and not the witnessing priest, are the actual ministers of the sacrament. In the Orthodox churches of the East, the presiding priest is the minister.

The covenantal nature of marriage is at the heart of its sacramentality. The Old or First Testament speaks of God's relationship with his people as a covenant. God binds himself to the people and expects their faithfulness but is bound to them through their periods of unfaithfulness as well. The mutual love and unconditional self-giving of a man and a woman through marriage is a symbol of God's love for all humanity. But as Isaiah reminds us, God's love is more faithful than the most faithful spouses or parents. The love between the spouses becomes for the Christian community another symbolic action of God's love and presence in the community and of Christ's love for his Church. The grace of the sacrament of marriage continually unfolds as the couple's relationship matures through the rough and tumble of everyday events. Because of the intensity of the relationship, the vulnerability of the individuals, the covenantal quality and symbolic value of Christian marriage, it is seen as a lifetime commitment.

The family created by the sacrament of marriage has been called the "domestic church" or the Church in miniature. The Church looks to the family for its way of welcoming others within its bonds, nurturing others, affirming others, forgiving and reconciling one another and healing others. On some level the sacraments are all experienced in the family before they are experienced in the Church community. The healthier the family, the healthier the community we call Church.

Parents may be children's first experience of God. It is in the faithfulness of parents to children that children first know there is a God who is all-loving, all-caring and all-forgiving.

At a marriage ceremony the priest invites the couple to make their marriage promises in the presence of the community. They promise to love each other in sickness and in health. They promise to love and honor one another. The priest prays in the name of the community that God will bless the newly married couple's love forever. A couple may exchange wedding rings. This symbolic action reminds them of their love and commitment to one another. The final blessing reminds the couple that they are to be willing and ready to comfort those in need and reach out in compassion to those who call for their help. The sacrament of marriage is not just for the couple but it is a sign for the whole community of God's love for each of us.

> *How do you see the grace of the sacrament of matrimony unfolding throughout the life of the marriage?*
> *How would you describe Christian marriage as a symbol for God's love for humanity and Christ's love for the Church?*
> *What are things we can do to promote healthy marriages?*

## WHAT IS LITURGICAL CATECHESIS?

Catherine Dooley, O.P., has provided many insights concerning liturgical catechesis. According to Dooley, the purpose of liturgical catechesis is "to lead communities and individual members of the faithful to maturity of faith through full and active participation in the liturgy which effects and expresses that faith." Liturgical catechesis is part of the larger catechetical endeavor. Liturgical catechesis happens in preparation for the sacraments, through the experience of the sacraments and in reflection on the sacramental experience.

Dooley describes four characteristics of liturgical catechesis: (1) it is *paschal:* it focuses on the death-resurrection mystery of Jesus Christ; (2) it is *ecclesial:* its point of reference is the whole Church, as seen as the assembly gathers to celebrate its identity in public worship; (3) it is *sacramental:* it aims to help those catechized discover the meaning of the sacramental symbolic actions so that they realize they are participating in the saving action of Christ; (4) it is *transformative:* it aims at conversion and the bringing about of the reign of God.

Liturgical catechesis helps people realize that the celebrations of the sacraments are celebrations of relationships to God and to one another in Christ through the Spirit. Liturgical catechesis should be part of all catechetical programs.

## PROMOTING JUSTICE

Striving for justice cannot be separated from the sacramental life of the Church. Sacraments are celebrations of God's sustaining life in the community through the power of the Spirit. God's Spirit is a spirit of justice. The Spirit is given to the community to continue building God's kingdom of justice. The renewed sacramental rites make us more aware of the communal nature of our lives and our relationship with God. No longer can we attempt to forge a "Jesus and me" mentality. We meet Jesus Christ in community; we are nurtured by the body of Christ; we are challenged by the whole body of Christ.

It is possible to look at sacraments as windows of awareness whereby, through the divine initiative, we are called to promote justice. Baptism-confirmation-Eucharist can be seen as welcoming nurturing sacraments whereby we are graced with God's sustaining presence in community. Flowing from this we are called and nurtured to welcome and care for others in the world who may be victims of hopelessness and hunger and have no one or no place to welcome them. We have been welcomed to the great banquet of the Lord; we in turn welcome others to come in off the street and be supported by good food and shelter. We do this because of what God has done for all humanity. We do this because of the dignity of each human being. In other words, we make real the presence of God to the victims of injustice.

In the sacrament of penance we ask a merciful God in and through the community for forgiveness. As recipients of God's plentiful mercy we are called to be compassionate to others. In reality, it may mean everything from visiting prisoners and supporting their rights, to advocating to abolish the death penalty and forgiving debtors. If we are working in the international financial industries it may mean supporting the reduction of debt or the forgiveness of debt of third world countries. If we are parents it may mean that justice calls us to forgive major transgressions of children. As catechists working with children it may mean that we promote forgiveness on the playground, at home and in peer groups. The areas are vast that need forgiveness as a way to promote justice.

Justice connected to the sacrament of the sick may mean advocating for health care related to the elderly, the homeless, or the uninsured. Care in time of illness is a basic human right. When people, especially the poor, do not have this, we are called to promote justice by supporting governmental or private agencies that provide this needed service.

Both the sacraments of holy orders and matrimony promote justice through service. In the rites of both of these sacraments there are summons to serve others. Bishops, priests and deacons are ordained to serve others. As preachers and promoters of the Gospel they are called to champion the cause of justice. Their just actions include taking the initiative and supporting diocesan and parish justice endeavors, promoting ecumenical, economic and global justice and working with governmental organizations to build a just world.

Justice also flows from the sacrament of matrimony. Living a life of love and fidelity is acting out of justice to one's marriage partner. Caring for children, both one's own and others, is an act of love and also justice. Children have rights to be loved, cared for and cherished. During the celebration of the sacrament, one of the prayers pushes the notion of justice beyond what is needed in the family. The blessing calls the couple to be ready, willing and compassionate to help all in need. Pope John Paul II has called the family "the Church in miniature." As such it takes on all the roles of the Church: proclaiming the Good News, praying and worshipping and being of service to God's community. Wonderful stories of families helping other families in need, of families taking in foster children and of families always having room for an extra hungry person for dinner abound. This is justice and charity in action.

Being a sacramental people cannot be separated from being a people of justice who work together to build a more just world. Our God is a God of justice, but some people will not know this unless we are visible signs of justice at work in everyday life.

> *Name specific activities you and those you catechize can do to promote justice based on the sacramental activities of the Church.*
> *What do you see as the connection between justice and charity?*
> *How is justice related to baptism?*

## PRACTICAL IMPLICATIONS

1. When catechizing, use symbolic actions and have the participants take part in these. This creates a readiness to understand and appreciate the power of the sacraments. Breaking bread, blessing oneself with holy water, sharing wine or grape juice from one cup, laying hands on one another's head and praying for them, and signing the hands with oil are all ritual actions which initiate those catechized into deeper knowledge of sacramental actions.

2. Depending on the readiness of the individuals being catechized, use some of the prayers or some of the wonderful imagery found in the prayers of the sacramental rites. Catechize from these; analyze them; probe their meaning; pray with them.

3. Provide opportunities for participants to reflect on their participation in the sacramental life of the Church. Use the process of the mystagogia as a framework.

4. Design activities which help those you catechize understand that grace is relationship, event, God's self-communication to us. Begin with sacraments to describe how grace, God's self-communication, is present in each one of them. Then invite descriptions of parallel situations in daily life where God is also present. Point out that in one way sacraments help us take life in slow motion so that we are more aware of God's presence in our life struggles, moments of joy, sickness, sinfulness, family meals, etc.

5. Work out justice activities that parallel the sacraments. What can we do to be more welcoming? more forgiving? more nurturing? more affirming? more healing?

6. Discern areas of injustice in your community. What needs to happen in these areas to prepare people for the Good News? What would be good news for these people to hear? What actions need to accompany the Good News so that it is authentic? How can you mobilize people to work for justice as a constitutive dimension of the Gospel?

## REFLECTION

Have a Bible enthroned with a lighted candle next to it. Have a large bowl of water and a towel for the ritual.

Sing an appropriate gathering song.

*Presider:* God, our Creator, you gave us your son Jesus, who lived, died and was raised from the dead for us. As signs of your continuous presence in our lives you gave us sacramental events which commemorate the paschal mystery of your son. Strengthen us as we attempt to help others appreciate the richness of these symbolic actions as they continue to build your kingdom of justice here on earth. We ask this through Jesus Christ our Lord.

*All:* Amen.

Have the gospel proclaimer and a candle bearer process with the Bible around the group and back to the front of the group.

*Reader:* Proclaim John 13:1, 4–9.

Have a period of silent reflection. Use the following questions for reflection:

> *In what ways am I like Peter? In what ways am I like Jesus? Washing the feet of the disciples was a symbolic action for service. In what ways do I serve others? Does this service create a more just world?*

Allow for sharing of the reflection.

As a symbolic action of our baptismal call to take part in the ministries of the Church, invite people to come forward, immerse their hands in water and after taking them out of the water make the sign of the cross. Have a towel available to dry hands.

General Intercessions

*Presider:* God, our loving Creator, you have given us many gifts; now we come to you with our petitions:

Invite participants to offer prayers of petition. All respond, Lord hear our prayer.

Examples: For those who are yearning for the "more" in life but do not know where to look, we pray to the Lord.

For the homeless and hungry…

*Presider:* Accept our petitions in the name of your son, Jesus Christ, our Lord.

*All:* Amen.

*All:* Pray the Lord's Prayer.

Close with an appropriate song.

## RESOURCES

Bausch, William J. *A New Look at the Sacraments.* Mystic, Connecticut: Twenty-Third Publications, 1986.

Dooley, Catherine, O.P. "Mystagogy: Ministry to Parents," in *Catechesis and Mystagogy: Infant Baptism,* ed. V. Tufano, 97-104. Chicago: Liturgy Training Publications, 1996.

Dooley, Catherine, O.P. "Mystagogy: Model for Sacramental Catechesis," in *New Directions in Sacrament and Spirituality,* ed. Mary Gray, 58-69. London: Geoffrey Chapman, 1995.

Dooley, Catherine, O.P. "From the Visible to the Invisible: Mystagogy in the Catechism of the Catholic Church," *Living Light* 31/3 (Spring 1995) 29-35.

Dooley, Catherine, O.P. "Liturgical Catechesis: Mystagogy, Marriage or Misnomer," *Worship 66* (September 1992) 386-97.

Galvin, John. "Grace for a New Generation," *Commonweal* (Jan. 25, 1985), 40-42.

Heschel, Abraham Joshua. *The Sabbath*. New York: Farrar, Straus and Giroux, 1979.

O'Donovan, Leo, ed. *A World of Grace*. New York: Seabury Press, 1980.

Rahner, Karl. "The Concept of Mystery in Catholic Theology," *Theological Investigations IV*. Baltimore: Helicon Press, 1966, 36-73.

Smith, Patricia. *Teaching Sacraments*. Wilmington, Delaware: Michael Glazier, 1987.

**"This cup is the new covenant in my blood, which will be shed for you."** (Lk 22:20)

# 8
# Celebration of the Eucharist

The Eucharist is the tapestry of Christian life. Its threads weave the Jewish stories and rituals into the Christian ones. Certain dimensions of the tapestry call forth the interconnections between the Word proclaimed and the lives of the believers. Other strands call the body of Christ to intensify its relationship to the death-resurrection mystery of Jesus Christ and to its members. Some of the pigments in the tapestry remind one of the challenge to recreate the earth and build the kingdom of God. The tapestry breathes with an invitation to unity and peace for all who participate in it. Catechists help those with whom they work to understand the tapestry, to contribute to its beauty, to receive from its magnificence and to celebrate its existence.

The celebration of the Eucharist is intimately connected to our identity as Roman Catholics. It truly makes us who we are. Three terms were used in the early Church to describe what we often call the Mass today. They were the Lord's Supper, the Breaking of the Bread and the Eucharist. "Eucharist" is a Greek term which means praise and thanksgiving. About the fourth century the term "Mass" began to be used. Mass actually means "to be sent." It came into use because the catechumens were dismissed from the Eucharist after the liturgy of the Word. This association led people to interchangeably use Eucharist and Mass for the ritual meal celebration remembering Jesus' death-resurrection.

## EARLY CHURCH CELEBRATIONS

As with all the sacraments, the Eucharist has evolved over the centuries. The earliest celebrations of the Eucharist were held on the day after the Sabbath, the first day of the week. It included the blessing of the bread and wine which was offered as communion in the body and blood of Christ.

The early Church was indebted to the Jewish traditions for its eucharistic celebration. The Jewish community had the custom of offering blessings over bread and wine at family Sabbath meals as well as at Passover. The Passover is the oldest of the Hebrew festivals. By Jesus' time, it had been celebrated in the Jewish community for more than 1000 years. It continues to be celebrated today. It commemorates two events, the freeing of the Israelites from the Egyptians and the beginning of the barley season which ultimately points to Israel's relationship to the land. The celebration of Passover with the Seder meal is both a wonderful catechetical event as well as a time to praise and worship our saving God. The celebration intertwines the following beliefs and experiences of the Jewish people at a ritual meal: God's call to the people plus the moral obligations that come with that call; solidarity with the poor; the Israelites experience of God in history; the mandate to pass on the story in an imaginative way to the next generation; the experience of oppression in the past as well as the present. The celebration itself involves drinking wine (or grape juice), sharing unleavened bread, eating sweet and bitter herbs, sharing a sweet salad, lighting a candle, eating lamb, blessing food and praising God and, most important, telling the story of why this night is so different from other nights.

> *What similarities do you find between a Passover meal and Mass?*
> *Consider doing more research on a Seder supper; share a Seder meal with those you catechize to help them have a better understanding of our Jewish roots. In preparation you may want to invite a Rabbi to talk about the meaning of Passover and demonstrate the elements used in the ritual.*

The early Jewish Christians, building on what they knew best, appropriated Hebrew customs and gave them new meaning. For the Christians the blessed bread and wine would become their sustenance as they remembered the life, death and resurrection of the Lord. It is assumed that in the early Church people first met to celebrate Eucharist in their homes. As the community grew they looked for bigger spaces. By the third century some of these larger spaces were called basilicas. The term was originally used to designate official buildings or courts of the Roman Empire. Basically, basilicas were big halls.

The foundation of all eucharistic celebrations is found in the Gospels. Matthew, Mark, Luke and John all have accounts of what we call the Last Supper, although John's is quite different from the others. While the accounts differ, it is clear that before Jesus died he celebrated a religious meal at which he offered blessings to God, blessed bread and wine and transformed the meaning of the Jewish ritual of Passover. By identifying the bread and wine with his own anticipated death of self-giving on the cross, Jesus began to nurture his community of followers in a way that remains with us today. While the Gospel of John does not have a Last Supper celebration of blessing bread and wine, it does have a supper where Jesus washed the feet of the disciples, thus symbolizing the meaning of his life and indirectly teaching the disciples to love one another. The seeds of eucharistic meaning in John's Gospel are found in his rendition of the feeding of the multitudes.

From an historical perspective, we find the earliest scriptural references to the Eucharist in Paul's letters. In his first letter to the Corinthians Paul admonishes the new Christians to wait to eat until all gather for the blessing. Primarily Paul saw the Eucharist as a sign of unity and a memorial of the great work of salvation that Jesus Christ had done. To begin eating before all the community had gathered was not a sign of unity and even suggested rudeness. Paul observes that the body of Christ is formed through the Eucharist. Paul describes the unity needed in a human body as the unity called for in the body of Christ. From early on there were two understandings. The first was that the community which gathered in the name of the Lord was the body of Christ. The second was that this same community was formed by the body of Christ received in the ritual meal.

Some scholars have pointed out that the synoptic tradition employs "taking, blessing, breaking and giving," while Paul assumes the practice of Jewish meal blessings with the addition of Christ's blessing of bread and wine. Some researchers think that the early Jewish Christians first went to the temple or synagogue to celebrate and then came home and had what amounted to a eucharistic celebration.

**EARLY DEVELOPMENT**

There was no such thing as a "Roman Missal" in the early Church. Depending upon what part of the Roman Empire one lived in, one had various prayers and ways of celebrating Eucharist. Jews and Gentiles adapted their celebrations to their particular cultural situations. Gradually prayers from different regions came to be written and passed on. During the persecution of the Christians the Eucharist was often celebrated in secret. Because of misunderstandings and distortions, some Church leaders said little about the meaning of the Eucharist until after people experienced the long initiation process (RCIA). After the experience of the Eucharist the community unpacked the meaning of the great prayer of praise and thanksgiving.

Despite the cultural variety in the way the Eucharist was celebrated in the first three centuries of the Church, it is fair to say that by the fourth century, four things could be said about the Mass. First, the Eucharist emphasized Christ's death and resurrection for all people. Second, there were moral implications for the lifestyle of those who participated in the Eucharist. Christians were expected to live by Gospel values and be signs of love and justice to the community. Anything other than that was scandalous. Third, the unity of the Eucharist was emphasized. The one bread of the Eucharist made Christians into the one body of Christ. Fourth, there was a relationship between Eucharist and preparing for death. People carried consecrated hosts on journeys. It is recorded that the brother of St. Ambrose took a host for a sea journey. This points to the early belief in the real presence of Christ in the consecrated host outside of Mass.

**SHIFT IN EMPHASIS**

After the fifth century, which witnessed the rich teaching on the Eucharist by the fathers of the Church, there was a decided shift in not only the emphasis on the teaching about the Eucharist but also in the historical context in which the Eucharist was celebrated. The barbarian invasions of the later centuries destroyed much of the religious culture of the old Roman Empire. According to the theologian Regis Duffy, O.F.M., this also influenced the teaching on the Eucharist. He says that the transitions from Augustine and Ambrose to the early medieval thinking could best be characterized as a "movement away from symbolic thinking about the Eucharist (i.e., why Christ gave the Eucharist to the Church) to an instrumental thinking (i.e., a practical "how" the bread becomes the body of Christ)."

This shift in emphasis led to the creation of miracle stories about the Eucharist and devotional practices that were not present in the Church prior to this time. There was a decrease in the reception of communion and a change from active participation to a passive piety focusing on adoring the "consecrated bread." In centering their attention on the words of consecration, people focused on what seemed almost like magic. There was also an increase in "private Masses," especially those for the dead. No longer was the Eucharist viewed as a whole event celebrating the death-resurrection of the Lord, nor was the celebration seen to challenge the moral, communal or individual behavior of the participants, nor was it as a sacrament of unity where the community came together as the body of Christ to be further formed and nurtured by the body of Christ. The custom of reserving blessed bread for the sick grew into the formation of elaborate tabernacles which became the center of eucharistic piety.

Thomas Aquinas in the thirteenth century, while retaining much of Augustine's symbolic understanding of the Eucharist, provided another framework for understanding it by employing the categories of Aristotle. Aquinas said that the bread offered at the Eucharist was substantially changed, while its "accidents" or outward appearance was not changed. Aquinas enhanced the understanding of the term "transubstantiation" used at the Fourth Lateran Council in 1215. While adding to the understanding of the Eucharist, Aquinas very importantly asserts that it is a mystery that no explanation can adequately define. Despite the work of Aquinas, abuses prevailed and fewer and fewer people partook of communion. The Mass was generally seen as a drama to be viewed, rather than a memorial of the Lord's supper in which the community was formed by the body of Christ.

## COUNCIL OF TRENT

The Council of Trent in the sixteenth century tried to stem the tide of some of the abuses of eucharistic practice by promoting a reformed celebration of the Mass and renewed catechetical efforts. While the reforms corrected blatant abuses they did not do much to promote participation in the action of the Eucharist. Before Vatican II, participating in the Mass even in this century often meant saying the rosary or reading from one's prayerbook while the priest performed the ritual with his back toward the people and in a language they did not understand. The reforms of Trent were in place until the Second Vatican Council's mandates.

> *From what has been briefly outlined above, what do you think was the most significant shift in the teaching about the Eucharist over the past centuries?*
> *Explain your response.*
> *How has this teaching influenced your thinking and experience of the Mass?*

While space does not permit even a thumbnail sketch of the history of the Eucharist in the East, it is important to note that for cultural, political and historical reasons the Eastern Catholic Churches developed their own eucharistic rites. Today there are four basic Eastern Catholic liturgical traditions: (1) the Syrian, which includes the Maronite rite; (2) the Byzantine, which came from Constantinople and is the most widely used of the Eastern Catholic rites; (3) the Armenian, which uses the eucharistic prayer of St. Athanasius; and (4) the Alexandrian, which includes the Coptic and the Ethiopian rites. While originally these rites were found mainly in geographical areas of their origins, today they are found worldwide. With the exception of the Maronite rite, which is celebrated only by Eastern rite Catholics, the others are used by both Orthodox and Catholic churches. There is also a difference in other sacramental rites, most notably the rites of initiation, between the Eastern Orthodox and Roman traditions.

## SECOND VATICAN COUNCIL

The roots of the liturgical renewal found in the results of Vatican II began in the late nineteenth century. Liturgical studies at that time started to focus on the relationship between liturgy and life. In the early part of the twentieth century Pius X encouraged frequent reception of communion and allowed children to receive communion at age seven. Pius XII shortened the hours for the eucharistic fast and wrote a foundational encyclical on the Mystical Body.

In 1963 the Vatican Council issued one of the most important documents to come from the council, the *Constitution on the Sacred Liturgy* (SC). This document was a watershed charter for liturgical renewal. The document and the revised rites which followed during the next decades renewed liturgical practices which reflected many of the early Church understandings. The eucharistic liturgy was described as the "source and summit" of Christian life. The document called for "full and active participation" of all the faithful in the sacramental life of the Church. The priest was seen as the presider over the assembly who *with the assembly* offers the Eucharist. The congregation was no longer a "silent spectator" but a true and vital participant (SC 14). To assist in making this possible permission was given for the Eucharist to be celebrated in the "mother tongue" instead of Latin (SC 36).

The *Constitution on the Sacred Liturgy* called for a simplification of the rites of the sacraments. Elements that had been added over time but had diminished in importance were discarded, and significant elements which were lost through the "accidents of history" were restored (SC 50). Before the Second Vatican Council there was a general understanding that the three most important parts of the Mass were the offertory, consecration and communion. One fulfilled one's "obligation to attend Mass" if one got to Mass by the offertory. Liturgical renewal since Vatican II has restored the understanding of the early Church that there are two parts of the Mass, the liturgy of the word and the liturgy of the Eucharist and, "together these form one single act of worship" (SC 56). The council did much to restore the importance of sacred scripture not only in the Church, but most especially in the sacraments. The council fathers remind us:

> "For it is from Scripture that the readings are given and explained in the homily and that psalms are sung;...it is from the Scriptures that actions and signs derive their meaning....It is essential to promote that warm and living love for Scripture to which the venerable tradition of both Eastern and Western rites give testimony" (SC 24).

God is present in the Word proclaimed in sacramental celebrations. God speaks to us in such proclamations.

*If you remember the celebration of Mass before Vatican II, how would you compare it to the celebration you experience today?*

*What is different?*
*What is the same?*
*What do you think is the greatest value of the Liturgy of the
Word to the community and yourself personally? (As you think
about this recall the earlier chapter on the power of story-
telling.)*

## NEW INSIGHTS ABOUT THE EUCHARIST FROM SECOND VATICAN COUNCIL AND SUBSEQUENT DOCUMENTS

The primary goal of catechesis is to help people to grow in faith.
Because the Eucharist is so central to our faith it is important to glean
all the insights possible from the liturgical renewal over the past thirty
years so that we can use it to awaken the faith of others. Peter Fink, S.J.,
discusses major ingredients to eucharistic faith: (a) the Eucharist as
seen from the perspective of its relationship to the Church; (b) the institution of the Eucharist by Christ; (c) the presence of Christ in the
Eucharist; (d) the Mass as sacrifice; and (e) the Eucharist as a sign of
hope, life and unity beyond our earthly existence. These insights are
based primarily on the work of the Second Vatican Council and the
renewal which followed it.

### 1) The Eucharist and the Church

The Second Vatican Council reversed the shift that had taken
place in the medieval period where the major emphasis was solely on
the priest. The new emphasis harkens back to the early Church where it
was understood that the action of the liturgy was done by the priest with
the people. The *Constitution on the Sacred Liturgy* states: "For the
liturgy…is the outstanding means whereby the faithful may express in
their lives and manifest to others the mystery of Christ and the real
nature of the true Church" (SC 2). The prayers which accompany the
preparation of the gifts illustrate the point. Before Vatican II the priest
said, "Accept…this spotless host which I offer unto you." Now he says,
"Blessed are you…we have these gifts to offer." The shift from "I" to
"we" is significant. The new emphasis is much more situated in the
Church community under the presidership of the priest. The priest now
acts with the people, not in place of the people.

## 2) Christ Instituted the Eucharist

The Second Vatican Council affirmed the foundational belief that Jesus instituted the Eucharist at the Last Supper (SC 47). But the Council enriched our understanding by reminding us that the Mass is not a remembrance of historical words Jesus used at the Last Supper, but rather it remembers the whole purpose of Jesus' life, death, resurrection and glorification (SC 48). Peter Fink says, "The full mystery of Christ lived first in his own life and given expression again and again in the Eucharist, is the event which Eucharist remembers, the event which brings the Eucharist into being." The originating event which the Eucharist remembers is the paschal mystery. The mystery focuses on Jesus' offering himself in obedience to God (offertory); his death that is transformed (consecration) into a life to be shared with all (communion). As we join in this offering, uniting our lives to that of Christ, our lives are also transformed as they are shared with others. Jesus did institute the Eucharist by his very life, death, resurrection and glorification with God, the source of all life.

## 3) The Presence of Christ

Usually when most people think about the "real" presence of Christ they refer only to the consecration of the Mass. Both the *Constitution on the Sacred Liturgy* (CS), and the *General Instruction on the Roman Missal* (GIRM) have broadened our understanding to include four distinct modes of Christ's presence. Christ is present in the assembly as it gathers to worship; Christ is present in the Word proclaimed to the assembly; Christ is present in the presider; and Christ is present substantially and permanently in the eucharistic bread and wine (SC 7, GIRM 7). By expanding our understanding of the presence of Christ, the Council did not take away from Christ's presence in eucharistic species, rather it gave us a broader context to understand this presence (SC 7). The *Catechism of the Catholic Church* affirms the Catholic belief in the real presence of Christ in the Eucharist by quoting from the Council of Trent (CCC 1376). Trent stated unequivocally that in the Eucharist "the body and blood, together with the soul and divinity, of our Lord Jesus Christ and, therefore, the whole Christ is truly, really and substantially contained." This doctrine is called transubstantiation.

The teachings of the council fathers gave us a renewed insight into the purpose of Christ's presence. Christ is present not primarily to be adored, but rather to be united to us (GIRM 54). Christ's presence gathers us as his body to worship God as Father (SC 48). Christ's presence in the blessed bread and wine nurtures us and unites us to go out and transform the world into the kingdom of God. Christ's presence in the Word proclaimed speaks to our hearts, connects us with his presence through history and sustains us on our journey to be fully united with him in our own death-resurrection. Christ's presence in the presider reminds us that Christ is the one united to us who offers the eucharistic sacrifice.

It is important to realize that the phrase "real presence of Christ" is not used interchangeably with the presence of Jesus. When we speak of the real presence of Christ we are referring to the anointed one, Jesus Christ, who was transformed by the death-resurrection-glorification experience and now lives in unity with the Father and Spirit. When catechizing about the "real presence," the emphasis is on the body of the resurrected Christ, rather than the body of Jesus who walked the earth.

It is significant to realize that each of the ways we experience the presence of Christ is important. Christ cannot be experienced immediately, but always through the deepest way of experiencing critical relationships, through symbolic actions. As described in the previous chapter, symbolic actions and words speak to us of the most profound relationships. The council fathers speak of it in terms of visible things symbolizing the invisible: "…and the visible signs used by the liturgy to signify invisible divine things have been chosen by Christ or the Church" (SC 33). Christ is really present in the assembly, in the Word proclaimed, in the presider, "but especially under the eucharistic species" (SC 7). The presence of Christ in the eucharistic species is unique and different from the other presences. The acknowledgement of this presence is at the heart of our Catholic identity and needs to be emphasized in catechetical settings. The other modes of Christ's presence need to be seen in relationship to his presence in the eucharistic species.

The question according to Fink is not how is Christ present, but rather how do we know Christ present? In other words, how do we meet the person of Christ present in the Eucharist. By looking at the Eucharist as a celebration of our redeemed lives in slow motion and by learning how to meet Christ in the Eucharist, we are preparing to meet and respond to Christ in the ordinary grace-filled moments of everyday life as we continue the work of Christ on earth today.

## 4) The Eucharist as Sacrifice

The Second Vatican Council reversed the medieval notions of sacrificial offering and restored the thinking of the early Church fathers during the first five centuries of the Church. The *Constitution on Sacred Liturgy* portrays Christ the priest identifying the Church with himself both in his worship of God and in his saving act for the world (SC 7). The sacrifice of the Eucharist is an action of Jesus Christ. It is neither repeated nor expanded in the Mass. It is remembered. In a beautiful passage the council fathers remind us of the richness of the sacrifice of the Eucharist:

> "At the Last Supper, on the night when He was betrayed, our Savior instituted the Eucharistic Sacrifice of His Body and Blood. He did this in order to perpetuate the sacrifice of the Cross throughout the centuries until He should come again, and so to entrust to His beloved spouse, the Church, a memorial of His death and resurrection: a sacrament of love, a sign of unity, a bond of charity, a paschal banquet in which Christ is consumed, the mind is filled with grace, and a pledge of future glory is given to us" (SC 47).

And in that remembering the unique offering of Christ to God on the cross is made present to God and the assembly through the eucharistic narrative so that all may be included in its saving power. The eucharistic activity is always related both to God in worship and to the assembly as a source of salvation. The entire paschal mystery, nuanced in terms of the sacrifice of the Eucharist, "is manifested by signs perceptible to the senses..." (SC 7). The once-for-all sacrifice of the cross is brought to expression in eucharistic celebrations so that God will remember what Christ did and so that all enacting the Eucharist (and all remembered at it) will be absorbed into the saving power of the cross. "...In the liturgy full public worship is performed by the Mystical Body of Jesus Christ, that is, by the Head and His members" (SC 7).

## 5) Eucharist as a Sign of Hope, Life and Unity

The Second Vatican Council gave a renewed focus to the future dimension of the Eucharist, referred to by theologians as the eschatological aspect. This understanding had been diminished in the Roman

Church since medieval times. By restoring images of pilgrim people on a journey it captured the notion that there was in the human condition a yearning for what is incomplete in this life. It reflected a hope and a waiting for a future that is yet unrealized. Phrases like, "we wait in joyful hope for the coming of our savior Jesus Christ," or the acclamation, "Christ has died, Christ has risen, Christ will come again," contribute to the sense that there is more to come, there is unfinished work to be done. The Eucharist in one sense is complete. In another sense it is incomplete because it has not been fully realized. We have a taste of what is to come. But the yearning and desire for unity of all humanity—and more than that of all creation—is yet to be attained. This future imagery is not a prediction of the future, rather it is an expressed hope in God's promise and pledge that God-Christ-the Spirit will always be with us, caring for us, supporting us on the pilgrimage as we continue to build the kingdom. It is the hoped-for banquet of spirit-filled unity and communion of all creation. Christ's presence in the Eucharist is the greatest sign of the hoped-for final transformation of all life into unity with God.

> *Review each of the five insights culled from Vatican II above and discern which are most life-giving to you at this point in your life. What difference do they make in your life?*
>
> *How are they a change from previous understandings of the Eucharist?*
>
> *Think about how they might be presented and experienced as part of the "tapestry of the Eucharist" by those whom you catechize.*

## CONSCIOUS ACTIVE PARTICIPATION

In order to promote conscious and active participation in the Eucharist it is important to know the parts of the liturgy, their function in light of the whole celebration, and the meaning of the gestures and symbols employed. What follows highlights some aspects of the liturgy and draws heavily on the ideas found in the *General Instruction of the Roman Missal* (GIRM). As noted above, the liturgy is divided into two major parts: the liturgy of the word and the liturgy of the Eucharist. Each of these parts has subparts. It should be noted that what we are talking about here is only the Roman rite. This is the predominant rite used in the Western world, but Eastern rites are also used. The rites have their own uniqueness and richness. There is not room to discuss them here, but the reader is encouraged to study them. A reference for such study is included in the resources cited at the end of this chapter.

## LITURGY OF THE WORD

### 1) Introductory Rites

Preceding the proclamation of the Word are the introductory rites (GIRM 24-32). These rites help the assembly become more aware that it is the body of Christ gathered in his name. It gathers to offer its life along with Christ to God in free and loving obedience so that its blessed life, made up of many individual lives, can be transformed and shared with all. The group that gathers for Mass is not just a crowd who happens to be free at the same time. Rather, it is and it becomes to a greater degree the body of Christ present to do the work of Christ, to worship God and partake in the works of salvation. The introductory rites include the entrance song, greeting, penitential rite, Kyrie, Gloria and the opening prayer. Not all of these rites are used at every Mass. The entrance song, the greeting and the opening prayer are the most significant of these rites. The entrance song has a marvelous quality of being able to bond people into a sense of community, thus making the reality that the assembly is the body of Christ more apparent. The greeting is always done by using our identity symbol, the sign of the cross, which further brings our character as the body of Christ to consciousness. In the greeting the presider proclaims to the assembly that Christ is present. Besides intensifying the assembly's sense of community, the entrance rites prepare the assembly for the word of God. In the opening prayer the priest invites the people to pray. Together they share a moment in silence to realize God's presence. This is followed by a prayer of petition addressed to God through Christ and the Spirit.

> *What do you think is the most significant aspect of the introductory rites?*
> *Do you think its purpose is well known to most people who participate at Mass?*
> *Explain your thinking. What can you as a catechist do to help others recognize the significance of the introductory rites?*

## 2) Liturgy of the Word

Readings from scripture and psalm responses, along with the homily, creed and general intercessions, form the liturgy of the word (GIRM, 33-47). Weekday masses may eliminate the homily and the creed. God speaks to the assembly in the scriptures proclaimed at Mass. The assembly is nourished by the stories of salvation that happened in the past. Through the homily, they are enabled to connect their own lives with the stories of salvation that continue to happen today. Christ is present in the Word proclaimed to support the assembly as it continues to build God's kingdom. By singing the psalm responses the assembly begins to integrate the Word of God into its life. By listening to the homily the assembly gets further insights into how it can live the message of the readings, especially the Gospel. The profession of faith or the creed provides another opportunity for the assembly to express its commitment to its beliefs. It is interesting to note that before Vatican II the priest proclaimed the creed with "I believe…" In the shift in emphasis the role of the assembly is accented now as the priest and people together proclaim "We believe…" Being fed by the Word of God, being confirmed in faith, now the assembly, along with the presider use their new energy to pray for the needs of the Church, for public authorities, for the salvation of the world, for those oppressed and for the needs of the local community. The general intercessions are initiated by the priest who invites the assembly to prayer. The actual petitions are proclaimed by a deacon, cantor or other person. The assembly as a whole is engaged in the prayer by its response after each petition. In some cases, petitions are offered directly from the assembled members.

A Vatican document, *Directory for Masses with Children,* issued in 1973, can be of great value to those who catechize children. It is written primarily for those participating in weekday Mass. There it is noted that the number of scripture readings may be reduced, but the reading of the gospel should never be omitted. The homily, which should have a preeminent place in the liturgy of the Word, may be given by a catechist or another adult with the consent of the pastor. However, as is true of all liturgies, the homily must be a reflection on the reading(s), not a catechetical lesson. The document supports children proclaiming parts of the readings much as is done for the reading of the passion during Holy Week. A dialogue homily with the children is also permitted. A thorough study of this document is a prerequisite for all who work with children, who prepare children for the celebration of Mass or who help them plan a eucharistic liturgy.

> *As you reflect on the liturgy of the word, what struck you as being very significant?*
> *In your experience of the liturgy of the word, what strikes you as a very positive aspect of it?*
> *What could be improved so that it is more effective?*
> *How would you get across to those whom you catechize the idea that God speaks to us in the liturgy of the word?*
> *What advice do you have for the homilist?*
> *After studying the* Directory for Masses with Children *name some ideas you will include in your next liturgy planning session with children.*

## LITURGY OF THE EUCHARIST

### 1) Preparation of the Gifts

This is the time when the altar is prepared, the gifts of bread and wine, financial contributions and other gifts for the Church and the poor are presented (GIRM 49-53). The altar is prepared by putting the corporal, purificator, missal and chalice on it. Then representatives from the assembly present the bread and wine which will become Christ's body and blood. This ritual is reminiscent of the times when the faithful actually brought bread and wine from their homes to be used at liturgy. Here they bring the fruits of the earth and the work of human hands, a symbol of creation and themselves, to be transformed into the body and blood of Christ. Song often accompanies the presentation of the gifts. Once the gifts are presented they are put on the altar. At this time the altar may be incensed, a symbolic action of the Church's prayer going to God. The priest washes his hands as a sign that he wishes to be cleansed within. The preparation of the gifts ends with an invitation by the priest to the assembly to pray that our sacrifice may be acceptable to God. After the assembly prays that God will accept the sacrifice for the praise and glory of God, for its own good and the good of the Church, the priest prays over the gifts. This part of the Mass was previously called the offertory. But this is misleading because the gift offered at Eucharist is Christ under the appearances of bread and wine. In the eucharistic prayer we unite with Christ to be offered to God. The purpose of this prayer is to prepare ourselves to be offered during the eucharistic prayer. It is our hope that as the bread and wine are transformed into the body and blood of Christ, we too will be transformed.

## 2) Eucharistic Prayer

This is the high point of the whole liturgy (GIRM, 54-55). In the eucharistic prayer, the priest prays that the assembly joins itself to Christ in recognizing the great things God has done and in offering the sacrifice. The action of the Eucharist happens in the taking, blessing and breaking. When communion services are used in the absence of a priest, this vital part of the Eucharist is missing. While a communion service will have the liturgy of the word, the praying of the Lord's Prayer and the distribution of communion, important actions of the Mass are missing. The taking of the bread and wine from the assembly, the blessing of the bread and wine, the memorial of Christ giving of himself totally to God and our union with him, and the breaking of the bread—all these are absent from communion services outside of the Mass. For these reasons, communion services can never take the place of the eucharistic liturgy.

There are eight important elements in the eucharistic prayer. The first of these is thanksgiving which is expressed especially in the preface. Here the priest thanks God for all the works of creation and salvation and highlights a special set of events corresponding to the feast or season. The second is the acclamation of the holy, holy, holy, where all join in praising God. The third is the special prayer calling on the Holy Spirit to take our gifts and transform them into Christ's body and blood and to transform the people who receive the body and blood of Christ at communion. The fourth aspect is the institution narrative and consecration. This part uses the words and actions of Christ as recorded in scripture at the Last Supper, where he offered his body and blood, gave them to his apostles to eat and drink and asked them to carry on this mystery. The fifth element is the memorial where we remember what Jesus did and continue in his stead united with him. The sixth element is the offering. In remembering the passion, death and resurrection the Church offers the "spotless victim," Christ, to the Father and Holy Spirit. In this offering we are united with Christ as our mediator in loving surrender to God. The seventh aspect of the eucharistic prayer are the intercessions. This is where the whole Church unites with the communion of saints in sharing the salvation wrought by Christ's body and blood. The final element is the doxology, a hymn of praise to God, where we all affirm our heartfelt praise in the great amen.

The three acclamations—the holy, holy, holy, the proclamation of Christ's death, resurrection and coming at the end of time in the institution narrative, and the great amen—are all times when we actively participate as the body of Christ to become more fully the body of Christ.

> *After reflecting on the preparation of the gifts and the eucharistic prayer, name three or four things which distinguish them.*
>
> *Name what is lost when we do not have a eucharistic celebration, but only a communion service.*
>
> *How would you explain this to people who think that a communion service is just a short Mass, and probably just as "good."*
>
> *Examine the four eucharistic prayers used in the Roman Catholic Church to find each of the eight parts named above.*
>
> *While Christ is present in four different modes in the Eucharist (the assembly, the presider, the word proclaimed and the blessed bread and wine), the Church teaches that Christ is present especially under the eucharistic elements of bread and wine (SC 7). Name ways you can highlight for those whom you catechize Christ's presence in the blessed bread and wine, while not diminishing Christ's presence in the other modes named above.*

### 3) Communion Rite

The communion rite consists of the Lord's Prayer, the rite of peace, fraction rite, commingling of the host and the wine, Lamb of God, personal preparation, prayer of humility, reception of communion, communion song, silence, and the prayer after communion. In preparation to receive Christ's body and blood, the assembly with the priest prays the Lord's Prayer. The priest alone extends the last petition of the Our Father by asking that we be further delivered from sin and anxiety. The people affirm this with the prayer of praise telling God that we want all power and glory to be with him now and forever. Affirming that sharing the bread of the Eucharist is a sign of unity, the assembly offers peace to one another. Sometimes the sign of peace is exchanged just prior to the liturgy of the Eucharist, pointing to the fact that there is unity among the faithful before the eucharistic offering is begun.

The breaking of the bread is rooted in the actions of Christ at the Last Supper. The ritual is an effective sign of our all eating from the one bread, the one body of Christ. It is also a sign of the brokenness which is healed through partaking in the Eucharist. In the commingling ritual the priest drops a part of the host into the chalice and prays that the mingling of the body and blood of Christ will bring us eternal life. The Lamb of God, a litany, accompanies the breaking of the bread. The priest prepares himself to receive communion by praying quietly to be freed from sin and to be ever faithful to Christ. He then holds up the host and the chalice and with the assembly prays in humility, acknowledging unworthiness, but at the same time expressing faith that Christ's word will heal us of any unworthiness. As people process to receive communion a song is sung which expresses the assembly's union in spirit. After communion the priest and people spend some time in silent reflection. In the prayer after communion the priest asks that the mystery just celebrated may be lived out in life. The assembly affirms this prayer with "amen."

### 4) The Concluding Rite

The eucharistic celebration is concluded simply by the priest's blessing and sending the assembly forward to do the works of the Lord (GIRM 57). A final hymn sends people home with joy and praise in their hearts.

## THE LITURGICAL YEAR

The liturgical year is the annual cycle of feasts that celebrate Christ's life, death, resurrection and ascension. The year begins with the season of Advent, which starts four weeks before Christmas. The period is one of preparing for the celebration of the Incarnation, the birth of Christ. This is followed by the Christmas cycle, which lasts from Christmas until after the celebration of the Epiphany on January 6.

The Easter cycle is preceded by six weeks of Lent. Lent is a time spent in prayer, fasting and almsgiving. Lent culminates in the celebration of the Triduum of Holy Thursday, Good Friday, the Easter Vigil and Easter Sunday. People are initiated into the Church at the Easter Vigil, where new fire and water are blessed, where the story of salvation is proclaimed and the mysteries of salvation are celebrated. It is a night of remembering the past, celebrating the present and expressing hope for the future. Easter Sunday is the most important of all the Sundays because it celebrates Jesus' being raised by God from the dead.

What is called Ordinary Time is celebrated throughout the year when Advent, Christmas, Lent and the Easter cycle are not celebrated. Ordinary Time includes more than thirty Sundays of the year. During this time the mysteries of Christ are unfolded in the readings of the liturgy of the word.

From year to year each Sunday the community gathers to celebrate its past, its present existence and its hope in the future. It does this by remembering and making present the life, work, insights, and actions of Jesus Christ so that they may continue to live on in the faithful gathered in his name today.

In celebrating the liturgical year, the Church draws from its artistic heritage. It uses specific colors to express the feelings of the season. It uses designated music to reflect the mood and thought of the season. It uses certain signs from nature to help form the assembly in its ambience of the time of the year.

## PROMOTING JUSTICE

The Eucharist in many ways can be called a celebration of liberation. Its Jewish roots remembered the Exodus, the First Testament's major liberating event. Eucharist celebrates our being liberated from the ravages of sin, our being saved from destruction and our being united with the Godhead through the death-resurrection mystery of Jesus Christ. Reflecting on what really happens to us as we celebrate Eucharist propels us to be just toward others and to create just systems. We are sent to "love and serve the Lord." All acts of justice flow from Eucharist, but several of those relating to liberation will be discussed here. Three forms of liberation will be presented: psychological, social and spiritual.

## 1) Psychological Liberation

Psychological liberation is needed for those addicted to drugs, alcohol, consumerism, materialism, computers, gambling, physical abuse, and other addictions. These kinds of addictions can be debilitating and harmful not only to individuals, but to families and communities. Because we do Eucharist we are called to work with people to liberate them from addictions. There are many professional organizations that have expertise in these areas with whom we may need to work. What is required is the ability to expose people to the tragedy of addictions, help them to recognize them in themselves and others and network with community agencies so that the addicted people get the needed help. There are other psychological diseases that enslave people. One of the most common is depression. Encouraging those who may be afflicted, walking with them, supporting them through difficult times is needed if we are to be eucharistic people.

## 2) Social Liberation

Social liberation is called for wherever we see oppressed people. Some of the oppression is due to racism, exploitation, greed and prejudice. Racism happens when the dominant culture oppresses the minority cultures. In the United States, African Americans, Hispanics and Asian Americans often experience racism. They are denied access to jobs and other resources which white people may have because of their racial heritage. The unity called for at the Eucharist does not allow for racism. We cannot come to the table of the Lord, become his body and then go out and oppress people who are different than we are. There is no integrity in such behavior.

Exploitation of the poor, of women, of the handicapped and other groups calls for works of justice from the eucharistic community. Justice demands that people be treated fairly and that the vulnerability of one group of people is not exploited by another. Poor people are often given only minimal opportunities for education and good jobs. Women are often paid less for doing the same work as men. Men are selected over women in the job market, even though women are equally qualified. The handicapped often do not have access to the same jobs and services as those who are not handicapped. The eucharistic community can be a means of strengthening us to look at ways we are just and ways we need to be more just. Moreover, the eucharistic community is empowered to engage in the struggles to build a more just economic and political system, not only locally but globally.

Greed is another root of injustice. Greedy companies and avaricious leaders exploit natural resources especially from third world countries, thus leaving the countries depleted of what could have helped them develop. Greedy companies go to third world countries to get cheap labor and they exploit workers by making them work under inhumane conditions. Lack of concern for the workers' welfare leads companies to make moves which increase the bottom line at the expense of the workers. Jesus Christ gives himself to us in the Eucharist in unbounded love; we who are the body of Christ and who receive the body of Christ have received a mandate to make a more just world.

Prejudice is another source of injustice. Prejudice can be found as we discriminate against gay people, people with AIDS, people who make less money than we do, those who lack the same kind of education that we have, those who have come from a foreign country, those who belong to another religious denomination or tradition, those who are heavy-set or those who come from another part of the country than we do. The Eucharist is a great celebration of unity. Exclusion of people in our daily routines has no place in the lives of people who come together to share in the sacrament of unity. As sharers in the body of Christ we must try to create a more just world by eliminating prejudice.

### 3) Spiritual Liberation

Spiritual liberation deals with the constant need to let go of old ways of thinking and be open to how God is working with us today. Yesterday's paradigms may not be appropriate for today. Yesterday's hopes may not be expansive enough for today. Yesterday's way of thinking may be harmful now. Spiritual liberation does not mean throwing out the baby with the bath water. We are a religious people with a long tradition. This tradition sustains us as we face the future. But our tradition has always been one that adapts to new situations and reads the signs of the times in the light of the Gospel. Spiritual liberation calls for us to be open to new ways of thinking, to be open to new models of Church, to be flexible and faithful at the same time. Jesus came so that we might see life differently and have an abundant life. If we get stuck in "old ruts" we are doing an injustice to the community and to ourselves. What is called for today are people who are open to the energy of the Holy Spirit to continually recreate the earth so that it better reflects the work of the Lord.

Striving for liberation from addictions, for global social liberation, and for spiritual liberation are but three small ways to look at the works of justice.

> *From your own experience think of what you can do to contribute to someone who is psychologically enslaved. How is this related to Eucharist?*
> *How can you and those you catechize work for social justice? How is this related to Eucharist?*
> *How can you contribute to the spiritual liberation of those with whom you work? How is this related to Eucharist?*

## PRACTICAL IMPLICATIONS FOR PARTICIPATION IN THE LITURGY

Throughout this chapter different ways of participation have been discussed. However, little has been said about the role of music, art and environment and the role of using our bodies to worship. These greatly affect the quality of worship.

### 1) Music in Worship

A document from the United States Catholic Bishops, *Music in Catholic Worship* (MCW), contains many insights about liturgy. The theological underpinnings of the document are rich. They cite the need to celebrate the signs and symbols of Christian life, otherwise they will die. Intuitively, the document says, "Faith grows when it is well expressed in celebration. Good celebrations foster and nourish faith. Poor celebrations may weaken and destroy it" (MCW 6). Active participation in the liturgy cannot be imagined without considering the vital role music plays. Music is a preeminent expression of faith. It forms an integral part of liturgy. Music both expresses faith and nourishes faith. Some of the earliest Christian writings tell us that the community came together to sing psalms, hymns and inspired songs (Colossians 3:16). Music helps form a sense of community. There is no substitute for good music in liturgy. Music has the power to transcend mere words and "touch" the divine.

Music for liturgy must be judged on three criteria. (1) The music must be good music from an expressive, aesthetic and technical standpoint. Only competent musicians can make a judgement on this. (2) The music must be suitable for liturgy and enhance the liturgical celebration. To enrich the celebration the cantor, choir and assembly all must be involved in their proper roles. Appropriate music must be sung at designated times. The role of the assembly in singing the entrance and communion songs is important in developing a sense of unity. The acclamations are to be sung because the involvement of the assembly brings to greater consciousness the work of the assembly and the faith of the assembly. Music may be used at other times during the liturgy, to enhance the liturgy as the work of the people. (3) Ultimately there is one judgement, pastoral judgement, which makes the choice of music for worship. The question which needs to be addressed for this criterion is whether the music selected contributes to nourishing the faith of the particular community in this place, at this time and in this culture. While not exhaustive, these three criteria provide a framework for choosing music.

In the catechetical setting music should be used generously. Listening to reflective music can quiet people for prayer. Singing can nourish faith. Playing instruments can add to the prayer of praise and thanksgiving. When catechizing children, one of the roles of the catechist is to be sure the young people know the songs the community sings at worship, feel comfortable singing the acclamations and understand their meanings.

## 2) Gestures and Bodily Movements

Because we are bodily people we use our bodies in prayer. We stand, kneel or sit at appropriate times. The uniformity of these bodily movements contributes to the sense of unity among the assembly. It expresses and nurtures the work of the assembly (GIRM 20). We sit to listen, to prepare, to reflect; we stand for attentiveness—we are becoming something new; we stand for the Gospel, prayer, praise and acclamation; we kneel to express humility and adoration; and we exchange a sign of peace to show solidarity. We are greeted with gestures of hospitality as we enter the worship space. We process to come together as the assembly, to present the gifts and to receive the body and blood of

Christ; and some professionals enact interpretive bodily movements or dance as ways to express faith and solidarity and to be nourished by symbolic actions of the liturgy.

When you pray with those you catechize, do not hesitate to use gestures. Beginning with pre-school and primary-aged children, young ones can be taught to use their bodies to praise and thank God for all blessings. Using their hands and arms to reflect postures of awe, humility and praise can greatly enhance their prayer life.

### 3) Art and Environment

*Environment and Art in Catholic Worship* (EACW) was issued by the United States bishops in 1978. This document is helpful in describing the design of the physical environment needed for worship, the pre-eminent role of the assembly, the role of the arts, body language, the furnishings and objects used in liturgical celebrations. One of the opening paragraphs describes poignantly the biblical and theological foundation of the document:

> "While our words and art forms cannot contain or confine God, they can, like the world itself, be icons, avenues of approach, …ways of touching without totally grasping or seizing. Flood, fire, the rock, the sea, the mountain, the cloud, the political situations…in all of them Israel touched the face of God, found help for discerning a way, moved toward the reign of justice and peace. Biblical faith assures us that God covenants a people through human events and calls the covenanted people to shape human events" (EACW 2).

This reminds us that God works through human people, events and things, always drawing us further into the mystery of who God is, but never allowing us to totally embrace the mystery.

While this document is primarily designed for liturgy committees, architects and designers, it does have some important implications for the artistry catechists need to employ.

First of all, in planning liturgies, catechists often can have some influence over the place in which they are celebrated. For example, when having Mass with a small group, it many be possible to rearrange the environment and to have the assembly gather around the altar for the liturgy of the Eucharist.

Secondly, the catechist often can have those catechized enhance the environment with plants, flowers, banners, altar and ambo coverings. Part of the preparation for the celebration is to study and reflect on the readings. Art projects often can be an expression of the assembly's understanding of the readings or liturgical symbolic activities.

Thirdly, the catechist needs to be selective in how much "art" is used to enhance the environment. There is nothing more distracting at liturgy than an environment that is cluttered. Knowing where to place art objects is also important. For instance, the altar is to be kept for the bread and wine and missal. Flowers, candles or crosses should not be placed on the altar.

It should be noted that criteria similar to what was described above for music can be used in the selection of art to enhance the environment. First, art should be good art. This does not mean, especially when dealing with children, that the art used to enhance a liturgical environment has to be technically sophisticated. It means that it should be displayed in a manner that represents harmonious colors, balance and attractiveness. Parish art and environment committees are often willing to help catechists in these efforts. Another source of expertise are school art teachers, who are often more than willing to be of assistance. Second, the art should be fitting for liturgical celebrations. The following questions can be used to discern the appropriateness of art for liturgy: How does it express faith or nurture faith? How does it contribute to the creation of an atmosphere that leads to prayer and worship? How does it define the worship space? Third, pastoral judgement has to be used in the selection and placement of art. Does it reflect the present community? Does it reflect the culture of the community? Does it reflect the global dimensions of the Church? Does it lead the assembly to better worship God and love one another? Does the art of hospitality permeate the environment? Does the environment provoke both a sense of the mystery of God and the "touch-ability" of God? Does the art foster a sense of the sacredness of worship?

### 4) Living the Gospel

Participation in the liturgy does not end with the final blessing. The Eucharist nourishes us, the body of Christ, to go forward and live the Gospel. Contributing to building the kingdom of God is part of the work of liturgy. Participation in the liturgy sustains us, energizes us, motivates us to be about giving our lives for the good of our families, the community, and not just our local community but the global community as well. The Eucharist enables us to be a Christian in the world. The Eucharist is celebrated not just for the building up of the Church but also for the building up of the world. The world needs to be more humane, more just, more peaceful, more sustainable because the Christian community is celebrating the Eucharist. The only way this will happen is if we consciously internalize the liturgy of the word and the liturgy of the Eucharist so that it becomes the very fiber of our existence. An extension of the offering of ourselves with Christ to God in the eucharistic prayer is seen as we help our young child to read, listen to our exhausted spouse, deal with an angry customer, lobby for the homeless, make political decisions that diminish profits but insure a better environment for future generations, stand up for racial justice and fight for economic justice for all. This is what eucharistic communities do. This is their identity.

## REFLECTION

Have a Bible enthroned with a candle lighted near it. Have a small loaf of bread and a cup of wine. Procure a small table on which to put the bread and wine, so that people can stand around it. Have appropriate recorded music.

Gather the participants with an opening song known by the group.

*Presider:* God, our Loving Creator, you have given us your son to show us how to live. You continuously give Jesus Christ to us in the Eucharist. Enable us to be more aware of the transforming power of the Eucharist in our lives and in the lives of all your people. We ask this in the name of Christ our Lord.

*All:* Amen.

*Reader:* Proclaim Luke 24:13–34.

Allow a quiet time for reflection. Use the following questions as a starter.

> *How do you think Jesus felt as he was walking with the disciples?*
> *What do you think he told them?*

*What elements of hospitality do you find in the story?*
*Have you ever had the kind of experience that the disciples had, where all of a sudden you realize something that should have been apparent before?*
*What is the significance of the disciples recognizing Jesus in the breaking of the bread?*
*Think of a significant family meal you have had. What made it significant?*

Allow for sharing of the reflections in small groups.

*Presider:* Invite participants to come and stand around the table with the bread and wine. Say the following or something similar: "Sharing the one bread and drinking from the one cup has been a sign of our unity with Jesus Christ. As we continue his mission on earth of evangelizing and catechizing let us be nurtured by one bread and one cup of wine." Break the bread so all share from the one loaf. Pass the cup of wine. Play appropriate music in the background.

General Intercessions

*Presider:* God, our Creator, as we have shared in a sign of unity with your community, we bring our petitions to you:

*Response:* Lord, hear our prayer.

Invite petitions from the group.

*Example:* For all those who will go to bed hungry tonight we pray…

*Presider:* We ask you to be mindful of these petitions and all the petitions in our hearts, in the name of Christ the Lord.

*All:* Amen.

All pray the Lord's Prayer.

Exchange a sign of peace.

Sing a final song.


## RESOURCES

*Constitution on the Sacred Liturgy,* Second Vatican Council, 1963, in *The Liturgy Documents.* Chicago: Liturgy Training Publications, 1991.

Dooley, Kate. *To Listen and Tell.* Washington, DC: The Pastoral Press, 1993.

Duffy, Regis, O.F.M. "Eucharist," in *The HarperCollins Encyclopedia of Catholicism.* San Francisco: Harper San Francisco, 1995.

Fink, Peter, S.J. "Theology of Eucharist," in *The New Dictionary of Sacramental Worship.* Collegeville, Minnesota: Michael Glazier, 1990.

Klenicki, Rabbi Leon. *The Passover Celebration.* Chicago: Liturgy Training Publications, 1980.

Marrevee, William. *The Popular Guide to the Mass.* Washington: The Pastoral Press, 1992.

Whalen, Michael. *Seasons and Feasts of the Church Year: An Introduction.* New York: Paulist Press, 1993.

"Directory for Masses with Children," "General Instruction of the Roman Missal" (GIRM),

"Music in Catholic Worship," and "Environment and Art in Catholic Worship," in Mary Ann Simcoe, *The Liturgy Documents.* Chicago: Liturgy Training Publications, 1991.

# 9
# Living the Christian Life

Today one hears a great deal about the moral fiber of our society. Some bemoan its disintegration, others see signs of hope as they witness groups coalescing to bring about a sustainable world. Catechists are called upon to pull together the strands of Christian moral teaching so as to help those catechized to develop a moral fiber that reflects the values of Jesus and builds the body of Christ both in the Church and in the world. The artistry of the catechist calls for two understandings: (1) the ability to select and intertwine the moral stands of the tradition in such a way that they make sense to those catechized; and (2) the skill to empower those catechized to embrace and contribute to the strong moral fiber of Christian life.

Throughout this book some of the aspects of social justice in Catholic moral teaching have been addressed. This chapter will focus on the law and moral values of Jesus, the development of conscience, what it means to live a virtuous life and how sin affects not only the sinner but also the community. It is acknowledged that personal morality and social morality cannot be separated in real life. They are separated in this book merely as a point for the sake of clarity.

Jesus lived as a Jew and accepted the prevailing moral teaching of his religious cultural tradition. However, Jesus did more than that. He selected the noblest strands from the Israelite tradition, put them in unique combinations and gave them an essentially new meaning. For instance, in Jesus' day a prevalent moral teaching was not to hate your enemies. Proverbs calls people to give food and drink to one's enemy. But Jesus takes that further and says love your enemies as well as those who treat you badly. Jesus pushes the Jewish tradition to new heights: Love your enemies; do good to those who hate you (Luke 6:27–30).

"…whoever drinks the water I shall give,
will never thirst…." (Jn 4:14)

While the law of the Gospel or the law of Jesus pushes the limits of the moral code of the day, it does not abandon the teachings of the Torah. Jesus assumed that people would be following the Ten Commandments. These were basic moral laws. The heritage out of which Jesus operated was steeped in a tradition almost two thousand years old. That tradition can be summarized by calling it the law. The law can be found in the first five books of the First Testament, but most especially in the books of Leviticus, Numbers and Deuteronomy. The myriad laws found in these books are rooted in the Exodus event in which Yahweh calls Moses and the people to a special covenanted relationship.

## THE COMMANDMENTS GIVEN TO MOSES

The sign of God's relationship was the law given to Moses. This has come to be called the Decalogue or the Ten Commandments (Exodus 20:2–17). The Decalogue was important to Moses and the people because it expressed a special relationship to God. The first three commandments were unique to the Israelite people. They spoke of God's relationship to them. God had called forth "the best" in the people as a personal response to God's saving presence.

### 1) The First Commandment

In the first commandment the oneness of God is declared. To us this may not be unique. But to the Israelites who lived in an environment where many of the people and tribes worshiped fertility gods, this declaration of one God, a God who was a caring person, was unique. Another unusual thing that God was requesting from the Israelites was to avoid having images that could be construed as a god. The neighbors of the Israelites had carved images of their gods. To placate the gods and receive their blessings, the tribes would worship the images. This was seen in the story of the Israelites ignoring the covenant and worshiping the golden calf. God did not want the Israelites to worship images. Worshiping God was very important; using an image of God to worship was forbidden (CCC 2084). For the first time, instead of using gods to placate their needs, the people through the grace of God were beginning to recognize, respect and appreciate a personal God, a caring God.

While the Israelites did not worship images of God, they revered the tablets of the law which symbolized their relationship to God and the presence of God with them. They carried the tablets through the desert in the Ark of the Covenant (Deuteronomy 10:1–5). Subsequently, when they built a temple in which to worship God, the Ark of the Covenant held a very special place (2 Samuel 6).

While today people may scoff at "false gods" as something tempting only the people who lived centuries ago, contemporary false gods creep into life today. Consumerism and materialism can become gods. People can focus so much of their lives on money and acquiring goods that they make these things their gods. They live for what they can gain materially instead of living to build up the reign of God or living to increase in love of God and neighbor.

### 2) The Second Commandment

The second commandment forbids using God's name in vain. The original intent of this commandment is not clear, but what is apparent is that the commandment is promoting reverence and respect for the name of God (CCC 2142). In the First Testament times, some observed this commandment by not ever using the name "God" for fear that it would violate this mandate. They would refer to God as the Holy One or other such phrases, but not use God's name.

Another use of the word related to proving one's credibility. The use of God's name was proclaimed to indicate that a person seriously intended to carry out a promise. In courts of law today people declare that they are telling the truth by adding the phrase "so help me God." Jesus warned against using God's name to increase one's veracity and promoted people using their own word to mean "Yes" or "No" (Matthew 5:33–37).

Today this commandment is interpreted as a warning against using God's name in anger or using it carelessly to make a point about what one is saying. God's name is to be used for praise, thanksgiving and adoration. Honoring the name of Jesus Christ is an extension of this commandment for Christians. Blasphemy is the word used to identify abusive statements against God, Jesus Christ or the saints (CCC 2148). Blasphemous and foul language is "killing language" and can be destructive in very pervasive ways. It can ruin relationships; it can diminish self-concepts.

The use of one's name always has a personal aspect to it. Being called by one's name implies a relationship. Isaiah tells us that God calls each of us by name to indicate an intimate relationship between God and each person. When we gather to worship we do so in the "name of the Father, Son and Holy Spirit." We can name God because we have a relationship to the Trinity. The naming acknowledges this connection.

### 3) The Third Commandment

The third commandment reminds us to keep the Sabbath holy. The roots of this commandment are found in the book of Genesis, where God rests after finishing creation (Genesis 2:2–3). God reminded us that rest is needed on a regular basis. God affirms the importance of rest and makes the day of rest a holy day in which to celebrate the works of creation. The second dimension of this command points to the relationship between the Exodus and keeping the Sabbath holy. While the Israelites were enslaved by the Egyptians, they had to work everyday. There was no day of rest. After God saved the people from their oppression, they not only had a renewed opportunity to rest, but they had another reason to keep holy the Sabbath: God had saved them. Therefore, the theological underpinnings of this commandment are rooted in both creation and redemption (CCC 2169, 2170).

For the Jews the Sabbath is celebrated from sundown on Friday—often with special prayers and a special family meal—to sundown on Saturday. The early Christians retained their Jewish celebrations and observed the Sabbath and then went on to remember the Lord's Day or Christ's resurrection on Sunday. Gradually, as the Church grew beyond the Jewish community, the Christians celebrated Sunday as their holy day, their day of rest, the day they remembered the resurrection, the day they worshiped God (CCC 2174, 2175).

Today this commandment is interpreted by the Church to mean that Catholics are to worship God through the celebration of the Eucharist and to refrain from hard labor on Sunday, the day of rest (CCC 2180).

*Name some contemporary challenges posed by each of these commandments.*

*In what ways can obeying these commandments contribute to a healthy society and a credible Church?*

*What do you feel are the hardest parts of obeying these commandments in relationship to those whom you catechize?*

## 4) The Fourth Commandment

The first three commandments were unique to the Israelite community since they concerned their relationship with God. The last seven commandments were found in different forms in the cultures of the Middle East before and after the time of Moses. In some ways they represent guidelines that people must follow if they are to live in communal structures. In other words it is reasonable to expect that one's property be respected; that one's life be respected; that one can trust what another says, and so forth. The commandments spell out these basic social expectations.

The fourth commandment calls people to honor their parents. At first glance this is often interpreted to mean that children are to obey their parents. While St. Paul does give this command (Ephesians 6:1–3), it is not the root meaning of the commandment. This commandment originally referred to children caring for their aging parents. In some primitive cultures people were valued for the children they could bear. After child-bearing years, they were considered less valuable and often neglected. The will of God is clear here: parents are to be respected and cared for especially when they are elderly or infirm (CCC 2218).

Today this commandment is used to help children understand their relationship to their parents and parents' responsibilities to their children. Children owe parents respect, obedience, assistance with chores, etc., and gratitude. But if this is to be, it must be reciprocal. Parents owe children the modeling of healthy Christian values, care and concern for their physical, social, educational and spiritual needs and the opportunity to grow up in a functional family (CCC 2250–52).

The importance of the family cannot be overstated. It is the backbone of society. Pope John Paul II has called the family the "church in miniature." It is in the family where a child first experiences the love of God through the love of parents. Forgiveness is first experienced in a family. A healthy self-concept is rooted in family relationship and is at the heart of a great deal of moral development.

### 5) The Fifth Commandment

The fifth commandment reminds us that we are not to take another's life or harm another. In the Israelite mentality this did not include just wars or capital punishment. Harming another, whether accidentally or in self-defense, was also covered by this commandment. Over time the command came to be understood as the unauthorized killing of an Israelite. Some principles of this thinking inform contemporary moral decision making, especially in the area of "just wars." The goal is that all life be preserved and that peaceful solutions be sought.

The commandment points to the sacred nature of all human life and is used in many kinds of moral decision making. For instance, abortion is morally wrong because it takes a human life (CCC 2270, 2271); euthanasia (the taking of a life to eliminate pain and suffering) is morally wrong because it takes a human life (CCC 2277); suicide is morally wrong because one deliberately takes one's life—a life given by God (CCC 2281). The culpability for any of these morally wrong actions can be diminished due to ignorance, grave psychological disturbances, fear, torture, and the like. From a catechetical perspective it is important to know the Church's teaching on these issues and to catechize about them in a way that informs and motivates those catechized to avoid making decisions that take or harm human life. It is also important to be pastorally sensitive to families where some moral injustices may have occurred and to offer the Church's support and forgiveness as people begin again to live lives worthy of their calling.

Jesus expanded the notion of not killing and put it in more proactive terms. He stated that we are to be peacemakers (Matthew 5:9). He also articulated the fact that even being angry at someone was in the same category as killing someone (Matthew 5:22). He told people that if they had a grudge against someone they had to be reconciled before they could participate in worship (Matthew, 5:22).

Taking care of one's health is also part of following this commandment (CCC 2288). Because God has entrusted all people with life, they are to do things that maintain their health. This includes eating well, exercising and avoiding things that harm one's health. It also means working so that others may have access to food, clothing, health care and the like, so that they too may maintain healthy bodies and minds.

### 6) The Sixth Commandment

The sixth commandment forbids adultery. In ancient Israel this commandment forbade a man from having sexual intercourse with a married woman. It showed a concern that a man would have a right to raise his own children. Early on, the commandment did not mean that a man needed to be faithful to his wife. Gradually the spirit of the commandment did apply to a husband's fidelity (CCC 2336). Jesus expands this further to include "lustful thoughts" (Matthew 5:28).

The Church teaches that pornography, fornication (heterosexual intercourse between two unmarried persons) and homosexual practices are contrary to the sixth commandment (CCC 2396). It is important to note that having a homosexual orientation is not sinful. The Church does not condemn homosexuals; rather, the Church forbids homosexual activity. When catechizing about these issues it is important to be pastorally sensitive: to hold up the ideals of the Church while at the same time avoiding a self-righteous judgmental attitude toward those who do not live according to the Church's standards.

Today, the challenge in teaching young people is to catechize them in an effective way to avoid pre-marital intercourse. Among the many ills that flow from this practice is the birth of babies to teen moms and dads who have little ability, emotionally or financially, to raise children in a healthy environment. Because the practice of chastity is counter-cultural, promoting it takes great know-how, experience and the ability to be able to relate well to youth.

Television, movies, the Internet all seem to expose young people to sexual mores which do not call for self-discipline or respect for the other person, or for anything but self-gratification. The values of the home and the Church seem to erode in the minds of the young people. If everyone is doing it, then it must be OK. The development of sexual mores that reflect the Church's teaching is one of the most difficult challenges facing those who catechize adolescents. However, it seems that promoting healthy families and family interactions, solid self-concepts, competence in all areas of readiness and keeping young people busy learning new sources of knowledge and new skills will help them see that they do not have to be sexually active to be accepted by others or to feel worthwhile about themselves.

*The fourth, fifth and sixth commandments have a lot to do with family life. How do you see them contributing to family life?*

*What are some forces that make obeying these commandments difficult?*
*What strategies can you use to promote the following of these commandments?*

### 7) The Seventh Commandment

At the time the Israelites received this commandment its meaning was quite different than it is today. Originally it prohibited kidnaping. The tenth commandment dealt with thievery. Kidnaping was punishable by the death penalty. Stealing goods was punished by fines and restitution.

Today the seventh commandment forbids unjustly taking the goods that belong to someone else (CCC 2401). It demands that contracts be respected (CCC 2410) and that the goods of another not only not be stolen but also that they not be damaged through abuse. The commandment also applies to respect for all creation including animals and plants (CCC 2415) and general stewardship of the earth. Economic and social justice are seen as flowing from this commandment (CCC 2419–2449).

### 8) The Eighth Commandment

The eighth commandment forbids lying. Any sort of misrepresentation violates this commandment. The lack of truthfulness is seen to undermine the covenant between God and God's people (CCC 2464). Perjury, rash judgement, detraction (the telling of someone's faults to someone who does not need to know them), gossip—all are contrary to the commandment which calls for truth and integrity (CCC 2475–2487).

For the Christian, martyrdom was seen as the ultimate witness to the truth (CCC 2506). The authentic Christian was exhorted to stand up and be counted as a person who belonged to the Lord even if it meant risking one's life. The social dimension of this commandment includes the right to truthful information from governments and agencies which control the well-being of society (CCC 2512).

### 9) The Ninth and Tenth Commandments

The ninth and tenth commandments are very similar. They differ only in their objects. The ninth forbids "coveting" (having an unreasonable desire for) the wife of another man. The tenth forbids an outrageous desire for another's goods. These two commandments go beyond the admiration of what another has, either in terms of relationships or wealth. They really refer to desires that are disordered and may lead to other immoral behaviors.

To overcome an unreasonable tendency to desire what does not belong to one, purity of heart is needed (CCC 2533). Purity of heart is situated in a strong desire to be one with God and to act with modesty and patience. To be honest and genuine with others means being honest and genuine about oneself. The tenth commandment calls for people to be conscious of their values. Jesus reminds people that where their treasure is, there too will be their values (Matthew 6:21). Envy and greed can play havoc on one's spiritual life. These two commandments strive to hold such tendencies in check.

> *Think of public examples of the seventh and eighth commandment not being followed.*
> *How has this led to the breakdown of some of the moral fabric of society?*
> *How can an inordinate desire for people or things lead to further immoral behavior?*

## THE LAW OF JESUS CHRIST

What laws were important in Jesus' life? Jesus was not interested in minute prescriptions or rigid adherence to the law. He was satisfied with a summary of the law that basically said that one was to love God with one's whole heart, mind and soul and one was to love one's neighbor as oneself (Luke 10:25–28). But Jesus pushed the boundaries of how people understood that. It was no longer good enough to love one's neighbor as oneself. The new mandate was to love one another as "I have loved you" (John 13:34). In other words, Jesus asked his disciples to love each other as much as he loved them. Such love was immeasurable. Jesus gave his disciples the hallmark of love as something that would identify them.

Throughout his life Jesus spelled out characteristics of what the law of love was all about. The beatitudes found in Matthew's and Luke's gospel are examples of this. Sometimes in catechetical settings these are melded together and called the eight beatitudes. The two versions have quite different styles.

In Matthew, Jesus praises people for developing certain virtues which indicate that they are striving to live a life as children of God: blessed are the poor in spirit; blessed are they who mourn; blessed are the meek; blessed are those who hunger after justice; blessed are those who practice mercy; blessed are the peacemakers, etc. (Matthew 5:3–12). Notice that there are no boundaries in these statements. Jesus was not saying how much comforting, peacemaking or justice was needed. He was speaking of qualities of life, not quantities of something to be done.

In Luke, Jesus consoles people who are living in less than ideal situations and promises a reward; then he issues threatening woes to those who miss the point (Luke 6:20–23). The Lucan beatitudes portray Jesus blessing people who are poor, hungry, sorrowful and despised, and telling them things will be better in the new life which he is about to bring. He then goes on to show a certain disdain for the rich, those who seem to "have it all" now, for they will not enjoy real blessings in the long term.

> *Explain in your own words Jesus' breaking the old boundaries of the law and demanding more than the law demanded.*
> *How would you explain that Jesus came to fulfill the law, not destroy it?*
> *How are the Ten Commandments included in the law of Jesus Christ?*
> *Compare how material things can increase only by addition, but "things of the heart" can increase only by giving them away.*

## LIVING A VIRTUOUS LIFE

### The Theological Virtues

A virtue is an habitual manner of acting in a praiseworthy way. Living a virtuous life has as its goal to become like God. As Christians we believe that we received the theological virtues of faith, hope and charity at baptism. These virtues are gifts from God but need to be exercised and developed, otherwise they wane. In reality the theological virtues are intertwined. They are separated here only for discussion purposes.

### a) Faith

The word faith is often used in two ways: that which we believe (We believe that Jesus is the son of God); and that by which we believe. The latter is the way we are using faith when we talk about it as virtue.

The gift of faith enables us to believe in a loving God, a God who gave his son Jesus Christ, who in turn sent the Spirit to be with us for our entire lives. Faith is the basis of our moral lives. Belief in the persons of the Trinity informs all we do and gives us values out of which to operate (CCC 1814). Faith is not against reason, but it goes beyond what reason is capable. Faith brings meaning to life. It helps people cope with the uncertainty of life, with life's tragedies as well as life's joys. Faith makes it possible to have an intimate relationship to a God whom we cannot see. Faith helps us believe in things which cannot be proved. Faith enables us to put up with the incongruities of life that we find in the Church and in society because we believe that there is something more important, something divine that cannot be controlled by human maneuvers; someone divine who loves us and empowers us and is not regulated by political power.

Faith calls us to respond to God's love as experienced and mediated through the Christian community. Faith, while being a personal relationship to God through Jesus Christ, is not a "Jesus and me only" relationship. It is a relationship to God that calls for building the kingdom in the world in communion with other people. Faith grows in community; faith grows through instruction; faith increases through struggling to believe; faith is a dynamic part of life because it is relational. It is a virtue because it is a habitual way of seeing the world, naming it and acting upon it. Faith helps us to see the "more" in life— the presence of the transcendent in the ordinary.

### b) Hope

The second of the theological virtues is hope (CCC 1817). Hope presupposes faith. It is a gift from God that enables us to imagine union with God. It is perhaps best understood by its opposites. Hope countermands despair and presumption. Hope diminishes despair by offering positive images and energy to live life with positive attitudes because of belief in a loving God. Hope counteracts the notion that salvation and union with God is impossible. Hope is the opposite of presumption. Presumption assumes that one is assured of salvation or that one can "earn" it through one's efforts. Presumption does not acknowledge one's dependency on God and God's ongoing presence in the lives of the faithful.

Today the need for the virtue of hope is recognized to a high degree. The rapid increase in the number of suicides, especially among young people, is alarming. With greater awareness of world problems, injustice, poverty, corruption, the possibility of ecological disaster, for example, some feel they cannot cope, that there is no hope and, thus, they take their own lives. This tragedy screams at the Christian community for solution. The needless loss of life reflects the lack of the practice of the gift of hope. Hope-filled people need to be symbols of hope for those who are struggling to believe and hope in a world that seems awry but in reality beckons us to union with God.

### c) Charity

The third of the theological virtues is charity. Together with faith and hope it forms the basis of Christian life. It too, is a gift from God. It has its source in God and its goal is union with God.

Charity's union with God also includes love, care and union with one another (CCC 1822). It is considered the most important of the theological virtues, but one cannot be charitable without also living by faith and hope. Charity functions as a symbol for all Christian life, the hallmark of what it means to be a Christian.

St. Paul, St. Augustine and St. Thomas Aquinas have all put charity in the prominent position of being pivotal to Christian life. They do this based on the teachings of Jesus Christ, especially those found in John's Gospel (John 15:15) and the first epistle of John (1 John 4:7–21). Because their ethical frameworks were so grounded in love, they also saw sin as an offense against charity.

Charity is always outward looking. It looks to God for sustenance. It engages in loving behavior toward others as a way of modeling the life of Jesus. It reaches out to strangers and enemies and strives to transform evil into good because it knows it has the power of the Spirit with it to make a difference in the world. The opposite of love is selfishness, that inward attitude that portrays a "me first" attitude and operates almost totally out of a self-centered perspective. A young child will be self-centered naturally, but gradually, through good role-modeling and the forming of habits which call for reaching out to others, self-centeredness gives way to other-centeredness. However, this side of heaven, there will always be a certain pull for the "self" and a desire to retreat into the self. The community of faith reaches out and beckons all toward other-centeredness.

While all the theological virtues are gifts from God, they are gifts that must be used. They are not magic. If a gift is not used, it atrophies and disintegrates, much as an unused body part does. A physical therapist knows how important it is to use one's legs, arms and hands well in order to keep them from weakening. So too with the theological virtues. Believing, hoping and loving are the lifeblood of the Christian community. They need to be used to enhance the vitality of the community.

> *In what ways do the theological virtues make life easier?*
> *Does it ever feel like they are not gifts but rather burdens?*
> *When? Why?*
> *Of the three virtues, which takes the least effort to practice?*
> *Which is the most difficult?*
> *Sometimes is it one, at other times, another? Explain.*

## 2) The Cardinal Virtues

Four other virtues permeate Christian life. They are prudence, justice, fortitude or courage, and temperance. They are called cardinal virtues because they are hinges upon which other virtues hang (CCC 1805). These virtues are also infused at baptism, but they need to be used or practiced so that they become second nature.

### a) Prudence

Prudence is the practical virtue (CCC 1806). It allows people to make a decision about a particular action that is needed in specific circumstances. It moves from the general to the specific. Parents are always trying to exercise this virtue as they struggle with the everyday situations of raising children. Questions such as "Is he old enough to go on his own?" and, "Did I prepare her well enough to drive alone, even though she has her license?" are but a few of the everyday decisions that require prudence.

### b) Justice

Justice empowers people to be fair in dealing with others (CCC 1807). Justice is applied not only to individuals but also to systems that may be unjust. Such systems may create classes of people, so that some get rich based on the work of others who remain poor. Justice is a social virtue demanding that people get their just due. The United States bishops, in their pastoral, Economic Justice for All, remind us that "the quest for justice arises from loving gratitude for the saving acts of God and manifests itself in the wholehearted love of God and neighbor" (39). In other words, because God has redeemed us and loves us, we need to be just and loving to others.

### c) Fortitude

Fortitude, or courage, enables people to pursue the good despite what could be enormous fears (CCC 1808). Courage motivates people to go through chemotherapy or radiation treatments in hope of a cure from cancer. Courage strengthens people to jump into a pool to save a drowning victim. Fortitude was the virtue the martyrs used by giving up their lives because of their faith in Jesus Christ. Courage is the virtue Jesus used by accepting the cross as the will of God. Today this virtue is needed especially when making moral decisions that are counter-cultural: not getting swept up in consumerism; standing up for what is right in the workplace; making hard decisions about sexual morality. In a culture where it seems that "anything goes," it takes courage to live a healthy moral life based on the values of Jesus Christ.

### d) Temperance

Temperance enables people to act with moderation (CCC 1809). It is a true sign of being Christian. The temperate person enjoys life, is self-disciplined, cares about others and does not go overboard on any behaviors. A temperate person is not obsessive, nor does the person have a laissez-faire attitude about the self-restraints needed to live a truly Christian life.

The four cardinal virtues interrelate with the three theological virtues and form a framework for living the Christian life. While these virtues are gifts given freely by God they must be exercised in order to contribute to the vibrancy of Christian life. These virtues animate the Christian community to live as Jesus did.

*How would you rank the cardinal virtues in terms of impor-*
*tance? Give reasons for your rankings.*
*At certain times in life different virtues become very important.*
*Reflect upon your life and describe when a virtue was particu-*
*larly important to you.*
*How do the virtues contribute to fighting sin and living a*
*healthy Christian life?*

### 3) The Importance of Conscience

The conscience is the whole person trying to make a judgment
about what is the right decision regarding a specific moral issue. Conscience is not a specific power, nor the effect of feeling guilty. It is not a
physiological, psychological or sociological factor. It is the thrust of
the whole person searching for a value to be applied to specific circumstances. Basically, conscience looks at the person as morally conscious.
The Second Vatican Council calls the conscience the place where one is
alone with God, the most secret core of one's being (GS 16). In one
sense conscience is subjective. It is the awakening and development of
a moral consciousness.

The formation of conscience is a gradual process which begins in
childhood and initially is based on reward and punishment. As the child
grows into adolescence, young adulthood and finally adulthood, the
person begins to interiorize the "law" or guidelines that had been
imposed externally. The development of conscience presupposes a loving environment where there has been emotional support and confirmation of a healthy self-concept. Ultimately, with the most highly
developed conscience one could operate beyond the law based on personal conviction rather than the law. People like Mahatma Gandhi or
some of our saints like Joan of Arc or Thomas More, are people who
had highly developed consciences that were not limited by law.
According to the Second Vatican Council, conscience is the place
where a person discovers, deep within, a law which the person has not
made individually, but one which must be obeyed; it summons the person to love what is good and avoid what is evil (GS 16). Following
one's conscience has always been important in the Catholic tradition.
St. Thomas Aquinas was a great promoter of being true to one's conscience. But he was always referring to a rightly formed conscience.

### 4) Formation of Conscience

As noted above, conscience formation is a life-long process because it is the formation of the whole person (CCC 1783). Conscience is influenced by family values, community mores, stories, information, study and response to God's grace. Catholics have the moral responsibility of forming their consciences by doing the following: (1) consulting sources of moral wisdom such as trusted people who may be able to act as mentors; (2) reading and reflecting on the New or Second Testament, especially the Gospels; (3) using a process of theological reflection (one is described in the next chapter); (4) carefully studying the teaching of the Church and looking for the underlying values supporting the magisterium's teaching; (5) consulting with and sharing the moral values of the local worshiping community; and (6) praying for grace and strength to make the right decision and carry it out. Conscience is not infallible. "In good conscience" it is possible to make a poor moral choice and have to deal with the consequences of that choice. Humility and openness to the possibility of having made a poor choice are necessary virtues in the formation of conscience. Discerning what is right and good and acting accordingly is the way to follow one's conscience. Living a virtuous life enhances the formation of conscience as it leaves its marks on the whole person (CCC 1794).

## WHAT IS SIN?

One cannot talk about living the Christian life without reflecting on sin. Sin is a reality of life. No matter how hard we try, we at times miss the mark, fall short of the goal. Sin has traditionally been looked at under three aspects: original sin, mortal sin and venial sin.

### 1) Original Sin

The term "original sin" was first used by St. Augustine in the fourth century. He used it in particular to deny the teaching of Pelagius, who asserted that infant baptism did not forgive sin, because tiny children could not have sinned. Augustine opposed this teaching by pointing out that baptism takes away "original sin," the sin all humans are born with because of Adam's sin.

While this explanation of original sin may not answer all the questions people raise about it today, one thing is certain—human beings experience a tendency not always to be their best selves, to act out of self-gratification and not in the best interest of God and the community. Augustine calls the effect of original sin "concupiscence." Concupiscence is the tendency to act out of self-interest; it is an inclination to sin (CCC 405, 406, 1264). Baptism gives people power over concupiscence. Living a virtuous life enables people to continue to struggle with the evil tendencies they endure as part of the human condition.

Rahner states that while there is certainly no lack of evidence of sin in the world, there is much more evidence of God's grace which prevails over sin. For Rahner the abundance of God's grace far surpasses the presence of sin and should be the focus of Christian gratitude. The grace of baptism gives us power over the effects of original sin.

### 2) Mortal and Venial Sin

All sin is evil and needs to be avoided. But some sin is more serious than other sin. Mortal sin involves a rupture in one's relationship to God. For mortal sin to occur, three conditions must be present: (1) very serious or grave matter; (2) full knowledge about the seriousness of the action; and (3) full consent of the will. A venial sin is one where there is less serious matter, or lack of knowledge about the seriousness, or lack of full consent of the will.

Some contemporary theologians like to make three categories of actual sin. Between mortal and venial they name serious sin. This has developed because some feel that mortal sin is a very rare occurrence, but some sins are more serious than venial sins.

Categorizing sin is not very helpful, in one sense, because all sin is harmful both to the individual and the community and to the manifestation of the presence of God on earth. It is hard to see God's reign amidst a sinful society and world. While sin needs to be acknowledged, time spent motivating people in a catechetical setting to live virtuous lives is a better use of effort than making distinctions about the kinds of sin there are. Whenever one catechizes about sin it is important to promote a nonjudgmental attitude towards one's neighbor. External acts are not always indicative of internal understandings or dispositions.

## FORGIVENESS

Any discussion of sin must always include forgiveness. Jesus talked about forgiveness in a way that set no limits. When asked how many times a person was expected to forgive, Jesus said the number of times was infinite (Matthew 18:21–22). Jesus gave up his life for the forgiveness of sins. The possibility of forgiveness abounds in the values of Jesus. Jesus knew people would miss the mark and fall short of the goal. The standards Jesus gave were high. Jesus expected his followers to be living signs of forgiveness.

Forgiveness reconciles people to God, to one another and to the community. We are called to act like Jesus: to pray that people will be forgiven (Luke 23:24); to forgive sins (Luke 7:36–50); to forgive debts (Matthew 6:12);to have pity on others (Matthew 18:33); to forgive our brothers and sisters (Luke 17:1–4); to be peacemakers (Matthew 5:9); to be merciful (Matthew 5:7). In catechetical settings, the possibility of experiencing forgiveness of our sins cannot be over-emphasized. The gravest of sins is forgivable. Reconciliation with God and the Church community is ever-present.

Jesus expected people to experience forgiveness in their everyday life experience. He demanded that people be reconciled with one another before participating in worship (Matthew 18:21–22). Catechists need to work with people so that they have the skills both to seek forgiveness of others and to offer forgiveness. Depression, despair and hatred are often the results of people being unable to forgive or ask to be forgiven. Skills such as conflict resolution, self-reflection, the ability to stand in another's shoes, along with the virtue of humility are all aspects of being able to participate in a process of reconciliation. Sometimes being able to forgive oneself is one of the most difficult aspects of forgiveness.

The sacrament of penance focuses on being forgiven by God and the Christian community. The sacrament is most effectively celebrated after one has come to an understanding of the relationship between sin and the community, sin and the individual and sin and God.


## PROMOTING JUSTICE

This chapter has focused on the law given to Moses, the law promoted by Jesus, living a virtuous life, the formation of conscience and an understanding of sin. Each aspect of the chapter has the potential to be a stepping-off point for promoting justice. The commandments are basic mandates for promoting justice and being able to live peacefully in society. By taking each commandment and having those catechized imagine a world where that particular commandment was not generally followed will help them see how integral to human life the commandments are. Using stories of gang "communities" who do not follow the commandments and contrasting those stories with some of people who are living according to the commandments will provoke interesting discussion and good consciousness raising.

Finding stories of those who follow Jesus' mandates even when the going gets tough and analyzing them for hints of the beatitudes in action can lead to an awareness that living by the beatitudes is possible even in the complexities of today's world. Using film or video can be effective in this regard.

While most of this book has dealt with social justice from a communal standpoint, it is important to realize that the community will only be as just and moral as its individual members. Motivating people to live just lives as individuals is paramount to building the kingdom of God.

## PRACTICAL IMPLICATIONS

1. Use lives of the saints to promote virtuous lives. Have participants learn about their patron saint or another saint that appeals to them. Depending upon the age of those catechized have the participants write or perform a skit about what a day would be like in their favorite saint's life. Encourage them to truly walk in the shoes of the saint they have chosen. This may call for some research into the saint's life and times.
2. Search through newspapers and magazines to find people apparently living virtuous lives. Define what this means in relationship to the article. Talk about what the hero or heroine in the article probably finds hard in his or her daily life. Make a connection with the lives of the participants.
3. Discuss the evil of sin and how it not only hurts the individual involved, but also how it diminishes the community and clouds the presence of God in the world. Depending on the abilities of those

catechized have the participants write or act out the results of one person's sin.

4. Take each of the virtues and portray a situation where they are lived out today.

5. Discuss some moral dilemmas that are age-appropriate. Show how the formation of conscience in the whole person will help the person make a good moral decision. Go through the steps listed above and give specific examples about how formation of conscience is achieved.

6. Develop contemporary examples of the beatitudes in action. Show what kind of moral fiber is needed to live them out. Connect these to the theological and moral virtues. Point to the interplay between the two.

## REFLECTION

Have the Bible enthroned with a burning candle next to it. Have a bowl of water and a small branch with leaves on it for sprinkling.

Begin with a familiar appropriate opening song.

*Presider:* God, our Creator, you have given us the Law of Moses and fulfilled it in the Law of Jesus Christ. You have given us the gifts of faith, hope and charity to empower us to build your kingdom here on earth. Send your Spirit to continually support us as we catechize those whom you love, and strengthen us to proclaim your Word so that it will be heard and lived. We ask this in the name of your Son and the Spirit who dwells in our midst.

*All:* Amen.

*Reader:* Proclaim Matthew 5:3–10.

Pause for reflection using the following questions:

> *How is Jesus calling us today to live out the beatitudes?*
> *Which beatitude do you feel could be the focus of your attention?*
> *How will you go about being conscious of that beatitude in your daily life?*
> *How can you empower others to live morally good lives?*

Allow an opportunity for sharing, if time permits.

*Presider:* Through the power of baptism we have received the wonderful gifts of the virtues. As we are sprinkled with water let us remember our baptismal commitment and pray that we will continue to grow in faith, hope and love.

Presider sprinkles the participants with water.

Invite participants to offer general intercessions. The response can be, "Lord, hear our prayer."

*Presider:* God, our Creator, we come to you with the following petitions:

(Petitions and response.)

*Presider:* Accept our petitions in the name of your Son, Jesus Christ our Lord.

*All:* Amen.

All pray the Lord's Prayer.

Exchange a sign of peace.

Sing an appropriate closing hymn.

## RESOURCES

Donnelly, Doris. *Putting Forgiveness into Practice.* Allen, TX: Argus, 1981.

Sloyan, Gerard S. *Catholic Morality Revisited.* Mystic, Connecticut: Twenty-Third Publications, 1990.

United States Catholic Conference. *Catechism of the Catholic Church.* Washington, DC: USCC, 1994.

Komonchak, Joseph; Collins, Mary; and Lane, Dermot, eds. *The New Dictionary of Theology.* Wilmington, Delaware: Michael Glazier, 1989.

McBrien, Richard, general editor. *The HarperCollins Encyclopedia of Catholicism.* San Francisco: Harper San Francisco, 1995.

# 10
# Catechesis and Pastoral Issues

Catechesis is not an isolated ministry. It is connected to all aspects of Church and parish life. Its strands are interwoven with evangelization and liturgy as well as social concerns. In order for it to be successful, it has to take into account many other concerns. Some of these are: family issues, parish pastoral issues, catechist training, recruiting and retaining those to be catechized and dealing with extreme groups.

## FAMILY ISSUES

Whether they recognize it or not, parents are the primary catechists of their children. Children and young people learn most from their parents' actions and attitudes. Sometimes catechists find themselves in awkward situations where they feel that to uphold the Church's teaching they are making negative statements about the parents or family members of those they catechize. For instance, while holding up the Church's teaching concerning restraint from sexual intercourse until marriage, they may be perplexing a child whose older brother or sister or a parent is "living with" someone to whom they are not married. Handling these and other moral situations in a pastorally sensitive way is imperative, while at the same time motivating those catechized to follow the ideals set forward by the Church.

There are several ways to approach situations like this. First of all, it is important to be as aware as possible of the family situations each child comes from. Are they from a single parent family? Are they being raised by a grandparent, aunt or uncle? If their parents are separated or divorced, do they have good relationships with both parents?

"I glorified you on earth by accomplishing the work
that you gave me to do." (Jn 17:4)

Do they know both parents? Some of this information can be obtained at registration, but the better way is by making home visits before cate-chetical sessions begin. At these visits the main message that the family should get from the catechist is, "My job as a catechist is to build upon what you are doing at home, for you are the primary developers of your child's faith life. What kinds of things would you like us to work on together?" Even if there are not family "structural" problems, the cate-chists will be more effective if they have a good relationship with the family before they start catechizing.

Second, if the family is in a new family relationship, is it a recent change in family structure? For instance, children who have just expe-rienced a divorce or the death of a parent may be much more sensitive to family issues than children who have been living with a single parent for years. Remember that single families are not unhealthy because they are single; in fact, they may be more healthy than two-parent fam-ilies that are dysfunctional. Research shows that what children need in order to grow into healthy adults is not to live in poverty and to have one parent who is "hooked" on them or devoted to them. That parent provides unconditional love and support, and challenges consistently by means of appropriate and reasonable discipline. That parent is the child's first experience of God.

Third, if the family is needy (emotionally, financially, spiritually) has there been any social outreach from the parish? If not, can there be? Sometimes single parents feel like second-class citizens in the Church and will not come forward. If the parish cannot reach out to them, can the family be connected to a local social service agency or a regional St. Vincent de Paul Society, if need be?

Fourth, when catechizing, be sensitive to the child's situation, not by watering down the Church's teaching, but by presenting it in a pas-toral way, so that the catechist is not making moral judgements on any-one's family. Whatever the person's family, whether it be adequate or inadequate in the catechist's eyes, that is the family of the person being catechized, and it is in that family that the person will find God's pres-ence manifested. It is the catechist's job to help the child discover this presence.

It is important when working with children of a newly divorced family to be aware that they may feel responsible for the divorce. It is not uncommon for children to think "If I had not been 'bad,' maybe mom and dad would not be divorced. If I behave well in the future, maybe mom and dad will get back together." Helping discredit these notions is important to relieve children of any guilt they may feel concerning the divorce. Also, it is important that newly divorced parents know how vulnerable children are at this time and that the best thing they can do for them is to reassure them that they are deeply loved and not responsible for the divorce.

Catechists need to be aware of several other family issues. If there are signs of physical, sexual or substance abuse, the catechist needs to consult with someone professionally competent to assess the situation, like a social worker or a nurse. This is usually done through the pastor or parish director of catechetics. Many states have mandatory reporting laws in cases of suspected physical or sexual abuse. In terms of alcohol and drug abuse, catechists need to know how to refer a family to the proper agencies to get help. Some education about abuse and abusive situations may be part of a catechetical program.

In some catechetical groups many of the children may have had no contact with their fathers; some may not even know who their father is. If this is the case, when talking about God, the first person of the Trinity, it is a good idea not to use exclusively the image of God as father. If children do not know a loving father, it is difficult for them to identify with a God who is like a loving father. Do not totally avoid the image because of its importance in Christian tradition. But expand upon it by saying something like "God is like a loving parent." Or ask the children to tell about the persons who love them just for who they are. After each child reflects on this and shares who this loving person is, then compare God to the person, noting that God loves them even more than whomever they named.

It is important that families be involved in the catechetical process. In some parishes this may mean family catechetical programs; in other parishes it may mean developing a hybrid program in which families participate in seasonal or traditional programs of the school or parish. It may mean that all sacramental programs are family programs. There are lots of options, but the most important catechetical question is not which textbooks will we choose, but how to get families involved in a substantial way in the catechetical process of awakening faith in their children.

*Think of ways you can get to know the families of those you catechize. What message do you want to leave with them about*

*your joint roles? How do you intend to involve them in the cat-
echetical process during the year?*

*Find out where you can get a list of community resources to
help assess difficult family situations and provide needed services.*

*From a pastoral perspective, what things do you need to take
into consideration concerning the families you are serving?*

## CATECHESIS AND OTHER PARISH MINISTRIES

Catechesis does not stand alone as a parish ministry. It involves
much more than what happens in catechetical sessions. Catechesis in
one sense is the work of the community. It is dependent on vibrant liturgies for its success; it requires good evangelization efforts for its effectiveness; it counts on parish outreach programs to be useful; it needs
good pastoral support to touch people; and it relies on a conscientious
staff who is committed to inter-ministry planning to be productive.

One of the phenomena that catechists have to contend with is
children attending parish or school programs but not participating in
the Sunday Eucharist. The reason they do not participate in liturgy is
because their parents do not. So while a child is being catechized on the
Eucharist as the source and summit of Christian life, they may have little opportunity to participate in it. The problem is a pastoral one, not
only a catechetical one. It calls for attention from liturgy planners, from
the evangelization committee and from the pastor as well as the catechetical leadership. Analysis is needed to determine the cause of the
family's absenteeism. Is it because the parents are not married in the
Church and think they cannot participate at liturgy? If so, a pastoral
visit that is very warm and welcoming may help clarify the situation
and perhaps even lead to regularizing their marriage in the Church. Is it
because one parent is not Catholic and the other is not very committed
to the Church? If so, working with the evangelization committee to do
some outreach to both parents might be helpful. Is it because the parish
liturgies leave a lot to be desired in terms of connecting with the real
issues in people's lives? Then the liturgy committee may need help in
designing prayerful and engaging liturgies which involve families. Is it
because the values of the family do not include Sunday worship? If so,
sensitive counseling with the parents may be needed so that they understand that sending their children to Catholic schools or parish religious

education programs and not following through with Sunday worship is very confusing to the children. In general, what is happening in the school or parish program is only as good as it parallels what is happening and promoted at home.

## RELIGIOUS INDIFFERENCE

Sometimes parents send their children to catechetical sessions only at times when the reception of a sacrament is the focus. It seems they know the importance of sacraments, even though they often do not regularly participate. Instead of bemoaning the less-than-ideal situation, one has to look at this as a catechetical and evangelization opportunity to involve the whole family.

### 1) Analysis of the Problem

If the quality of the sacramental programs is high and involves parents and if there is a process for parents to look at their own faith without being made to feel guilty, then the family may experience a "change of heart" and become more active in the parish and in their children's programs. In other words, even though there may be problems and apparent indifference, the fact that parents care enough to send their children for sacramental preparation needs to be seen as an opportunity for further evangelization efforts or adult catechetical growth. Ignoring families that are marginal participants in the liturgical life of the parish will only further alienate them. Having rigid rules for attendance will have the same effect. We need to be a warm and welcoming community, not one which sits in judgement and welcomes only the choir members!

### 2) Evangelization Efforts

Most would admit that within the parish boundaries there are probably many more children who are not being catechized—or who are not even baptized—who should be, because at least one of their parents was raised a Catholic. This calls for good collaboration with the parish evangelization committee. Sometimes doing a door-to-door census helps identify families that need to be welcomed back into active participation into the Church. For these efforts to be effective the canvassers need to be well-trained to be open, welcoming and non-judgemental. Good follow-up from pastoral staff is often needed. Campaigns to welcome back "those who have been away" have been effective in many parts of the country. When people do return to active participation in the Church, they often need a lot of encouragement to stay active. Inviting sponsor-families to stay in touch with the family and do social as well as religious activities with the family often is effective in helping the returning families feel a sense of community.

### 3) Adult Participation

Another issue related to religious indifference is the difficult time parishes have getting adults to be part of catechetical efforts. Parishes need to look at the kinds of programs they plan, who is involved in the planning, how they are scheduled, and the like, before they conclude that people do not come because they are apathetic. Sometimes the planning, marketing and scheduling are done poorly and these factors lead to meager participation. Sometimes people equate adult catechesis with lectures on Church topics. While lectures may be one form of adult education, they certainly are not the most effective because they usually do not take into consideration the need to build community, the need to know to whom one is lecturing and what the audience's questions are. Lectures often provide little interaction among group participants and little follow-through after the presentation.

Small groups meeting in homes, and often involving prayer and scripture study, have been successful, if the leaders are well-trained. Parish retreats which involve some presentations as well as interaction and prayer are another form of adult catechesis which can be successful. Using the opportunities provided by children's sacramental programs for parents to examine their own faith and get up-dated on theological concepts is valuable adult catechesis, if done according to the principles of adult education. Another form of adult catechesis is having a parish library with print materials and videos for parishioners to check out for use at home either alone or with family and friends.

### 4) Electronic Media

The electronic media, such as the Internet, is opening all sorts of opportunities for distance learning. The parish, if it has a homepage, can do mini-courses via the Internet. Caution has to be taken about everything in the electronic media because not all of it is of good quality or adequately reflects Church teaching. However, there is no doubt that this is a vehicle for communication and catechesis that parishes would do well to explore.

## CATECHIST TRAINING

Consider catechist training as leadership training for some of the best and the brightest people in your parish. Catechist training is one of the best opportunities for adult formation in any parish. It also can provide opportunities for family enrichment. It needs to be a parish priority and sufficient resources need to be allocated to it. In recruiting, catechist formation must be part of the package and it can be presented as an advantage to being a catechist, especially if it includes personal enrichment and family enrichment.

### a) Scheduling Problems

One of the biggest challenges to parish and school catechetical programs is how and when to train catechists. In Catholic schools many teachers have not been trained in theology or catechetics. In the parish most catechetical programs are implemented by generous, well-meaning volunteers who live very busy lives. The problem centers on designing ways to involve all those in the catechetical ministry of the Church in formation programs. The major difficulty to this is to find time for catechists, both in schools and in parish programs, to come together for training. Volunteers are stretched by the time it takes to prepare and implement their sessions. Many of them are working full-time and raising families. Catholic school teachers often are so bombarded by many other curriculum priorities and inservices that they feel they cannot add one more thing to their schedules.

## 2) Terminology

The terms "catechist and catechetical ministry" apply to both school and parish programs and personnel. When Catholic school teachers participate in the ministry of catechesis—helping children and young people to grow in faith—they act in the role of catechists. This is an official ministry in the Church and while related closely to teaching, it is a different ministry because the process is one of faith formation and involves building community, leading people to pray, proclaiming the message and motivating people to serve others. Therefore, it is not accurate to associate the term catechist only with parish volunteers who participate in catechetical programs.

## FORMATION OPPORTUNITIES

The following suggestions for formation can be adapted for both school and parish catechists.

### 1) Building Community

Some opportunities need to be provided for catechists to build community among themselves. When there is a good *esprit de corps* among catechists, the attrition rate goes down. By getting to know one another, by sharing meals and stories, a bond is formed which sustains catechists when discouragement sets in. The enthusiasm generated by a group of catechists is reflective of the Spirit at work in their midst.

One way to bring catechists together for formation programs is to have a light supper for them and their families. Do not make it a potluck because they should not be expected to do something extra. Include a common shared meal prayer and a brief family experience at the supper. After supper have other parish volunteers, e.g., mature adolescents, monitor the children by providing a homework room or a video showing or athletic games or board games. Depending on the number of children and their ages, adult volunteers will be needed to supervise high school students who may be helping in the program.

Parents who are catechists can relax and learn more about their ministry if they know their children are fed, safe and happy for a couple hours. This same idea can be applied on Sunday or Saturday mornings depending upon when the catechetical sessions are scheduled. Catechists are more likely to come to monthly sessions for training if some of their other home responsibilities are alleviated.

Some directors of catechetics have been successful in planning and implementing summer camping excursions for their catechists and their families. Such events can lead to a lot of creative "religious activities" that build community, foster prayer, proclaim the message of God's everlasting presence and motivate people to service.

Christmas parties and end of the year celebrations for catechists and their families are wonderful ways to build community and enhance family life.

### 2) Providing a Theological Background

For catechists to be able to proclaim the message of Jesus Christ effectively, they need a solid theological background. Using a book like this one or videos or engaging speakers are all aids in achieving this. What is important is not to attempt to pump a great deal of information into catechists, but to use the catechetical resources of the Church in a process that will help them reflect on their own faith life and to integrate this with more knowledge about the Church, the Bible, the liturgy and the lifecycles of those whom they catechize. In helping people to be effective catechists, we, in reality, are nurturing them to grow in faith. Some group sessions are needed to build community but also to share faith and ask questions concerning the theological content presented. A good process for this is called theological reflection. One way to do it is:

(1) to reflect on one's experience, one's questions, one's curiosities about a certain topic;

(2) to investigate relevant information from the disciplines of scripture, liturgy, the teachings of the Church, the lives of the saints, church history and social justice issues, and so forth.

(3) to be aware of the culture and what is currently happening in the news, in society, in the world and to discern how these events influence one's thinking and understanding;

(4) to process the information in light of one's experience, one's beliefs and one's insights and the group's experiences and beliefs;

(5) to implement some action as the result of the theological reflection process. In this case the action would involve the work of catechesis.

### 3) Transference of Learning and Experience

One of the problems with many catechetical training programs is that there is no transference of learning from the formation session to the catechetical session. The fourth step in the theological reflection process points to this. Often this step is not well defined in terms of practical help for the catechists. The connection to the particular catechetical session one is being trained for needs to be made explicit. For example, the training session might be on how the scriptures were formed. For the catechists of young children this may seem irrelevant to what they do. However, if there is a connection made by all the catechists about how they use scripture in their sessions, the origin and type of scripture used, then the catechetical sessions with others, not to mention the catechists, will be enriched. For instance, if the formation session included how the psalms were formed, all can find verses of the psalms to use in prayer with those whom they catechize. Because the catechists have just studied the psalms, they will approach praying with them in a different way than if they had not been given the background. However, transference of learning cannot be taken for granted. In the training session itself, efforts must be made to have the catechists make the connections between what was learned or experienced and what is the focus of the catechetical material they use in their sessions. Sometimes this can be done by examining catechetical materials, finding connections or adapting the materials to include what was learned and experienced in the formation session.

### 4) Catechetical Textbooks

Catechetical materials such as textbooks need to be seen as resources, one of the artistic tools that the catechist uses. The danger is that some people are enslaved to the textbooks. No textbook can be designed or written for a particular parish. Textbooks are generic in nature. In examining them one should look at what the underlying assumptions are about catechesis and compare them to the parish's or school's belief about catechesis. Each parish should have an articulated set of assumptions and beliefs about catechesis and be operating out of them. They should also have a set of curriculum guidelines for children's and adolescent's programs. Diocesan offices often have general guidelines which pertain to the whole diocese. Parishes should design their own, based on the diocesan ones, but adapted to local situations. For instance, if the parish has a large Mexican Hispanic population, certain feasts will be of particular importance. The curriculum guidelines should reflect the ethnic character of the parish, while at the same time not losing the global nature of the Church. Textbooks are meant to be supplemented by materials and processes that reflect local parish priorities and needs as well as the artistry of the catechists.

### 5) Communal Prayer

Communal prayer is essential for a catechetical training program. Sharing of the scriptures, praying prayers of praise, thanksgiving and petition in common, participating in rituals, and singing hymns are at the heart of formation programs. Every formation session should provide an opportunity for communal prayer. After initial formation some of the catechists themselves can plan the prayer. Days or evenings of reflection, where the focus is not on practical details of catechetical sessions, are needed to enrich the spiritual life of catechists. Consideration should be given for the catechists to invite their spouses to such experiences so that the whole family can be enriched. If this is done, meals and child care must be provided and some family interaction should be built in for a short period of time to enhance family life.

### 6) Service

Service is integral to catechetical ministry. The ministry itself is one of service to the Word of God. However, other service opportunities need to be explored as possibilities for those catechized. This can be done in collaboration with the parish social outreach or human concerns committee. Part of catechist formation is to present possibilities for service that the catechists can use with the participants in their sessions.

### 7) In-service on the Human Growth Life Cycles

In-service for catechetical ministry needs to include key points about the growth and development of those catechized. The first chapter in this book refers to some of the salient characteristics. Considering the life cycle is important because over- or under-challenging those to be catechized can be disastrous.

### 8) Discipline

Discipline can be a chief concern of those catechizing children. There are some rules of thumb that can prevent major discipline problems.

#### a) Be well prepared

Have all materials ready. Have an outline of the sessions so you do not have to rely heavily on copious notes.

#### b) Design a variety of activities

Children do not like having to sit still too long. They do not like a lot of reading out loud. Small children need to be given activities which are short in duration because their attention span is very limited. The activities need to be varied: drawing, singing, appropriate body movement, cutting and pasting, listening, praying, acting out a skit.

Older children also need a variety of activities. In an hour session there should at least be three different kinds of activities. Some might include reading or listening, discussing with peers, doing an art project with a partner, praying, planning a service project, singing, helping younger children, creating through music and video, etc.

#### c) Know the names of those you catechize from the first day you meet them

This may include having them wear name tags for the first couple of sessions. For the older ones, place-cards with their names on them can be effective.

#### d) Try to have a helper or aid with each catechist to be of general assistance as well as to expedite discipline problems

The assistants can be see as interns being trained by a "master catechist." With younger children, have a mischievous one sit next to you in a circle. When you are reading a story the child can help turn the pages. Keeping children busy helps prevent discipline problems. With older children, especially for the hyper-active ones, have activities like passing out papers, distributing the markers, hanging up the artwork, and the like.

If all else fails, have the aid work with the disruptive person on a one-on-one basis. If things continue to be problematic, discuss the situation with the director of the program or the child's parents. However, remember that the primary responsibility for discipline is the catechist's.

### e) Have the children or young people being catechized participate in setting ground rules for the time they are together

Be sure that what the catechist thinks is important is on the list of these guidelines. Review these at the end of a session and each time you convene. Positive reinforcement of good behavior is more beneficial than focusing on failures. Point out when the guidelines all have agreed to have been broken. Haranguing about discipline issues is not effective. Looking at the causes of them can be helpful if strategies can be developed to overcome the problems.

### 9) Programs for Special Needs

Be sure to provide programs for children and adults with special needs. Some of these children may not have the intellectual ability to be in regular sessions. Some may be deaf or blind. Whatever keeps them from being able to participate with other children should be addressed so that special catechetical programs are designed for them. Often one-on-one catechetical efforts can be successful in helping people with various intellectual, physical and emotional disabilities.

### 10) Ecumenical Dimensions

Ecumenical marriages, where one spouse is Roman Catholic and one is not, can present a catechetical challenge. In some parts of the country close to 40 percent of the marriages are ecumenical. In many of these cases both parties continue to practice their faith in their separate denominations, or one party does not practice in any denomination at all. There are three areas that should be considered regarding ecumenism.

First, when dealing with children from an ecumenical marriage, invite the non-Catholic party to participate fully in parent catechetical programs. This may require extra effort on the part of the catechetical leaders to reach out to all parents. Non-Catholic parents have a role to play in the sacramental preparation of the children and should be encouraged to participate.

Second, be sensitive to ecumenical issues, but at the same time clearly explain Catholic doctrine. Watering down the Catholic Church's beliefs in order to encourage ecumenical relations is non-productive for all parties. When presenting information about other Christians, do it with adequate knowledge of the issues and the history which led to the division. Be aware that in many ways the Reformation exposed practices which had gone awry in the Catholic Church and needed to be addressed. Avoid a sense of elitism and the "we are better than you" mentality. Invite leaders from other denominations to dialogue in your catechetical sessions. Ask your pastor and/or the diocese for help in designing processes for greater ecumenical understanding among those you catechize. Highlight the central beliefs that are shared by the entire Christian community.

Third, encourage prayer and dialogue for Christian unity. Ask your pastor or director of catechesis to help design a prayer service where the minister from a neighboring congregation and the children and families from that denomination come together with your pastor and families of the children you catechize to pray for unity. Share a potluck supper with people from both congregations.

## 11) Relationship to Other Religions

Besides ecumenical dialogue, relationships and understandings need to be developed with people from other religions. In catechizing it is important that you correct misunderstandings that people may have, especially about Jews or Muslims. Christ's suffering and death "cannot be blamed on all the Jews then living…nor upon Jews of today" (NCD 77). The Church deplores all hatred of the Jews or signs of anti-Semitism. We share much with the Jewish people. Our roots are Jewish. We share much of the Bible with the Jewish people. Catechesis must make strong efforts to repair years of misinformation and prejudice against the Jewish people.

Muslim people are those who follow the teachings of Muhammad. They are also called the people of Islam. Today, unfortunately, Muslims are often associated with terrorism because a very small segment of Muslims embrace terrorist tactics to bring about change. Muslims, however, have many things in common with Christians and try to promote peace as much as Christians do. Muslims believe in God as the creator of all things; they believe in Abraham as the patriarch and a key person in the history of salvation; they believe in the prophetic role of Jesus Christ; they believe in Mary as the virgin mother of Jesus; they also believe in the disciplines of prayer, fasting and almsgiving. There is a long history of quarrels and wars between Christians and Muslims. To have a better working relationship with Muslims today it is important to know about and acknowledge the struggles of the past, but then to continue to build collaborative and peaceful relationships based on shared values of peace and justice.

Two other major world religions are Buddhism and Hinduism. Buddhism began in Asia about five hundred years before Christ was born. It strives for universal perfection. A Buddhist is one who stands in the circle of the Buddha or the Enlightened One. Buddhists accept people where they are and are very tolerant of differences. They believe that through supreme human effort there is the possibility of experiencing freedom in perfect existence. The practice of Yoga, a meditative practice which has become popular in the United States, has its origins in a form of Buddhism.

Hinduism originated in India about fifteen hundred years before Christ. It is a very complex and rich religion. Sometimes Hinduism is called the religion of renunciation; sometimes it is identified with the worship of the cow; sometimes it is recognized for its influence on the Indian caste system; sometimes it is known for its belief in rebirth or reincarnation. For the Hindu there are no absolute lines separating the sacred and the secular. Life is looked upon as a rite. To understand Hinduism one needs to comprehend the immense network of symbolism which underlies Indian thought. There are many sects in Hinduism. Some have political and social orientations. Mahatma Gandhi and his nonviolent peace movement is one example of such an orientation.

Christianity shares values with Hinduism and Buddhism and, at a time when the world is getting smaller, it is important to be informed about world religions so that collaborative efforts can be shared to build a more just and peaceful society. When catechizing about world religions three things are significant.

First, it is important to give accurate information. One of the best ways to do this is to invite someone from that specific world religion to dialogue with those catechized. If this is not possible, search for videos which give accurate information in a visually enticing way.

A second consideration is to help those catechized appreciate the insights and contributions of that world religion. This calls for sharp analysis and should be challenging to middle school, high school and adult participants.

A third factor is to be attentive to the possibility of doing joint social justice projects with people of other religions (NCD 79). Such projects build relationships and help break down prejudices and barriers to peaceful coexistence.

## 12) Dealing with Those Who Do Not Agree with Your Thinking

A lot of time and energy is sometimes spent in dealing with people who represent rigid thinking and are opposed to any sort of change in how worship is done and how catechesis is done. These people usually fall into two categories: those who are uninformed through no fault of their own and those who are informed to some degree but refuse to be open to any other thinking outside their own adamant stances. The latter group is usually well organized and often influences more than one parish.

With the right strategies, the people who fall into the first category can be informed about the Second Vatican Council's views and beliefs. Several steps need to be taken to be successful with this group. First of all, be sure to treat the people with utmost respect, so that they do not feel put down or stupid. Bonding on some affective level is important. Share some of your own faith journey, without dominating the session. Invite them in a non-threatening way to share theirs, if they wish.

Second, begin slowly so that they are not overwhelmed to discover or reveal their real questions, fears and anxieties. For instance, if their questions deal with the Bible, begin by helping them understand the formation of scripture. (See some of the ideas in Chapters Two and Three of this book.) You might start with the story of the boy who discovered the first of the Dead Sea Scrolls in the 1940s. Gradually move to such things as the two different creation stories. Use the Gospels as examples of different views by different communities of Jesus' life and mission. Through all this, especially if you are working with scripture, consider the spiritual sense of the Word as well as the literal sense. In other words, what are the scriptures saying to us today? In adult groups, be sure to include the building of community among the participants, along with prayer, study and dialogue.

Third, be prepared to work with some people individually or in small groups because their questions and concerns may be different from others. This can be done formally or informally over a cup of coffee or tea. Don't hesitate to call upon other resources or experts to help deal with their questions. You do not need to have all the answers, but you do need to be encouraging and welcoming of questions and fears.

Fourth, have various resources available, in print and video, for people to take home and read and watch.

Fifth, have an attitude of "walking with" the people on a faith journey. They are on a conversion journey, looking for new insights, new ways to bring meaning to their lives. You have the privilege of accompanying them on their journey.

The second group of people are much more difficult to deal with. Many are self-righteous and have no intention of changing. They are often not willing to see things from another point of view. Some of these people are misinformed and are overly influenced by others in the group; others seem to be psychologically incapable of changing or growing when it comes to issues of faith. When they see the world changing so fast in so many areas, they cannot afford to have a faith that is anything but an immutable rock that they can hold on to in the midst of massive change. Some sincerely believe that God is calling them to be a force of truth in a changing world.

In working with fundamentalists several things should be considered: first, the people who appear rigid and self-righteous may have some insights which we may benefit from hearing; second, the people need to be treated with respect and not be engaged in shouting matches, no matter how enraged we may feel at any given moment; third, if possible try to engage the people in a reasonable dialogue which is controlled by rules set up ahead of time; fourth, emphasize points of commonly held beliefs rather than points of divergence; fifth, try to present the more recent understandings of the Second Vatican Council from an historical point of view, showing how much of what is considered new really is a renewal of older practices in the Church, some of which go back to the time of the apostles; sixth agree to disagree; seventh, allow as much diversity in your programs as you can and still have integrity, so that many needs can be met and one point of view is not being forced on people; and lastly, compromise where and when it is appropriate, but within a framework of sound catechetical and theological principles.

Many other pastoral issues face parishes, such as the mobility of families, the return of families to active participation where the children have had no catechesis, lack of financial and professional resources, over-worked pastors and pastoral staffs and bi-cultural or tri-cultural catechetical needs in one parish. These and other pastoral issues form the threads of the fabric of catechesis which are being woven by the artists of this century and the next. The strength of the tapestry is found in the interwoven strands of the Spirit's presence.

## REFLECTION

Have the Bible enthroned. Light a candle before beginning the prayer service. Have strands of different colored yarn or ribbon to make a rough weaving. Prepare a small table with a light-colored tablecloth for the weaving project. Have a small crucifix to give each catechist.

Begin with a familiar opening song.

*Presider:* God, our loving Creator, you have called us to assist others to grow in faith. You have charged us with the task of spreading the Good News of Jesus Christ in such a way that both children and adults become avid disciples. Strengthen us and give us courage to strive for greater clarity and creativity as we continue the mission of Jesus on earth. We ask this in the name of Jesus Christ our redeemer, brother and friend, through the power of the Spirit.

*All:* Amen.

*Reader:* Proclaim Luke 16:15–18.

Allow time for reflection. The following questions may be used to initiate faith sharing.

> *In what you do as catechists and/or parents, how are you following the mandate of Jesus as found in this passage?*
> *What talents has God given you to help you in this ministry?*
> *What do contemporary times have in common with the time Jesus and the apostles walked the earth? What is similar? What is different?*
> *In what way do you consider catechesis an art?*

After allowing time for faith sharing, invite each catechist to think about one or two tools or talents he or she has or needs to continue creating catechesis as a form of art. Have participants choose one or two strands of yarn or ribbon to represent the tool or talent they need or have. Ask them to present their thread on the table and tell the group what their thread represents. *Example:* "I chose yellow because it reminds me of the Church and we need the Church to have effective catechists." Or, "I chose red because it reminds me of the Old Testament's story of God saving the Israelites from the oppression of the Egyptians. To be effective catechists we need to know our Jewish history." As the threads are presented have each person intertwine his or her thread with those presented before so that the end result resembles a loose weaving. Of course, each person may present more than one thread.

*Presider:* God, our Creator, you have called us to continue your creative work on earth by presenting your Son and Word in such a way as to make him relevant to people today. We ask you to hear our petitions as we continue your work:

Invite petitions from the group. Response: "Lord, hear our prayer."

*Presider:* Hear our prayers and answer them in the name of Jesus Christ your Son and our redeemer.

*All:* Amen

*Presider:* Invite each catechist to come forward to receive a crucifix as a sign of commitment to the mission and ministry of Jesus Christ.

> *Say: I present you_____, with a crucifix, the sign of your commitment to continue the catechetical ministry of Jesus Christ. May you do it creatively so that the Word of God is recognized as being alive today in the hearts and minds of those with whom we work.*

*Catechist:* Amen.
*All:* Pray the Lord's Prayer.
Exchange a sign of peace.
Sing a closing song familiar to the group.